Studies in the History of Law and Justice

Volume 29

The purpose of this book series is to publish high quality volumes on the history of law and justice. Legal history can be a deeply provocative and influential field, as illustrated by the growth of the European universities and the *Ius Commune* , the French Revolution, the American Revolution, and indeed all the great movements for national liberation through law. The study of history gives scholars and reformers the models and courage to question entrenched injustices, by demonstrating the contingency of law and other social arrangements. Yet legal history today finds itself diminished in the universities and legal academy. Too often scholarship betrays no knowledge of what went before, or why legal institutions took the shape that they did.This series seeks to remedy that deficiency.

Studies in the History of Law and Justice will be theoretical and reflective. Volumes will address the history of law and justice from a critical and comparative viewpoint. The studies in this series will be strong bold narratives of the development of law and justice. Some will be suitable for a very broad readership.

Contributions to this series will come from scholars on every continent and in every legal system. Volumes will promote international comparisons and dialogue. The purpose will be to provide the next generation of lawyers with the models and narratives needed to understand and improve the law and justice of their own era. The series includes monographs focusing on a specific topic, as well as collections of articles covering a theme or collections of article by one author.

Aniceto Masferrer

The Making of Dignity and Human Rights in the Western Tradition

A Retrospective Analysis

Springer

Aniceto Masferrer
Faculty of Law
University of Valencia
Valencia, Spain

ISSN 2198-9842 ISSN 2198-9850 (electronic)
Studies in the History of Law and Justice
ISBN 978-3-031-46666-3 ISBN 978-3-031-46667-0 (eBook)
https://doi.org/10.1007/978-3-031-46667-0

Translation from the Spanish language edition: "Dignidad y derechos humanos. Una análisis retrospectivo de su formación en la tradición occidental" by Aniceto Masferrer, © Tirant lo blanch 2022. Published by Tirant lo blanch. All Rights Reserved.

This Springer imprint is published by the registered company Springer Nature Switzerland AG
The registered company address is: Gewerbestrasse 11, 6330 Cham, Switzerland

Paper in this product is recyclable.

Acknowledgements

To Alfredo Obarrio, for his generous and loyal friendship over two decades.

To Francisco Carpintero Benítez, from whose work I have learned so much and I still have so much to learn.

To Alejandro Guzmán Brito (†), part of whose work I was reading at the time of his death.

This study has been carried out within the framework of the Project "Tradition and foreign influences in the Spanish Criminal Codification: Contribution of jurisprudence in the evolution of the Special Part (1870-1995)" (PID2019-105871GB-I00), funded by the Spanish Ministry of Science and Innovation.

This book is a modified English version of the monograph entitled *Dignidad y derechos humanos. Un análisis retrospectivo de su formación en la tradición occidental* (Valencia: Tirant lo Blanch, 2022).

I'm immensely grateful to Zheng Hong See (Oxford University) and to my colleague and friend Miguel Martínez López (Valencia University) for having revised the English text and to my outstanding student Patricia Plana de Juan for her wonderful job in adjusting the footnotes and references of the manuscript to the requested style of the publisher.

Contents

Chapter 1
From Human Rights to Natural Rights

1.1 Introduction

The tragic consequences of the Second World War gave rise to a new stage in public international law, based on the protection of and respect for human rights.

Indeed, the aftermath of this horrendous tragedy, with the loss of 50 million human lives, in addition to other damages, both personal (prison riots, after-effects of the concentration camps, family dislocation, hunger and difficulties of the soldiers in adapting to civilian life), and patrimonial (destruction of cities, railways, roads, bridges, industrial plants, as well as the damage to the most fertile fields), made the leaders of many States reflect on the need to find new bases on which they could found new foundations on which they could build a new world order, as well as the position of each individual and the whole community vis-à-vis its political power.

In this context, shortly after the end of the Second World War, the *Charter of San Francisco* (or *Charter of the United Nations*) was signed on 26 June 1945, with the aim of internationalising the recognition of fundamental rights whose national protection, that is, by the various states or nations, had proved insufficient. The creation of the *United Nations Organization* (UN) was, therefore due to the repudiation of Nazi crimes (inside and outside Germany) and the desire to establish a basis for a just and peaceful coexistence between individuals in a political community, as well as between states.

This founding treaty of the UN, ratified by the original 51 member countries—193 since 2011, that is, the majority of nations—begins with a Preamble reaffirming "faith in fundamental human rights, in the dignity and worth of the human person, in the equal rights of men and women and of nations large and small."[1]

[1]Preamble to the *Charter of the United Nations* (26 June 1945): "We the peoples of the United Nations determined to save succeeding generations from the scourge of war, which twice in our lifetime has brought untold sorrow to mankind, to *reaffirm faith in fundamental human rights, in the*

A. Masferrer, *The Making of Dignity and Human Rights in the Western Tradition*,
Studies in the History of Law and Justice 29,
https://doi.org/10.1007/978-3-031-46667-0_1

A few years later, and under the initiative of the same body, the *Universal Declaration of Human Rights* (UDHR) (10 December 1948) was drafted to establish human rights as the basis, and cornerstone of law in general and of international public order in particular, and its Preamble made the primordial role of human rights even clearer:

> Whereas recognition of the inherent dignity and of the equal and inalienable rights of all members of the human family is the foundation of freedom, justice, and peace in the world;
>
> Whereas disregard and contempt for human rights have resulted in barbarous acts which have outraged the conscience of mankind, and the advent of a world in which human beings, freed from fear and want, shall enjoy freedom of speech and belief and freedom from fear and want has been proclaimed as the highest aspiration of the common people;
>
> Whereas it is essential, if man is not to be compelled to have recourse, as a last resort, to rebellion against tyranny and oppression, that the rule of law should protect human rights;
>
> Whereas it essential to promote the development of friendly relations between nations;
>
> Whereas the peoples of the United Nations have in the Charter reaffirmed their faith in fundamental human rights, in the dignity and worth of the human person and in the equal rights of men and women and have determined to promote social progress and better standards of life in larger freedom;
>
> Whereas Member States have pledged themselves to achieve, in co-operation with the United Nations, the promotion of universal respect for and observance of human rights and fundamental freedoms;
>
> Whereas a common understanding of these rights and freedoms is of the greatest importance for the full realization of this pledge.

This clear and forceful Preamble was followed by 30 articles enshrining respect for and protection of civil, political, economic, social, and cultural rights. The text does not contain a definition of 'human right' as such, nor does it deal with its basis, a matter on which there was no unanimity. Still, it does contain a series of elements whose origin and historical development are easily recognisable. Thus, for example, art. 1 provides as follows:

> All human beings are born free and equal in dignity and rights. They are endowed with reason and conscience and should act towards one another in a spirit of brotherhood.

---

dignity and worth of the human person, in the equal rights of men and women, and of nations large and small, to establish conditions under which justice and respect for the obligations arising from treaties and other sources of international law can be maintained, to promote social progress and better standards of life in larger freedom, and for these ends to practice tolerance and live together in peace with one another as good neighbours, to unite our strength to maintain international peace and security, and to ensure, by the acceptance of principles and the institution of methods, that armed force shall not be used, save in the common interest, and to employ international machinery for the promotion of the economic and social advancement of all peoples, have resolved to combine our efforts to accomplish these aims. Accordingly, our respective Governments, through representatives assembled in the city of San Francisco who have exhibited their full powers found to be in good and due form, have agreed to the present Charter of the United Nations and do hereby establish an international organisation to be known as the United Nations"; Loewenstein (1945), p. 275: "...the Second World War taught us that human liberty, like peace, is indivisible, and that no stable world order is possible as long as any government, claiming the sovereignty of its state, can trample underfoot the liberties of its own citizens"; see Arendt (1968), Ch. 9; Moyn (2018).

The notion of 'fraternity' came from the French Revolution, although—as is well known—it was not the French Revolution that invented it. That men are born 'free and equal in dignity and rights' was not something new either; it came from the natural law doctrines, both pre-Christian and as the fruit of a Judeo-Christian tradition that would reach its peak in the seventeenth century, in which several thinkers such as Hugo Grotius, Samuel Pufendorf, Christian Wolf, or John Locke, who notably developed the pre-political character of the fundamental rights, precisely because 'every human being is born free and equal in dignity and rights', would stand out.

As its very name indicates, this Declaration was a mere declaration, lacking legal force or binding force upon the States that have been ratifying it. It would, however, be the starting point for many other national and international legal instruments, which would have legal force and whose violation would allow recourse to the courts—national or international—to render the protection of human rights effective.

Indeed, this *Declaration* was to be followed by the 'International Covenants on Human Rights' (or 'New York Covenants'), the name given to two crucial International Covenants, namely the 'International Covenant on Civil and Political Rights' (ICCPR) and the 'International Covenant on Economic, Social and Cultural Rights', both adopted by the United Nations General Assembly by Resolution 2200 A (XXI) of 16 December 1966. However, the latter entered into force 2 months earlier (3 January 1976) than the former (25 March 1976).

These 'International Covenants on Human Rights', together with the aforementioned *Universal Declaration of Human Rights*, comprise what some have called the 'International Bill of Human Rights'.

The UDHR, in addition to being the starting point for these 'International Covenants on Human Rights', served as a model for other regional (in Europe, America, Africa and Asia) and national texts, to the extent that many state constitutions around the world adopted similar or even literal precepts from it.

The emergence of human rights in the twentieth century, particularly in its second half, led Norberto Bobbio to describe this historical period as the 'age of rights.'

We say 'historical' because, according to some thinkers, in this context of crisis in which the political powers do not seem to be able to sustain the model of the Social State and the Rule of Law created after the Second World War; the viability of this State, the guarantor of an increasing number—up to unsuspected limits—of social benefits, is uncertain. It is also unclear whether each and every one of the social benefits that the public authorities have been guaranteeing, from a retirement pension to the financing of an abortion drug or a surgical intervention for a gender reassignment, can be considered 'human rights'. Are all of these social benefits enforceable against the State because they respond to the demands of human dignity, because they are, in short, 'human rights'?

The second half of the last century indeed saw an eruption or explosion of human rights, but the twentieth century cannot be credited with their invention or discovery. Human rights were neither discovered nor invented in the city of San Francisco in 1945: it was only there that the dire consequences of the violation of these rights became apparent, and 3 years later, it was solemnly declared that "disregard and contempt for human rights have resulted in barbarous acts which have outraged the conscience of mankind", as the Preamble to the UDHR begins.

The two World Wars of the last century were not due to a lack of knowledge of human rights, nor even due to their scant formulation and legal development: they were due to their absolute disregard, even by States whose governments managed to come to power by the requirements of a democratic political system.[2] Once again, a sad chapter in the history of mankind was being repeated: the abusive exercise of political power by those who wielded it, the use of the machinery of the State for purposes unrelated to the common goods, with contempt for the dignity of individuals, their sacredness and their inviolable and inalienable rights.

History repeats itself. One might think that 'there is nothing new under the sun', but this sad episode presented a new physiognomy regarding its particular features and circumstances. While the violation of human rights could be understood within the framework of absolutist political systems, typical of the *Ancien Régime*,[3] this case had been different: it had taken place after the establishment of a political and legal system which, based on the notions of fundamental rights (human rights) and sovereignty (power resides in the nation, that is, in the group of individuals who make up the national community), was supposed to safeguard and guarantee respect for human dignity. Indeed, by setting limits to the power of the State, by creating a private sphere of the individual whose entry was forbidden to political power (thus giving rise to individual liberties and rights), it was intended to move from the 'liberty of the ancients' to the 'liberty of the moderns', as Benjamin Constant pointed out in a famous lecture delivered in 1819.[4]

Seen in this light, one might think in the following terms: while it is understandable that human rights were violated in pre-liberal absolutist states, whose power lacked limits and was exercised despotically, it is less understandable that such violations took place in the context of constitutional political systems (liberal and democratic), whose basis and raison d'être was—after the painful experience of the absolutist monarchies of the eighteenth century—the protection of fundamental rights. This statement is only partially true because neither the political power of absolutist states was completely without limits (at least in theory), nor were the theoretical bases of constitutional political systems, both in their liberal (nineteenth century) and democratic (twentieth century) phases, able to guarantee the respect and safeguarding of human rights. History has only confirmed this truth.

---

[2]However, it is worth remembering that Hitler came to power by a compromise made by Hindenburg in view of Germany's ungovernability. In the elections of 5 March 1933 his Nazi Party (NSDAP) won the most votes. Failing to achieve a majority, Hitler had to reach a coalition agreement with the Zentrum-led (the Centre Party) and DNVP in order to break the parliamentary deadlock. It took Hitler only three weeks to arrest all the Communist deputies and most of the Social Democrats, and on 23 March he passed the Enabling Act, ending parliamentary democracy and establishing the notorious totalitarian regime.

[3]This does not mean that the Ancien Régime lacked fundamental laws; in this respect, see Coronas (1998), pp. 218–310.

[4]Constant (1988).

Since, as Cicero said, "history is the teacher of life and the witness of the times", and since human rights were not a discovery of the twentieth century but rather the product of a long historical tradition, let us examine it below to understand the process of formation or shaping of a reality that is so important today. Since we can't present here a complete development of the history of human rights, whose origins can be found in various cultures and traditions far removed from our own, we have chosen to adopt the method of retrospective history, which, instead of going from the most ancient to the most modern, goes the other way round: from the modern to the ancient. This makes it possible to highlight which modern elements came from previous periods, while simultaneously exempting us from an exhaustive analysis of a merely descriptive history of human rights, devoid of life and critical analysis, like a body without a soul.

1.2 The Recognition of Fundamental Rights in Modern Constitutionalism (Nineteenth Century)

1.2.1 Fundamental Rights as a Reason for and Limit of the Liberal State

Modern constitutions, promulgated in the West to enshrine the triumph of liberal revolutions, became the ideal legal and political instruments for setting limits on political power.

It was precisely the establishment of limits to the—then generalised—absolutist political system that was the raison d'être of the modern notion of constitution, which sought to safeguard the individual from the excessive power of the State, that was identified with monarchical absolutism.

In this line, the *Declaration of the Rights of Man and of the Citizen* (1789) clearly stated what was required to be able to speak of a society with a Constitution:

> Any society in which no provision is made for guaranteeing rights or for the separation of powers, has no Constitution (art. 16).[5]

In reality, both the separation of powers and the guarantee of fundamental rights were aimed at a common objective: establishing and guaranteeing a space of freedom for the individual and of non-interference by the State in it. To this end, the new public power, structured in distinct—but not completely independent—

---

[5] Article 16 of the *Declaration of the Rights of Man and of the Citizen* (1789); the basic constitutional texts cited throughout this study have been extracted from the following editions: with respect to the comparative field, Varela (1998); regarding Spain, Tierno (1984); and Esteban (2000).

powers, was required to defer to the law (the rule of law in the United States),[6] or to legality (principle or legislative supremacy in France).[7]

The deference of all public powers to the law (the rule of law) or to legality (supremacy of the law, understood as the expression of the general will), as well as the safeguarding of fundamental rights (also understood as subjective rights),[8] rested on a previous and fundamental principle: the principle of national sovereignty. In other words, the ownership of power no longer resided in the monarch but in the nation,[9] although the monarch could later share its exercise as head of the executive power.

The principle of national or popular sovereignty was thus a creation or invention of modern constitutionalism,[10] without which there could be no actual constitution.[11] The first American constitutional texts enshrined the principle that "all power belongs to the people, and therefore derives from the people,"[12] giving the people the power to dismantle existing political ties with another,[13] as well as the authority, proper to all people, to enact and promulgate their own Constitution.[14]

The first French constitutional texts did the same, declaring that "the representatives of the French people, constituted in a National Assembly (...), have decided to set forth, in a solemn declaration..."[15] art. 3 of this same *Declaration* clearly and solemnly enshrined the principle of national sovereignty in these terms:

---

[6]Loughlin (2003), p. 75; on this question, see also Kriegel (1995).

[7]On the supremacy of the law in the French Revolution, see García de Enterría (1994), pp. 108 ff.; for a comparative analysis between the supremacy of the law in the French Revolution and the Anglo-Saxon *rule of law*, see García de Enterría (1994), pp. 145–152.

[8]On the notion of natural rights in modern Constitutions (particularly in the United States and France), see Loughlin (2003), pp. 117–125; on the declaration of rights in the first French constitutional texts, see Duguit (1937), pp. 203 ff; for a summary of the evolution of the concept of subjective law from Roman law to the French Revolution, see García de Enterría (1994), pp. 47–96; on the interconnection between law and rights in the French Revolution, see García de Enterría (1994), pp. 114–124; Varela (2007), pp. 114–124; Varela (2007), pp. 109–119.

[9]For a general overview of the substitution of the nation for the king in the ownership of power or sovereignty in the French Revolution, see García de Enterría (1994), pp. 102–114.

[10]The idea of popular sovereignty as an "invention" is described and defended in Morgan (2006).

[11]According to the opinion of Tomás y Valiente—and in accordance with his prescriptive definition of Constitution contained in footnote n. 4—, "...from these postulates [of the democratic ideological position] it is lawful to separate the line of our authentic Constitutions (that of 1812, that of 1969, the republican of 1931 and the current one of 1978), that of the degraded Constitutions (those of 1837, 1845 and 1876) and that of the sham constitutional texts (those of 1808, 1834 and those initiated by the New State, created after the military rebellion against the Second Republic)...." (Tomás y Valiente (1980), p. 13).

[12]Art. 2 of the *Virginia Declaration of Rights* (June 12, 1776).

[13]Preamble to the *Declaration of Independence* (July 4, 1776).

[14]Preamble to the *Constitution of the United States of America* (1787).

[15]Preamble of the *Declaration of the Rights of Man and of the Citizen* (1789); for a historical synthesis of national sovereignty from the French perspective, see Hauriou (2003), pp. 268–306.

> The principle of any Sovereignty lies primarily in the Nation. No corporate body, no individual may exercise any authority that does not expressly emanate from it.[16]

The first French Constitution, that of 1791, again enshrined this principle in its first article, as follows:

> Sovereignty is one, indivisible, inalienable and imprescriptible. It belongs to the Nation; no section of the people nor any individual may claim to exercise it.[17]

The first Spanish Constitution, the Cadiz Constitution of 1812, in the wake of French constitutionalism, included this principle,[18] which later exerted a notable influence in Europe and America.[19]

The ancient Roman principles according to which the will of the monarch has the force of law (*quod principi placuit legis habet vigorem*), [20] which, moreover, did not bind the monarch, who was above it (*princeps legibus solutus est*), [21] were thus repealed. A new system was introduced which, attributing sovereignty to the nation, established the principle of legislative supremacy, by which the law, in addition to being the expression of the general will, without discrimination of any kind,[22] guaranteed the freedom and natural rights of individuals,[23] set the limits of what was and was not enforceable,[24] indicated who could be prosecuted and convicted for the commission of a crime,[25] and allowed any public agent to be held accountable for the exercise of their office.[26]

---

[16] Art. 3 of the *Declaration of the Rights of Man and of the Citizen* (1789).

[17] Art. 1 of the French Constitution of 1791.

[18] In this regard, see my study Masferrer (2011), pp. 639–672.

[19] In this regard, see the work Escudero (2011), pp. 459–763.

[20] *Institutions* 4, 1.

[21] *Institutions* 3, 31; on this subject, see the now classic study Wyduckel (1979).

[22] Art. 6 of the *Declaration of the Rights of Man and of the Citizen*: "The law is the expression of the general will (...). All citizens have the right to take part, personally or through their representatives in its making (...). It must be the same for all, whether it protects or punishes. All citizens are equal before it..."; on this subject, see the studies Carré de Malberg (1931, 1998).

[23] Art. 4 of the *Declaration of the Rights of Man and of the Citizen*: "Liberty consists in being able to do everything that does not harm others: thus, the exercise of the natural rights of each man has more limits than those which assure to the other members of society the enjoyment of these same rights. These limits can only be determined by law".

[24] Art. 5 of the *Declaration of the Rights of Man and of the Citizen*: "The law can only prohibit actions harmful to society. Whatever is not forbidden by law cannot be prevented, and no one can be compelled to do what the law does not command".

[25] Art. 7 of the *Declaration of the Rights of Man and of the Citizen*: "No man may be accused, arrested or detained except in the cases determined by law, and in the manner prescribed by law (...). It is only when a citizen is called upon to obey by virtue of the law that he must obey immediately". Art. 8: "No one may be convicted except by virtue of a law established and promulgated prior to the offence".

[26] Art. 15 of the *Declaration of the Rights of Man and of the Citizen*: "Society has the right to call every public official for an accounting of his administration".

Now, just as the recognition of national sovereignty was a more than sufficient title for the organisation of the State with its various powers, it being understood that these had been "created" or constituted by the people or the sovereign nation, the same could not be said, however, concerning fundamental rights. These were understood not to emanate from sovereignty but from nature and could therefore only be recognised or declared, making it clear that such rights were natural, that is, corresponding to nature or inherent to the human being and, in any case, not susceptible to deprivation or alienation by means of any pact. This was expressed in Article I of the *Virginia Declaration of Rights*:

> That all men are by nature equally free and independent and have certain inherent rights, of which, when they enter into a state of society, they cannot, by any compact, deprive or divest their posterity; namely, the enjoyment of life and liberty, with the means of acquiring and possessing property, and pursuing and obtaining happiness and safety.

The text of the American *Declaration of Independence* went even further by affirming, after insisting on their inalienable character, "that to secure these rights, governments are instituted among men, deriving their just powers from the consent of the governed,"[27] that is, that it is the function of governments, whose power derives from the consent of the governed (sovereignty of the people or nation), to secure or guarantee such rights. Now, which rights were considered natural and, therefore inalienable? The *Declaration of Independence* expressly referred to the rights to life, liberty, and the pursuit of happiness. Four years later, in the ten articles of the first amendment to the American Constitution (1791), after enumerating some rights, it was expressly warned that "the enumeration in this Constitution, of certain rights, shall not be construed to deny or disparage others retained by the People."[28]

In the French context, the *Declaration of the Rights of Man and of the Citizen* stated in its very Preamble its purpose to "set forth, in a solemn declaration, the natural, inalienable and sacred rights of man, so that this declaration, constantly present to all members of the social body, may permanently remind them of their rights and duties." Finally, after pointing out that "men are born and remain free and equal in rights" (art. 1), it used a formula similar to the American *Declarations* of 1776:

> The aim of all political association is the preservation of the natural and imprescriptible rights of man. These rights are liberty, property, security, and resistance to oppression (art. 2).

The content of this precept is straightforward and leaves no room for interpretation. It is not in vain that it has been recognised that "respect for natural rights is objectively imposed on the social pact, thus marking its limits and giving it meaning" since "the affirmation, defence and protection of such rights (...) as the authentic *prius* and foundation of society, will constitute the criterion of the legitimacy of all

---

[27] Paragraph II of the Preamble to the *Declaration of Independence of the United States* (July 4, 1776).

[28] *The Ninth Amendment to the American Constitution* (December 15, 1791).

human coexistence, the limit and, at the same time, the meaning of the social pact."[29] Precisely because such rights were declared natural and imprescriptible, the French Constitution of 1791, in guaranteeing several of them in its Title I, provides that "the legislature may not make laws that infringe upon or obstruct the exercise of the natural and civil rights set forth in the present title and guaranteed by the Constitution."[30]

1.2.2 The Fragility of 'Fundamental Rights' in the Face of 'National Sovereignty' and the Law as 'Expression of the General Will'

As we have seen, it was precisely the protection of the fundamental rights of the individual that gave the liberal State its raison d'être while at the same time advising both the new structuring of the State into different powers (legislative, executive and judicial) and its deference to the Law.

The fact that the deference of all public authorities to the *rule of law* or legality (supremacy of the law, understood as the expression of the general will) and the safeguarding of fundamental rights were based on a fundamental political principle, the principle of national sovereignty, did not mean that the people or the nation could, in the use of its powers, restrict those fundamental rights which, being rooted in the nature of man, constituted a pre-political reality not only unavailable to the people or the nation, but also to the nation itself, which obliged the State to recognise and protect them.

While the recognition of national sovereignty was a more than sufficient title for the organisation of the State with its various powers, it being understood that these had been "created" or constituted by the people or the sovereign nation, the same could not be said, however, concerning fundamental rights. These rights were understood to emanate not from sovereignty but from nature and could therefore only be recognised or declared, making it clear that such rights were natural, that is, belonging to nature or inherent to the human being and, in any case, not susceptible to deprivation or alienation by means of any agreement.

Following this line of thought, all the first constitutional texts and Declarations—both European and North American—started from the existence of rights that, having their origin in nature and being 'inherent' to human beings, had a natural pre-political character, so that men, once they had constituted themselves in

---

[29] Díaz (1997), p. 238.

[30] It should be noted, however, that the French Revolutionaries quickly became "less revolutionary". In the various declarations of rights, the right of resistance to unjust government was soon suppressed, which is surprising because the first doctrines, which maintained that "power resides in the people", tended to start from the right of resistance to the prince who acted unjustly. They were soon dominated by the idea of the State as a finished "totum".

(political) society, could never be deprived or dispossessed of their inherent rights by means of any pact. This was expressed in Article I of the *Virginia Declaration of Rights*:

> That all men are by nature equally free and independent and have certain inherent rights, of which, when they enter into a state of society, they cannot, by any compact, deprive or divest their posterity; namely, the enjoyment of life and liberty, with the means of acquiring and possessing property, and pursuing and obtaining happiness and safety.

As we have seen, the text of the American *Declaration of Independence* went even further by affirming, after insisting on their inalienable character, "that to secure these rights, governments are instituted among men, deriving their just powers from the consent of the governed,"[31] that is to say, that it is the function of governments, whose power derives from the consent of the governed, to secure or guarantee such rights.

The Declaration of the Rights of Man and of the Citizen stated the same thing in its Preamble, setting out its raison d'être:

> ...to set forth, in a solemn declaration, the natural, inalienable and sacred rights of man, so that this declaration, constantly present to all members of the social body, may permanently remind them of their rights and duties.

As if that were not enough, after stating that "men are born and remain free and equal in rights" (art. 1), art. 2 provided:

> The aim of every political association is the preservation of the natural and imprescriptible rights of man....

Precisely because such rights were declared natural and imprescriptible, the French Constitution of 1791, in guaranteeing several of them in its Title I, provided:

> ...the legislature may not make laws which impair and interfere with the exercise of the natural and civil rights set forth in this title and guaranteed by the Constitution.

As can be seen, the idea that fundamental rights, being rooted in the very nature of the individual, are not available to the public authorities or to the people or nation in which sovereignty resides was at the basis of modern Western constitutionalism. So much so that later declarations and constitutional texts unequivocally embraced this same principle.

Thus, for example, the *Universal Declaration of Human Rights* (1948), in the first Recital of its Preamble, provides:

> ...recognition of the inherent dignity and of the equal and inalienable rights of all members of the human family is the foundation of freedom, justice and peace in the world.[32]

---

[31] Paragraph II of the Preamble to the *Declaration of Independence of the United States* (July 4, 1776).

[32] And in its 3rd Recital it qualifies as essential that "... human rights be protected by the rule of law, so that man may not be compelled to have recourse to the supreme remedy of rebellion against tyranny and oppression"; therefore, only in a State of Law in which such natural rights are effectively recognised and legally protected, should the individual not feel 'compelled to rebel

Article 1, in stating that "all human beings are born free and equal in dignity and rights. They are endowed with reason and conscience..." recognises that the dignity and the rights that derive from it do not derive from their status as political citizens but from their birth. Thus, the birth, dignity and rights of the human being constitute natural pre-political realities that the State is responsible for recognising and protecting.[33]

The current Spanish Constitution, whose Preamble contains a clear reference to the "Rule of Law that ensures the rule of Law as an expression of the popular will,"[34] with a final clause of apparent Rousseaunian influence—law as an expression of the general will—, expressly mentions both 'human dignity' and 'the inviolable rights that are inherent to it.'[35]

While it is true that modern Western constitutionalism harboured no doubt about the existence of natural rights, of a pre-political nature, whose recognition and protection constituted the raison d'être of the State, the question of which rights should be considered as natural was less clear.

Thus, for example, as we have seen, while the *Declaration of Independence* had expressly referred to the rights to life, liberty and the pursuit of happiness, a few years later, in the first ten Amendments to the American Constitution, after enumerating some rights, it expressly warned that "the enumeration in this Constitution of certain rights shall not be construed to deny or disparage others retained by the People."[36] For its part, the *Declaration of the Rights of Man and of the Citizen*, after

---

against tyranny and oppression'. Otherwise, that is, if the state were not capable of legally recognising and protecting such natural rights, then the individual could feel compelled to do so; see Stuurman (2017), Ch. 9, defending that the Universal Declaration of Human Rights was a product of thorough consideration and cross-cultural compromise that was agreeable to almost all the signatories. For Stuurman, the Declaration was not a "Western" document, even though its language about individual rights were mostly drawn from Western philosophy. In his view, the fundamental views of common humanity and personal dignity have always been shared throughout the world, even if the individualistic conception of the human person is somewhat of an European peculiarity.

[33] The idea that the Declarations and constitutional texts are limited to recognising the existence of rights, and not to 'creating' them according to the historical situation or the existing consensus at any given time, is another characteristic feature of modern constitutionalism. Along these lines, and by way of example, the European Convention on Human Rights (1950) provides, in its 2nd Recital, that "this declaration aims to ensure the universal and effective recognition and enforcement of rights...".

[34] Spanish Constitution of 1978, Preamble: "The Spanish Nation, desiring to establish justice, freedom and security and to promote the good of all its members, in the use of its sovereignty, proclaims its will to: guarantee democratic coexistence within the Constitution and the Laws in accordance with a just economic and social order; consolidate a State of Law that ensures the rule of Law as an expression of the popular will; protect all Spaniards and peoples of Spain in the exercise of human rights, their cultures and traditions, languages and institutions".

[35] Article 10.1 CE 1978: "The dignity of the person, the inviolable rights that are inherent to him/her, the free development of the personality, respect for the law and the rights of others are the foundation of political order and social peace".

[36] Art. 9 of the *Amendment to the American Constitution* (December 15, 1791).

affirming—in its Preamble—the existence of 'natural, inalienable and sacred rights of man', and pointing out—in its art. 2—that "the aim of every political association is the preservation of the natural and imprescriptible rights of man", states which are such rights: "These rights are liberty, property, security and resistance to oppression." Clearly, as the American constitutional text warned, the enumeration of such rights could not imply the denial or disregard of others.

This was not, however, the most fragile point of the fundamental rights and freedoms recognised at the very origins of modern constitutionalism. The most damaging and corrosive aspects—as the passage of time has shown—were the specific notions of sovereignty and law as 'the expression of the general will' introduced in the Declarations above and constitutional texts. These two concepts, by progressively losing their limits or their relative scope,[37] would end up being absolutised to the point of subverting the order established by our primitive modern constitutionalism, changing the natural and unavailable character of the fundamental rights on the part of the State into rights lacking any other foundation and legitimation than the one coming from the exercise of the sovereignty itself which, political reflection of the affirmation of the complete autonomy of the will,[38] without limits or pre-political referents of any kind, goes from recognising rights to 'creating' them through the law, on which, being the expression of the general will, there is no room for dissent. The individual can no longer invoke any right, however fundamental it may be, if it lacks express legal expression, regulation or recognition.[39]

This was the poisoned germ contained, in a latent way, in the first declarations and modern constitutional texts. And the passage of time has only confirmed its pernicious effects, introducing totalitarianism into the democratic State and the Rule of Law itself. This seed, present in the beginnings of modern constitutionalism in the West, came from the doctrine, both previous and contemporary. Its origins were remote but can be found in the philosophical context that goes through Descartes, Newton and Marx. Its effects were evident both in the philosophy of Law and in political philosophy, as well as in classic authors—some of them already mentioned—such as John Stuart Mill, Thomas Hobbes, John Locke, Jean-Jacques

---

[37] In relation to the need to establish limits, it has been said—and rightly so—that violence appears "as a denial of the respect due to the human person, who is reduced to a being to be exploited, humiliated or eliminated. The denial of respect is the result of excess, of *hybris*, of the lack of a sense of limit, which in each case arises as the unconditional primacy of profit, pleasure or the will to dominate" (Ballesteros (2006), p. 107).

[38] In this regard, see the study Cotta (1974), p. 14, in whose introductory study Jesús Ballesteros points out that "the connection between Sastre's denial of all essence, prior to existence, and his famous phrase in *Huis Clos*: 'hell are the others' is significant. If my freedom lacks intrinsic limits, imposed by my nature, it is the other who appears as a brake and limit to my freedom and therefore as an enemy".

[39] On the falsity of the principle according to which the fundamental rights of individuals necessarily require their express legal or constitutional embodiment in order for the legal system to be able to guarantee their effective safeguard, see Masferrer (2005), pp. 515–544.

Rousseau, Voltaire (François-Marie Arouet), Christian Wolff, Johann Gottlob Heineccius and Daniel Nettelbladt, among others.[40]

It is not that the theses of all these authors coincide in this respect. Still, they do show a gradual evolution whose outcome would be the denial of the (pre-political) dignity of the human being or, better, the rejection of the pre-political nature of fundamental rights and in the consequent absolutisation of both society and political power (State), denying the existence of a pre-political social dimension of the human being constitutive of an objective natural referent, setting itself up as an insurmountable barrier or a limit to the exercise of public power in the framework of a democratic State under the rule of law.[41] When this reality or pre-political dimension is denied, public power becomes all-embracing and absolute, leaving the individual defenceless and unprotected against a collective interest (embodied in the State and crystallised in the law) whose force is overwhelming. When this reality is denied, the thought arises that "the individual can be freed from all evil and reach his perfection *in* society and *by the work* of society", which ends up embodied in the State, this being *le grand tout* (Rousseau) or the *Totalität (*Hegel and Marx).[42]

This is particularly evident in the doctrines of Thomas Hobbes and Jean-Jacques Rousseau, the latter being probably—and in this respect—the author whose influence on the origins of our modern constitutionalism was most pernicious.[43] While a good part of modern thought maintains, starting from an Augustinian approach, that the political structure is necessary but provisional and imperfect (Locke, Montesquieu, Constant, Tocqueville and Rosmini, among others), appreciating "a healthy distrust of political power and stressing the need for its limitation and control, to make it responsible,"[44] other authors, as in the case of Rousseau, led to "the mythification of political power." [45]

Indeed, the Rousseauian notions of sovereignty and law as the expression of the general will introduced in the first Declarations and constitutional texts carried the germ above. A careful study of his work is enough to examine to what extent the State and the law are given an absolute value, placing them above—and not at the

---

[40] Regarding German or Central European authors, see the study Carpintero (2016a), pp. 35–58; I do not want to—and cannot—fail to take advantage of that first quotation to Professor Carpintero to thank him expressly for his patient reading of my manuscript, as well as his valuable comments on some of its parts; logically, any errors ('*errare humanum est*') are entirely mine.

[41] According to Thomas Hobbes, "individual rights-bearers do not possess rights because they are inscribed in nature or because they can be understood to be expressions of human reason, but only because they have been conferred by the sovereign's legislation" (Loughlin (2003), p. 86); these theses, which are still prevalent today, are defended by authors such as John Rawls and Ronald Dworkin, among others; in this regard, see the suggestive study Rhonheimer (2005), pp. 1–70.

[42] Ballesteros (1974), p. 16.

[43] In this regard, see the study Gearty (2010), p. 8, who attributes to Hobbes the fragility of fundamental rights and freedoms in Western legal culture: "...there is no doubt that Hobbes remains hugely influential (...). Hobbes's residual theory of liberty has proved of immense influence".

[44] For a manifestation of this conception, see López Ulla (1999); Pardo (1991), pp. 243–258.

[45] Ballesteros (1974), p. 16; on this subject, see also several studies by Cotta (1963, pp. 171–189; 1964; 1965).

service of—the individual. On the one hand, Rousseau presented the notions of sovereignty and law as closely linked[46] and defended, on the other, the superiority of the law as an expression of the general will, conferring on the law the force of democratic legitimacy.[47]

Now, what is the point of affirming that "the exercise of the natural rights of each man has no limits other than those that assure the other members of society the enjoyment of those same rights"[48] or that "the law can only prohibit actions that are harmful to society,"[49] if sovereignty has no limits and is precisely that which, at each historical moment, shapes—in the strict and absolute sense of the term—society, since neither limits imposed by the very dignity of the human being nor a social dimension of man prior to the political community are recognised?

This question, posed in this way, requires distinguishing two realities of different genesis, the one proper to modern natural law and the Rousseauian one.

About the first, modern natural law jumped directly, so to speak, from the individual to the State. This happened very clearly with Fernando Vázquez de Menchaca, who, following a line of thought very present in the *ius commune*, showed individuals dissatisfied with the '*status naturae*', fundamentally because they saw their 'natural freedom' restricted.[50] All these Romanists, from the eleventh to the sixteenth century, went from isolated individuals to a single political society, i.e., the state. For jurists before the sixteenth century, this was not real but rather the fruit of imagination. Still, this exercise of imagination permeated deeply into philosophical-political and legal culture: hence the scholastic defences of the individual liberties of the Indians.

The doctrine of the nominalist philosopher-theologians of the fifteenth century added to this legal jargon, namely that of John of Gerson—of extraordinary influence—Conrad of Summenhart and Gabriel Biel. Both lines—that is, the legal and the philosophical-theological—converged in Vázquez de Menchaca.[51] For these

[46] In Rousseau's view, the notions of sovereignty and Law as an expression of the general will were closely linked: "...sovereignty being nothing but the exercise of the general will, it can never be alienated, and the sovereign, who is nothing but a collective being, can only be represented by himself; power can be transmitted but not the will (...). For the same reason that the will is not alienable, it is also indivisible: because the will is general or it is not (...). It is important, then, for the formulation of the general will that there should be no partial society in the State and that each citizen should express his opinion exclusively according to his own understanding" (Rousseau (2007), p. 29).

[47] "Sovereignty cannot be represented for the same reason that it cannot be alienated; it consists essentially in the general will, and this cannot be represented: it is itself or it is another; there is no middle ground (...). Any law not ratified in person by the people is null and void; it is not a law. The English people believe they are free, but they are wrong, they are only free during the election of the members of Parliament" (text included in Jiménez (2003), p. 71); see also Jiménez (2001).

[48] Art. 4 of the *Declaration of the Rights of Man and of the Citizen* (see footnote n. 23).

[49] Art. 5 of the *Declaration of the Rights of Man and of the Citizen* (see footnote n. 24).

[50] In this regard, see Carpintero (1981).

[51] On this author, see the book—already classic—by Carpintero Benítez, F., on Vázquez de Menchaca, see Carpintero (1977).

authors, the important thing was the will because they understood that it was the only capacity of man capable of modifying his environment. All of them went 'directly', as has been said, from the individual to the State. They drew an imaginative straight line so that, *ex terminis*, whatever might lie between each individual and the political power, lacked explanation. It was not in vain that this new trend in the Modern Age received the name '*mos geometricus*': the family, religious confessions, and associations among citizens were understood as matters of "private law", which is the branch of law that deals with the utility of private individuals, that is, the egoism of private individuals. In his opinion, "public law", whose task is to attend to the public good, does not have to deal with these "intermediate" or "partial" societies. This line was followed by Francisco Suárez, in whom, as in Menchaca, the notion of subjective law as a proto-epiphany of the legal was united with nominalism. This whole procedure was confusing and plagued by contradictions.[52]

About the second, the Rousseaunian, this author started from a fabricated chassis on which he could build: the individuals in the *status naturae* that give rise to a unique political power. His anthropological vision was rather pessimistic in presenting the *status naturae* as composed of individuals indifferent to each other who lacked morality: they were neither good nor bad.[53] In his opinion, social life began with the private appropriation of land and, after a succession of changes, the current situation was reached: cowardly men without manhood, who hide behind their positions, money or titles. Faced with this reality, he sought a criterion or principle for justice.[54] He proposed to "universalise the individual", that is, to look for a common nerve in all the subjects in which each one of them recognises himself and realises himself. This is a difficult objective, because in the diaphanous transit from each man to the Power, there are "intermediate" societies that necessarily vitiate what he called the *volonté générale*. He did not trust the existing votes, which in his opinion, gave rise to what he called *volonté de tous*: they are rotten by money and by the influences of intermediate societies. Once the *volonté générale* was achieved, it deprived the existing wills of all their particular or egoistic notes, leaving only one will, the fully human will.

[52]For example, Vázquez, mocking the opposite opinion, declared Roman Law to have no legal value. Still, at the same time, he was a Romanist who based a good part of his opinions on this law and on jurists who were or had been Romanists. On the other hand, as a Jesuit, Suarez considered the validity of Canon Law absurd. But, at the same time, he strongly reinforced the existing order, understanding that everything that exists is the result of the contingent will of God, but He, being perfect, cannot contradict Himself and change the reason by which He has created us. Moreover, he left the legislative power so exclusively in the hands of the national Sovereign that he even denied that custom had the force of law, something that Vázquez de Menchaca did not do, who repeatedly affirmed that "*Vox populi, vox Dei*".

[53]The interpretation of some was that, in contrast to Hobbes' "*Homo homini lupus*", Rousseaun's anthropology was optimistic, and this does not quite fit in with the other sources.

[54]Let us bear in mind the importance of the "*principium unicum, evidens et adaequatum*" in modern ethico-political theories. In fact, this requirement was initially present, in the sixteenth century, in several Spaniards. According to this view, justice cannot be broken down into several principles because then there would be different versions of justices.

How to get to know this mystical *volonté générale*? It is certainly not easy if one wants to dispense—as Rousseau advocated—with real voting. In fact, he did not finish answering this question, although he implied that, if the State is *républicain*, the state will was the true general will.[55]

It could be said that with Rousseau absolutism was not banished, but simply changed venue, passing from the absolute monarch to a—supposed but unaffordable—general will that, without any theoretical limit, was doomed to a totalitarianism clothed in democratic legitimacy. [56]

In this sense, it is eloquent his defence of "...a form of government that puts the Law above Man", in which the individual would find freedom in the law.[57] In our opinion, Rousseau related the notions of sovereignty, law and freedom in a fictitious and unreal way, generating contradictions that are not easy to solve.

First of all, it is worth mentioning that the contradictions of the very concept of national sovereignty, described as a 'dogma' not infrequently,[58] with a 'supernatural force.' [59] A dogma or myth that, together with the cult of individual freedom,[60] could only end up denying and violating the rights of individuals,[61] since the general will

[55] There was an interesting discussion in the early twentieth century between Jellinek and Boutmy on the subject. Jellinek maintained that Rousseau had designed a totalitarian state. Boutmy, using more French esprit, reminded Jellinek of the Rousseauian pathos for liberty. It would be naive to think that this tendency ended in Rousseau. José Luis Díez-Picazo y Ponce de León, for example, understood that any political doctrine that placed any intermediate instance between the individual and the State was "totalitarian".

[56] Ballesteros (2006), p. 115: "Indeed, totalitarian democracy is possible and the revolutionary Convention proves it. It arises where the general will claims to be the supreme norm of justice, in such a way that it is necessary to alienate personal rights to the collective entity, to the whole, which results from such a general will. This absolutisation of the general will also lead logically to the elimination of dissidents, of those who oppose it, considering them as close to delinquents"; on totalitarianism and democracy in relation to Rousseau, see Talmon (1956), pp. 41 ff.

[57] In this line, Rousseau pointed out: "A free people obeys, but does not serve; it has chiefs but no masters; it obeys the laws, and it is by the force of the laws that it obeys men (...). A people is free, whatever the form of its government, when those who govern it do not see man, but the organ of the Law. In a word, liberty always follows the fate of the laws, it reigns or perishes with them; I know nothing that is more certain" (Rousseau (1964), p. 842); see Rousseau (2007); on the identification of wills between individual and Nation, of Rousseaunian origin, see Paine (1962), p. 243: "Every citizen is a sharer in sovereignty and as such cannot acknowledge personal subjection, but only obedience to the Law".

[58] Duguit (1922), p. 56; on Duguit's work and his critique of the notions of sovereignty (with respect to public law) and liberty (with respect to the sphere of private law), see the study Grimm (1973) (a review of this study can be found in the *Anuario de Filosofía del Derecho*, 1975, written by Jesús Ballesteros); see also Duguit (1913); for a reading of this book, see Loughlin (2016).

[59] Duguit (1922), p. 57.

[60] Duguit (1922), pp. 57–58: "Alongside the myth of national sovereignty, the cult of individual liberty was instituted".

[61] Duguit (1922), pp. 213–214: "Many theologians of individualism have endeavoured to explain it, but without succeeding, because they necessarily came either to make the sovereignty of the State disappear for the benefit of individual freedom, or to sacrifice the freedom of the individual completely to the sovereignty of the State, whatever the sophistry employed to keep the sovereignty

of the nation, contrary to the cliché of the liberal revolution,[62] should prevail over individual choices.[63] Hence, after the First World War, the French constitutionalist Jean Duguit fiercely criticised the liberal dogma of sovereignty and its primary author, Rousseau,[64] whom he called the 'pontiff of national sovereignty.'[65]

In reality, it was true that continental European Constitutionalism, unlike the North American, had not managed to protect the rights of individuals properly. It would be from the first half of the twentieth century, when a new European constitutionalism would emerge, recognising the normative value of the Constitution, and of which the Constitutions of Austria (1920), Italy (1947) and Germany (1949) would be precise exponents. However, these reforms did not resolve the question of the protection of fundamental rights in the State of Law, which continues to be weighed down by the paradoxes and inadequacies of the original principle of national sovereignty,[66] which allows the State or political power to tend to absolutise itself and cover everything, reducing the scope of freedom of the individual to unsuspected limits. It is the era of a constitutional State which, undermined by the utilitarian and relativist currents, was proven to be incapable of enforcing the fundamental rights of the individual in the face of an excessive exercise of public power which, protected by a supposed democratic legitimacy, lacks limits and bursts

---

of the State intact, while trying to maintain the rights of the individual"; see, in this respect, the following texts of Rousseau: "It is agreed that whatever each one alienates from his liberty is only that part whose use is of importance to the community. It must also be agreed that only the sovereign can judge this importance" (Rousseau (2007), Book II, Ch. IV); "The union [resulting from the social contract] is as perfect as it can be, and no associate has any claim to it, for if any right were left to the individual, as there would be no common superior who could stand between them and the public, the association would necessarily become tyrannical or vain" (Rousseau (2007), Book I, Ch. IV).

[62] A synthesis of the myth of a self-sufficient society as a reaction against the absolute State can be found in García de Enterría (1981), pp. 13–31.

[63] This means that "the individual, finding the fullness of his being only in the State, the State can be all-powerful without the autonomy of the individual being diminished. Rousseau does not say otherwise when he affirms that by virtue of the social contract which creates the collective will, individuals, obeying this will, obey only themselves. The more powerful this collective will is, the more powerful are the individuals themselves, since it is made up only of individual wills. To affirm the unlimited sovereignty of the collective will of the State is thus to affirm the unrestricted sovereignty of the individual. Individual autonomy acquires reality in the sovereignty of the State and exists by reason of this sovereignty" (Duguit (1922), pp. 215–216).

[64] Duguit (1922), p. 214: "The initiator of these sophisms is, indisputably, J.J. Rousseau, who by a singular error is often cited as the inspirer of the liberal doctrines of the Declaration of Rights promulgated in 1789, when, on the contrary, he is the initiator of all the doctrines of dictatorship and tyranny, from the Jacobin doctrines of 1793 to the Bolshevik doctrines of 1920 (...). It is enough to open the *Social Contract* to see how J.J. Rousseau unreservedly sacrifices the rights of the individual to the omnipotent power of the State".

[65] Duguit (1922), p. 285.

[66] In this regard, see Kotzour (2003).

into the sphere of individual liberties. Relativism, by denying the universality of human rights,[67] ends up decisively conditioning their content and scope.[68]

1.3 The Defence of Human Rights in the Early Modern Period (Sixteenth to Seventeenth Centuries)

The human rights claimed after the Second World War had their precedent-and most direct reference—in the liberal Revolutions and the Enlightenment thinking of the eighteenth century. However, these rights did not emerge from the Enlightenment, nor was this current of thought the cradle where they were born since they had already been defended and developed in the sixteenth and seventeenth centuries. Three major events took place in these centuries, the circumstances of which gave a decisive impetus to the defence of human rights. We refer to the following:

1. Spanish colonisation in America and the contribution of Bartolomé de las Casas and the school of the Second Scholasticism (with Francisco de Vitoria, Domingo de Soto, Fernando Vázquez de Menchaca, Francisco Suárez, etc.);
2. The Peace of Augsburg (25 September 1555) did not prevent the Thirty Years' War, with the signing of the Peace of Westphalia (with its two peace treaties of Osnabrück and Münster, signed on May 15 and October 24, 1648), thanks to which a space of freedom and religious tolerance was established in a social and political context that envisages division, discrepancy and confrontation for religious reasons
3. The Glorious Revolution (1688) in the United Kingdom and its corollary with the approval of the '*Bill of Rights*' of 1689, which the English Parliament imposed on Prince William of Orange in order to succeed the monarch, James II. Let us now look briefly at the contribution of these events and texts to the formation and development of human rights in the West

1.3.1 Spanish Colonisation in America: Natural Rights and Their Universal Nature

After the discovery of America by Christopher Columbus (1492), and by the four bulls that Alexander VI, at the request of Queen Isabella, granted to Castile (1493), the colonisation of the New World began and, with it, a new historical phase began,

---

[67] See Goodale (2011); Morsink (1999); Kotzour (2005).

[68] See, in this regard, some of the works of Ernst-Wolfgang Böckenförde, Böckenförde (1987, 2002, 2007); see also Renteln (1985); Kleinig (1981); more specifically and in relation to terrorism, see Kleinig (2007).

that is, the Modern Age. Expectations and hopes were placed on the American territories, whose population needed to be evangelised (religious objective: 'God'), whose lands had to be explored and exploited if necessary (economic and scientific objectives: 'Gold' & 'Glory').

It soon became clear that the economic interest ('Gold') of some colonisers and *encomenderos*, who treated the natives—the indigenous or Indians—who worked on their properties (called '*encomiendas*') in an ignominious and inhuman way, was a more important objective than their evangelisation, education and culturisation. In some cases, the mistreatment of the Indians was not only due to the excessive greed and desire for the economic benefit of the *encomenderos* but also to the lack of recognition of the dignity of these people, who were considered more like slaves than free people.[69]

This attitude, so little in keeping with the Christian spirit that was supposed to inform the whole colonising enterprise, was noticed by some colonisers, whose voices were soon heard. This was the case of Bro Antonio Montesino who, on Sunday, December 21, 1511, after reading the passage from the Gospel of St. John where it says: "I am a voice crying in the wilderness" (Jn 1, 23), pronounced, from the pulpit of a church in Santo Domingo—and in the name of the whole first Dominican community in the New World—a memorable sermon (known as the 'Advent Sermon'), of which we only mention here its forceful beginning:

> I am the voice of one crying in the wilderness. In order to make your sins known to you I have mounted this pulpit, I who am the voice of Christ crying in the wilderness of this island; and therefore it behooves you to listen to me, not with indifference but with all your heart and senses; for this voice will be the strangest, the harshest and hardest, the most terrifying that you ever heard or expected to hear... This voice declares that you are in mortal sin, and live and die therein by reason of the cruelty and tyranny that you practice on these innocent people. Tell me, by what right or justice do you hold these Indians in such cruel and horrible slavery? By what right do you wage such detestable wars on these people who lived mildly and peacefully in their own lands, where you have consumed infinite numbers of them with unheard of murders and desolations? Why do you so greatly oppress and fatigue them, not giving them enough to eat or caring for them when they fall ill from excessive labors, so that they die or rather are slain by you, so that you may extract and acquire gold every day? And what care do you take that they receive religious instruction and come to know their God and creator, or that they be baptized, hear mass, or observe holidays and Sundays? Are they not men? Do they not have rational souls? Are you not bound to love them as you love yourselves? How can you lie in such profound and lethargic slumber? Be sure that in your present state you can no more be saved than the Moors or Turks who do not have and do not want the faith of Jesus Christ.[70]

---

[69] This was not the same in all cases, in fact far from it, and the treatment of the indigenous population by the Spanish colonisers was not worse than in other countries, despite what an anti-Spanish and anti-Catholic historiographic current has wanted to show. Thus, for example, Hernán Cortés was motivated by a sincere desire for evangelisation. He did not trust the secular clergy and eventually brought religious Franciscans, even though the Spanish Crown was not based on the Franciscans, but on the Augustinians.

[70] For a version of the sermon with language appropriate to the historical moment, see the one given in the main text of footnote n. 147 in Part II; see Loewenstein (1945), p. 273: "Western civilization

Such a clear and forceful sermon in a church packed to overflowing, and before such a qualified audience (which included the main colonial authorities, among them Admiral Diego de Colón, son of the conqueror, as well as the clergyman Bartolomé de Las Casas, in his capacity as *encomendero*), produced in many a reaction of anger and open rejection. After the Mass, Diego de Colón and several royal officials went to the Dominican convent to reprimand the preacher for the scandal sown in the city, accusing him of 'making a disservice of' the King and demanded that he recant in public the following Sunday. A week later, Fray Antonio Montesino took the pulpit again, but not only did he not recant, but he delivered a much more belligerent speech in favour of the Indians, in which he defended five principles: (1) that the laws of religion are above the laws of individuals and the State; (2) that there are no racial differences in the sight of God; (3) that slavery and servitude are unlawful; (4) that the Indians should be restored to their liberty and property; and (5) that the Indians should be converted to Christianity by example. Such a sermon provoked an even greater feeling of revulsion than that of the previous Sunday, and the royal officials sent letters of protest against the friars to the king.

Fray Antonio Montesino was sent to Spain to give account and reason to the king for the content of his sermon. Overcoming the impediments, he finally managed to meet with King Ferdinand, to whom he presented an extensive memorial of the grievances of the conquerors against the Indians: launching a war on peaceful and meek people, entering their homes and taking their wives, daughters, sons and farms, imposing forced labour in the mines and other delirious acts and violations against their lives and physical integrity.

King Ferdinand, after listening to Fray Antonio Montesinos and a representative of the *encomenderos*, Fray Alonso de Espinar, ordered a board to be made to study the situation of the Indians. In this board meeting (*Junta*), which was held in Burgos in 1512, the first regulations were approved—sanctioned by the aforementioned king on 27 December—in defence of the natives, and concluded that, although the Spanish monarchy enjoyed the just titles of dominion of the American continent, the Indian had the legal nature of a free man with all the rights of property, and that, therefore, he could not be exploited, although he should work in favour of the crown as a subject, with the Spaniards settled there, for which purpose two Indian institutions had been created: the '*requerimiento*' and the '*encomienda*'. This conclusion, although not entirely satisfactory, did constitute a notable advance, since the Indians were recognised as free human beings and, therefore, with the right to property. The conclusions of the board meeting in Burgos (Junta de Burgos) were the final result of two conflicting legal-theological positions, namely (a) that which established the supremacy of a supernatural—or spiritual—right to the point of invalidating natural law, so that pagans could be subjected to force because, being in original sin and outside the grace of God, they lacked rights; and (b) that which upheld the autonomy of the supernatural from the natural, so that man could not be deprived of his natural

of our day is predominantly determined by the values of individual liberty, inherited from Greek philosophy, Roman law and the teachings of Christianity."

attributes, of political rights, of property and of cultural determination, which always accompany man, inasmuch as original sin does not change human nature or invalidate man's rights.

On August 15, 1514, Bro Bartolomé de las Casas (1484–1566), after a process of conversion by the example of some (like that of the Dominican Montesino) and the impact of other episodes (like that of the massacre of Caonao, 1513), pronounced, at the age of 30, he gave a sermon in *Sancti Spíritus*, in which, besides criticising the treatment of the Indians by the Spaniards, he announced—to everyone's astonishment—that he was giving up all his *encomiendas* (which, at that time, were substantial). In just 3 years, De las Casas went from supporting the interests of the *encomenderos* and other colonisers—even showing his most heartfelt rejection of Montesino's sermon—to being the staunchest defender of the Indians in America. De las Casas was a staunch critic against the enslavement of the Indians, pointing out that, since they had the use of reason and were, therefore rational creatures, they were as human beings as the ancient Greeks and Romans. And as human beings, the Indians were protected by natural law and were, consequently, entitled to the right to liberty and to govern themselves, being able to appoint their own authorities.

From then until his death in Madrid in 1566, De las Casas devoted himself completely to the defence of the Indians. In addition to meeting with King Ferdinand, when he was already very old and in poor health, he also met with Charles I in 1540. This one, worried by the situation of the Indians in America that De las Casas exposed and having knowledge of the new ideas of the law of nations spread by Francisco de Vitoria, chose to summon the Council of the Indies through the *Board of Valladolid* (*Junta de Valladolid*) (1542), for which he gave appointment to the most important European theologians and jurists. According to the conclusions of that Board, contained in the *New Laws*, approved by the aforementioned monarch on November 20, 1542, the slavery of the Indians was prohibited, and it was ordered that all were free from the *encomenderos*, remaining under the direct protection of the Crown. In addition, it was stipulated, in relation to the penetration of hitherto unexplored lands, that these enterprises should always involve two religious, who would ensure that contacts with the Indians were carried out peacefully, leading to a dialogue that would lead to their conversion. *The New Laws* were undoubtedly one of Charles I's greatest contributions to the law of nations, thanks in large part to the influence of Fray Bartolomé de las Casas and Francisco de Vitoria.

Bartolomé de las Casas's contribution to the theory and practice of human rights is contained in his *Brevísima Relación de la Destrucción de las Indias*, a work that, completed in Valencia in 1542, and is considered by some to be the first modern account of human rights. There he described the atrocities to which the Indians in the Americas were subjected by the Spanish *conquistadors*. In his *History of the Indies* he further developed the abuses described in the *Brevísima*. Some have claimed that the Dominican exaggerated in his description of the abuses. Others have demonstrated the veracity of such abuses. In any case, it is indisputable that this stark—and, at times, impudent—way of describing such abuses and atrocities was intended to capture and attract the attention of the monarchy and other authorities who could change the course of events.

Was the opinion of Bartolomé de las Casas shared by the other ecclesiastics, as well as by the highest authority of the Church? The answer is that it was not with regard to the former, but it was with regard to the latter. In fact, not all the ecclesiastics shared the opinion of the Dominican De las Casas, who earned the enmity of many who had previously considered him as a friend, as he himself relates in his work. Some ecclesiastics, following the Aristotelian arguments on slavery, argued that it was not convenient to recognise the freedom of the Indians. This was the case of Pedro Mártir de Anglería, as he wrote in a letter to the Archbishop of Cosenza in 1525:

> Long experience, indeed, has shown the necessity of their being slaves, and not free, those who by nature are prone to abominable vices, and who, lacking guides and tutors, return to their impudent errors. We have called to our Council of the Indies the two-coloured Dominican friars and the Franciscan discalced friars, who have long resided in those countries, and have asked their mature opinion on this point. All, in agreement, agreed that there was nothing more dangerous than to let them go free.

However, it was Juan Ginés de Sepúlveda who was the best-known author in the Aristotelian defence, especially in his second essay (*Demócrates Segundo*).[71] He and Bartolomé de Las Casas met in Valladolid in 1550 to discuss the great problem concerning the American Indians, and Sepúlveda was "the opponent of Father Las Casas". The disagreement centred on the causes that could justify the war against the Indians. Juan Ginés de Sepúlveda proposed four: (1) "Natural servitude of the Indians", (2) "Obligation to eliminate the human sacrifices and anthropophagy practiced by the Indians", (3) "Obligation, by natural right, to free the innocents sacrificed in such rites", and (4) "To favour the preaching of Christianity". All of them were rejected by Las Casas.[72] Regarding the first, Sepulveda stated:

> There are also other causes which justify wars; one of them, the most applicable to these barbarians vulgarly called Indians, is the following: that those barbarians whose natural condition is such that they must obey others, if they refuse the rule of the latter and no other recourse remains, should be subdued by arms, for such a war is just according to the opinion of the most eminent philosophers, among them Aristotle.[73]

This was not, however, the opinion of the pontiff, who in the first half of the sixteenth century made a clear pronouncement in this regard. In this regard, Pope Paul III, responding to a consultation of the Mexican bishop Julian Garces, published in 1537 the bull 'Sublimus Dei' or 'Sublimis Deus' and the brief *Pastorale Officium*,

[71] de Sepúlveda (1984).

[72] In this regard, see Maestre (2004).

[73] This reasoning was not accepted by Las Casas, who replied: "One cannot generalise the argument of "barbarism" without further ado and, relying, as Sepúlveda does, on the authority of Aristotle, apply it to the Indians of America.... First of all, it is necessary to define the concept of 'barbarism'... 'the different classes of barbarians' and to see in which of these the Indians fall, if they fall into any"; texts collected by Maestre (2004), pp. 117–118.

which were a milestone and managed to settle, at least from a theoretical point of view, the controversy. These pontifical documents recognised the human nature of the Indian and the right to his freedom, prohibiting the enslavement of the Indians. In addition, they emphasised the eminently voluntary character that conversion had to have, proposing new methods of penetration and evangelisation. This is how a fragment of the 'Sublimis Deus' (2 June 1537) read:

> We hereby determine and declare that the said Indians, and all peoples who in the future shall come to the knowledge of the Christians, although they live outside the Christian faith, may freely and lawfully use, possess and enjoy their liberty and the dominion of their property, that they shall not be reduced to servitude, and that all that would have been done otherwise is null and void.

Although the Catholic monarchies did not always manage to implement this pontifical doctrine—even in spite of the legislation passed along these lines—, nor did some ecclesiastics and many laymen who were not willing to diminish the substantial benefits that their ruthless attitude towards the natives brought them, the fact is that the pontifical magisterium in this regard was already very clear from that time on.

To the contribution of Bartolomé de las Casas in the defence of the indigenous in the political and social sphere of colonisation (which in Portugal would have its homonym in the Jesuit António Vieira), we must add that it was carried out, in the academic and cultural sphere, by some authors of the Second Scholasticism, whose influence had an even greater reach than that of Bartolomé de las Casas. This is the case of Fernando Vázquez de Menchaca, Francisco de Vitoria and Domingo de Soto, among others. Outside the scope of this doctrinal current, although impregnated with the theses of some of these authors, it is worth mentioning the figure of Hugo Grotius, who is considered, together with Francisco de Vitoria, Fernando Vázquez de Menchaca and Alberico Gentile, the founder of the modern Law of Nations or International Law.

Francisco de Vitoria (1483–1546) supported, logically, the theories of De las Casas on the existence of an essential humanity common to all men independently of their indigenous character, defending, therefore, the human condition of the Indians, and the possession of an autonomous original power, from which other rights were derived, such as that of property over their lands. In his works *De Indis prior* and *De Indis posterior sive de Iure belli* (1539) he denounced the excesses committed in the American lands.

His *Relectio de Indis*, a short work that he delivered orally at the University of Salamanca around January 1, 1539, contains the fundamental keys to his vision of overcoming a medieval theocracy based on legal principles that tended to identify the natural order with the supernatural and to transpose the attributions of temporal power to the spiritual. According to Vitoria, dominion is not based on grace—as the Waldensians, among others, defended—but on human nature, on man as the image of God that he is. And being the image of God corresponds to the natural order, by virtue of his rational nature, not to the supernatural order or the order of grace. It is precisely the rational powers that allow man to have dominion over his acts, since, following Thomas Aquinas, whom he quotes, "a person is master of his acts when he can choose this or that" (S.Th. I-II, 82, I, ad 3). Thus, if man's capacity for mastery derives from his personal condition—self-mastery—no sin or infidelity—which causes him to lose supernatural goods, but not his personal condition—prevents man from being master of his goods. This doctrine, besides disqualifying the theory of grace as a title to natural dominion, also denied the alleged Aristotelian thesis—supported by some authors—of natural slavery. At that time, to base the title of legal dominion on the nature of the human person, without using any argument of a supernatural nature, was a novelty although, in reality, it was not.[74] Vitoria had based himself on the doctrine of Thomas Aquinas, but his coherent systematisation applied to a concrete case constituted, without any doubt, a novelty.[75]

The consequences of this novel approach to the question were not minor, given that it affected the rights granted to the Catholic Monarchs through the papal bulls of Pope Alexander VI (1493). In other words: if the Indians were the true owners, the donations by means of such bulls lacked legitimacy. In fact, Francisco de Vitoria denied the legitimacy of such rights to the Catholic Monarchs. And the reason was quite simple: the world must be governed by natural law, and war is governed by a law of *ius gentium*. In this sense, if the Indians were forming their own organised states, war could only be declared against them if they denied other peoples the rights of the natural order, as would be the case if they prevented trade, evangelisation or peaceful relations between peoples. If the titles granted by the Pope to the Catholic Monarchs were not legitimate, Vitoria explained why such legal titles did not legitimise the occupation of America, and which, being just (hence, 'Just Titles'), could really justify the presence of the Spaniards in America.

Among the non-legitimate titles were—in the opinion of the Dominican from Burgos—that of the universal dominion of the Emperor and that of the universal temporal dominion of the Pope.

Disagreeing with jurists of the stature of Bártolo de Sassoferrato and Baldo de Ubaldis, the professor from Salamanca claimed not to find in natural, divine and human rights any title that attributed to the emperor the dominion over the whole universe. In his opinion, if all men are free and equal, the foundation of public powers could only be found, together with the social nature of man, in the agreement of free human wills and in positive law. Hence, as history shows, the consensus of

[74] In fact, it was not really a novelty. This doctrine had been held by Valdo and Wycliffe and, more recently, by Armachanus (Richardus Fiztralph), bishop of a French diocese. It was not accepted by any Catholic other than Armachanus. And, before him, it is worth mentioning that the nominalist current, which followed the theory of "*In puris naturalibus*", according to which men have two ultimate ends, the natural and the supernatural. This current led to a human-rational knowledge that led to sustaining the rational validity of the natural law with the well-known formula *Etiamsi Deus non daretur*, which many attribute to Hugo Grotius, but which was already very present before the thirteenth century, for example, in John Duns Scotus. That is why Thomas Aquinas chose to be so concerned with combating it in his youthful work (*The Commentaries on the Sentences*).

[75] In this regard, see Fazio (2006), pp. 33–38, in particular, pp. 33–34.

the members of a community has been a decisive element in the process of the formation of nations.[76]

On the other hand, with regard to the Pope's supposed title of universal power, Vitoria denied that the Pope had such secular power throughout the world, and even less that he could transmit it to the secular princes. What the Pope did have, according to the Dominican master, was the temporal power in order to spiritual things, that is, that which was strictly necessary to administer spiritual goods. Consequently, the Pope had no temporal power over barbarians and infidels, and he could not make war against them or occupy their goods, even if they were unwilling to recognise any power over him:

> The pope is not the civil and temporal lord of the whole world, speaking of civil dominion and power in the proper sense (...); since the supreme pontiff would have such secular power over the whole world, he could not transmit it to the secular princes (...); the pope has temporal power over spiritual things, that is, insofar as it is necessary to administer spiritual things (...).(...); the Pope has temporal power in order to spiritual things, that is, in so far as it is necessary to administer spiritual things (...); the Pope has no power over those barbarians or over the other infidels (...); even if the barbarians do not wish to recognise any dominion of the Pope, one cannot therefore make war against them or occupy their goods.[77]

It might be surprising to note how Vitoria arrived at anti-theocratic conclusions, using arguments of reason and resorting to theological sources (Sacred Scripture and the Fathers of the Church). But that is how it was. His Christian humanism led him to distinguish the permanent elements from the circumstantial ones, that is, from those that came from the historical or circumstantial political tradition, and the result was an important and novel contribution in its formulation: he showed that rights (natural or human) come from the natural order (nature), and that they are not—nor can they be—suppressed by the supernatural order (grace), although they are—or can be—incorporated and elevated by grace.

His defence of the natural order allowed him to reject coercion in matters of faith. In this sense, for Vitoria the act of believing, besides being a gift of God, should be completely free. Following the doctrine of Thomas Aquinas, he warned that Christian truth could not be compelled or imposed by force, since this would violate the intimate sphere of personal conscience. This had obvious consequences for American colonisation, to which he made express reference:

> Even if the faith has been proclaimed to the barbarians in a probable and sufficient way and they have not wanted to receive it, it is not lawful, for this reason, to make war against them or to deprive them of their goods.[78]

In spite of everything, Vitoria was not against the Spanish presence in America, but the titles that justified colonisation had to be different. It was in the development of

[76] In this regard, it is useful to bring up the well-known distinction between title and cause: the ultimate title of political society was the necessity and the will to live together, while the proximate cause on which the prince could base his power was the consent of his subjects.

[77] de Vitoria (1960), pp. 678–682 (text collected by Fazio (2006), p. 36).

[78] de Vitoria (1960), p. 695 (text taken from Fazio (2006), p. 36).

these 'just titles' that he laid the foundations of an international law, non-existent until then. Breaking with the medieval vision of a Christendom, composed of the various Christian nations of Western Europe, Vitoria argued for the existence of an international community (which he called *Totus Orbis*) made up of all peoples and nations with equal rights, and governed by a law of nations (*ius gentium*) that came from natural law.[79]

What, then, were the just titles that could legitimise Spanish colonisation in America?

According to Vitoria, the natural right of communication came first. As both Spaniards and Indians were part of the same community, the Spaniards could settle in America—as the Indians in Spain—as long as no rights of the Indians were infringed. If "friendship among men is of natural right, and it would be contrary to nature to refuse the company of men who do no wrong," it would be unjust for the Indians to oppose that natural right of communication. Along with this title, he also defended others such as freedom of navigation and trade—which, in this case, came from the law of nations—, the right to equal treatment and reciprocity, the right to choose nationality, the right of evangelisation—respecting the freedom of the Indians—, or that of 'humanitarian interference', among others. With regard to the latter, it states:

> Another title may be the tyranny of the barbarians themselves, or tyrannical laws against the innocent, such as those which command the slaughter of innocent men, or the killing of guiltless men to eat them.

According to the Dominican from Burgos, above the positive laws of a nation are the laws of humanity, framed in the sphere of natural and divine law. There would be no justification, therefore, for the passivity of other nations when the positive laws of a nation were tyrannical and oppressed its citizens. This title could legitimise the intervention of the Spaniards, on behalf of the international community, to safeguard the innocent from an unjust death, but it should cease immediately when the injustices that caused it were put to an end.

> For Francisco de Vitoria, these were the legitimate titles of conquest of new territories:
>
> 1. Men are not born slaves but free.
> 2. By natural right no one is superior to the others.
> 3. The child does not exist because of others, but because of himself.
> 4. It is better to renounce one's own right than to violate the rights of others.
> 5. It is lawful to man, private property, but no one is an owner who must not, at times, share his things... and in extreme necessity, all things are common.
> 6. The perpetually insane, who neither have, nor can hope to have, the use of reason, can be owners... they have rights.
> 7. It is lawful for a man condemned to death to flee, because liberty is equated with life.
> 8. If the judge, not observing the order of law, were to obtain the confession of the accused by torture, the judge could not condemn the accused, for in so doing he is not a judge.
> 9. You cannot put to death a person who has not been tried and convicted.

[79] Fazio (2006), p. 37.

10. Every nation has the right to govern itself and can accept the political regime it wants, even if it is not the best.
11. All the king's power comes from the nation, because the nation is free from the beginning.
12. The whole orb, which in a certain sense constitutes a republic, has the power to give just and convenient laws to all mankind.
13. No war is just, if it is known to be waged for more harm than good and for the good of the nation, no matter how many titles and reasons there may be for a just war.
14. If the subject is aware of the injustice of war, he cannot go to war, not even by the prince's command.
15. It is not man the wolf for man, but man.

In his work *De potestate civili* (1528) he had already laid the theoretical foundations of modern international law. There he proposed the idea of a community of all the peoples of the world based on natural law, while rejecting the use of force as the basic instrument for the articulation of international relations. Moreover, by basing this global community on a natural law that set moral limits, he distanced himself from the thesis of Niccolò Machiavelli. According to Machiavelli, the state was a morally autonomous entity, so that, since it could not be judged according to external norms, its power was omnipotent or unlimited, everything being considered valid as long as power was maintained or, in other words—and even changing its meaning—as long as it remained in power. Hence the expression 'Machiavellian', whose meaning refers to the cunning or absolute lack of scruples that someone exhibits in pursuing what he intends.[80]

After his death, De las Casas and other of his disciples (Melchor Cano, Domingo de Soto, Bartolomé de Carranza) used these arguments of Vitoria against Juan Ginés de Sepúlveda in the Junta de Valladolid (1550–1551), distinguishing, within the framework of the so-called 'polemic of the natives', the just titles from the unjust ones with respect to the conquest of America.

In short, with the affirmation that the Indians were not inferior beings, but possessed the same rights as any human being, and that they were, consequently, owners of their goods and lands, the modern Law of Nations or International Law began, and its author became one of its founders.

Hugo Grotius (1583–1645), considered by many to be the father of international law, also addressed the question of the Indians in America in his works *De Indis* (*On the Indies*) written in 1604–1605 and published in 1868 with the title *De Jure Praedae* (*On the Right of Capture*). He agreed with Vitoria's doctrine regarding the rights of the Indians to the ownership of their lands, as well as in relation to their condition as human beings, although he emphasised the existence of notorious differences with the rest of human beings. In his most important work, *De jure belli ac pacis* (*On the Law of War and Peace*), first published in Paris in 1625 (and shortly afterwards reprinted for a second time in Amsterdam, 1631), he also argued

[80]The RAE includes the following three meanings of this adjective: 1. Belonging or relating to Machiavelli or Machiavellianism; 2. For its part, www.wordreference.com is even more explicit: "Having characteristics considered characteristic of Machiavellianism, such as perfidy, unscrupulousness or cunning".

that in international relations there was no distinction to be made between Christian and infidel nations, for they were all part of the same international (or global) community, which was to be governed by a law of nations that came from right reason and whose existence could be proved rationally, without recourse to God or to the supernatural order or grace ('even if we were to concede that God does not exist', or '*etiamsi daremus (...) non esse Deum*'). According to Grotius, this natural right "would take place even if we were to concede—something that cannot be conceded without committing the greatest crime—that God does not exist or that He is not concerned with the human."[81]

> This text has been the object of some interpretations far removed from its meaning, having gone so far as to manipulate the literal tenor of the text, changing the concessive conjunction *etiamsi* (although) for the modal conjunction "as if" (*ut si*), introducing a further simplification: "as if God did not exist" (*ut si Deus non existeret*), when the literal text reads as follows: *locum aliquem haberent, etiamsi daremus, quod sine summo scelere dari nequit, non esse Deum, aut non curari ab eo negocia humana. Therefore the literal expression would be 'etiamsi daremus (...) non esse Deum'*. The most widespread version is *etsi Deus non daretur*.

Grotius did not deny that this natural law also found its foundation in God or in the divine will, but in dealing—as Francisco de Vitoria did—with an international law that was composed of Christian and non-Christian nations, thus overcoming the medieval vision of the world as Christendom or Christian Empire, and to establish the natural order common to all mankind, it should be this natural law or law of nations, coming from right reason, the proper foundation for this new order *orbis*, and not a superior order (divine or supernatural) that did not have to be shared by all. For his part, Vitoria's novelty, for which he is called the father of international law, was that he went from considering the law of nations as a legal order that is

[81] Grotius (1625b), *Prolegomena*, n.11; it should be noted, however, that this approach to ethics and law did not originate with Hugo Grotius (1583–1645) or, therefore, with Protestantism, but almost two centuries earlier with authors such as John of Gerson (1363–1429) and his disciple Conrad of Summenhart or Gabriel Biel (1420–1495), among others. The latter, a notably active Catholic thinker, wrote: "Nam per si impossibile Deus non esset, qui est ratio divina: aut ratio illa divina esset errans, adhuc si quis ageret contra recta rationem angelicam, vel humanam, vel aliam aliquam, si qua esset, peccaret. Peccatum est voluntaria carentia conformitatis ad rationem rectam debiti voluntati" (Biel (1574), L. II, Dist. 28, quaestio unica, p. 165-E). In short, in posing the question of what would happen if God were dispensed with, Biel already held that the ethical or moral contents of reason would remain the same even if God did not exist—a sin against what reason shows would be a 'rational' sin—so that what is good is good and what is evil is evil "even if God did not exist" ("*Etiamsi Deus non daretur*"); in this regard, see Carpintero (2017), where he argues that "the thesis of the validity of natural law *Etiamsi Deus non daretur* was a creation of the Nominals who, since they denied that natural law could consist of a "real" or metaphysical order, maintained that it existed only under formal or modal mode. In this way it undoubtedly exists in the heads of men, and whoever denies any of its precepts opposes God, who is the one who gave us the reason we currently have" (Carpintero (2017), pp. 184–185); on this doctrine in Gabriel Biel, two centuries before Grotius, see also López Hernández (1998), p. 226; for another view, see Hervada (1987), pp. 266–268, for whom Grotius was the first to defend this thesis, because previous theologians had shown, in his opinion, an "analogised" being, so that human reason could change by being only analogous to divine reason.

universally in force, to expounding it as a *jus "inter" gentes*. The new context, as well as the problems that arose with the conquest and colonisation of the New World, led to the emergence of international law or law of nations, to move from a national to a global law, from an *ius urbi* to an *ius orbi*, for which the concepts of (national) sovereignty and positive laws were insufficient. The theologians, philosophers and jurists of this time had to face this challenge and the result was the creation of an international law that was to protect all people equally, regardless of their origin, ethnicity or religion. These rights, also known as natural rights, would be the object of study throughout the sixteenth and seventeenth centuries, would be at the basis of the great revolutions—such as the American and French—of the eighteenth century, and would be embodied—as fundamental rights—in the nineteenth-century constitutions, which were—as we have seen—the most direct and closest precedent of the 'human rights' of the twentieth century.

Unfortunately, the theses regarding the Indians held by the abovementioned authors did not enjoy much popularity, and remained, to a large extent, without practical application, or even falling into oblivion. On many occasions, some well-intended laws enacted in the sixteenth and seventeenth centuries in order to safeguard the rights of the Indians, were hardly applied. Not infrequently, States continued to treat Indians in a discriminatory manner, violating their rights. It would take several centuries to move from theory—as set out here—to practice and, in many territories, that was not achieved until the second half of the twentieth century. Note that even today, in quite a few territories and countries—both uncivilised and already civilised and culturally and economically well developed—, human rights are in practice ignored, violated and even scorned.[82]

1.3.2 The Thirty Years' War and the Peace of Westphalia: Towards Religious Freedom

If with the discovery of the New World the medieval idea of Christianity or Christian Empire collapsed, giving rise to a new Law—international or of peoples—which,

[82]The divorce between theory and practice might—at least, partly—explain such undeniable, paradoxical reality. In the same vein, today is notably discussed the rise of colonialism and slavery under natural law in the sixteenth/seventeenth century—the very same natural law out of which the idea of human rights would grow. One might wonder how the rise of the ideas on natural rights could go hand in hand with exploitation of thousands of Africans, Asians and native Americans. History shows that ideas and laws not always go hand in hand with the practice. Some ideas might not have any influence over laws, and some laws might be hardly enforced or perfectly ineffective. However, this does not preclude the possibility of studying the history of ideas and see how they were introduced in the legal order, as I'm doing here, even though some of them did not have much impact in the laws or, if they do, were not appealing enough to make such laws effective, as it somehow happened with the Native Indians; the abuses towards Indians led to the creation of the protector of Indians in some Spanish colonial territories, as scholars show: Cutter (1986); Ruigómez (1988); Bonnett (1992); Novoa (2016).

based on the natural order—or natural law—sought to safeguard the natural rights of all (whether Christian or barbarian), the Protestant Reformation (Lutheran, Zwinglian, Calvinist and Anglican) and the consequent Counter-Reformation (Catholic) put an end to the unity of that same Christianity in the West (the Eastern Schism had already occurred in 1054). And the subsequent Counter-Reformation (Catholic) put an end to the unity of that same Christianity in the West, Calvinist and Anglican) and the subsequent Counter-Reformation (Catholic) put an end to the unity of that same Christianity in the West (the Eastern schism had already occurred in 1054), bringing about a new political and social context of bitter division and confrontation, to the point of provoking several wars of religion in various countries of central Europe, especially in Germany and France.

The Lutheran Reformation was based on theological presuppositions that would have important consequences in the political sphere. Luther, following William of Ockham, rejected natural law—and with it, the natural order and reason—because, after the original sin, according to him, nature had been corrupted and could not set itself up as a norm or moral point of reference in the individual or social sphere. Thus, the only referent was the divine will, and this could only be imposed with the support of secular power or lay princes, which contributed to a process of theocratisation of Protestant territories.[83] Thus, a double morality was introduced: that of the Sermon on the Mount in the spiritual realm, which was ruled by God with his mercy, and that of the secular realm, which was ruled by God through the political power or the lay prince.[84] And the Christian had to submit to this secular power if he really wanted to fulfil God's will. Luther thus ended up giving the secular force the power to restrict the principle of freedom or free examination that he had denied to the Church and its pontiff. This undoubtedly contributed to consolidate the absolute power of modern monarchies, while at the same time it made religion a shaping or structuring element of the civil and political unity of States, a determining factor of social cohesion and a distinctive sign of each nation. *Cuius regio, eius religio* ('to such a king, such a religion' or 'whose [is] the region, his [is] the religion'): with this principle, originating in antiquity but taken up in the 'Augsburg Confessions' of 1530, the problem of the coexistence of people with different religions in the same territory or German principality was solved at its root. (It should be borne in mind that the German Empire was made up of more than 300 territories).

The solution arbitrated by the 'Peace of Augsburg' (25 September 1555), signed between Emperor Charles V and the Schmalkaldic League, was quite simple: the

[83] On this, see Figgis (1998).

[84] In practice, the "theocratic states" tried to impose God's law by all means, and in a short time they succeeded in controlling urban life more tightly than the Church did in Catholic cities. However, also in Catholic areas this mentality was gradually introduced through "Jansenism", a religious movement initiated by Jansenius (1585–1638). Although condemned as heretical by the Catholic Church, it enjoyed a certain popularity in Europe. Denying the contest of human freedom, it emphasised original sin, human depravity, and the necessity of divine grace, which saved only the predestined. It was, undoubtedly, a puritanical and intransigent doctrine.

religious confession of the prince was to be applied to all the citizens of the territory, the religion of the prince determined the religion of his subjects; and those who did not share—or wanted to share—that religion, had to emigrate to another territory. Only in this way could the political power guarantee social peace and political stability in its territory.

Luther's denial of the natural order had a serious consequence, namely, that since political power could only be based on the supernatural order or theological truth, there could be no division or compromise on this point, and any hint of toleration or religious freedom for the citizens, who had to follow the religion of the prince who ruled their territory, was rejected.

The doctrine on which the Peace of Augsburg was based did not prevent the various conflicts and wars of religion that ravaged much of Europe for almost a century, the Thirty Years' War (1614–1648) being the most tragic and best known of them all. The doctrine of some authors on the 'just war', which declared the unlawfulness of war for religious reasons, was of no use.

In this sense, it is worth mentioning Francisco de Vitoria. In his *De Jure belli Hispanorum in barbaros* (1532), where he analysed the limits of the use of force to settle disputes between peoples, he pointed out that it was lawful to wage war, provided that it was initiated to respond proportionately to an aggression. It was not lawful, therefore, to wage war simply because of differences of religion or to increase territorial dominance.

The Peace of Westphalia (with its two peace treaties of Osnabrück and Münster, signed on 15 May and 24 October 1648) put an end to the Thirty Years' War (Germany) and the Eighty Years' War (between Spain and the Netherlands), seeking to establish an area of freedom and religious tolerance that would guarantee social peace (among individuals) and political peace (among the various territories and states).

Apart from other consequences, this Peace brought with it the recognition of religious freedom between territories or states, which were able to adopt the religion of the time as their own and official (Title 49). This meant the disintegration of the *Christian respublica* and, with it, the rupture of the unity of Western Europe.

In contrast to the Spanish and Holy (German) Empire's vision of a *universitas christiana*, the French idea prevailed, which exalted the *raison d'état* as the justification for international action, making the state the ultimate authority in international relations, replacing other supranational or transnational institutions. In reality, this meant that the state was no longer subject to moral norms external to itself, and was given a quasi-limited power to do whatever it saw fit to do for its own growth and consolidation.

It also meant the end of the European wars that, since the Protestant Reformation and the Counter-Reformation, had been unleashed for both religious and geopolitical reasons. After the Peace of Westphalia, war could no longer find any justification in religion or, if you prefer, religion could no longer be wielded as a *casus belli*.

In Westphalia, a new order was established in Central Europe based on the concept of national sovereignty. According to some authors, the Peace of Westphalia introduced the principle of territorial integrity as the basis for the existence of states, thus overcoming the feudal conception of territories and peoples as mere hereditary patrimony and giving rise to the nation state. Alongside the principle of 'territorial integrity' or 'territorial sovereignty',

> Westphalia also brought with it the principles of 'non-interference in internal affairs' and equal treatment of states irrespective of their size or power. In practice, the application of these principles was uneven for different states.

In short, although the Peace of Westphalia was a step forward with regard to the freedom of states in religious matters, putting an end to the wars of religion, the scope of religious freedom as well as freedom of conscience was, to say the least, limited. First, because it affected princes and rulers more than subjects, who had to leave their territory if they did not share the religious denomination of their prince; second, because Luther attributed to the political power the power to limit free examination or freedom of conscience, which would lead to a notable intervention of the State (of course, confessional) in religious matters, using the coercive force of law to impose religious practice (this would be particularly accentuated in the territories of Calvinist influence: Switzerland, Holland, Scotland, England—puritanism, in its English version, which would later spread in the United States, especially in New England); and third, because the consolidation of sovereign States without any subjection to moral norms external to itself, with quasi-limited powers and without supranational or interstate institutions that could restrain them or exercise a minimum control over them, constituted a dangerous seed that would not take long to germinate, bearing detestable fruits. The absolute monarchies of the seventeenth and eighteenth centuries served as good proof of this and the liberal revolutions came to put a timely remedy to such excesses, but they only succeeded in part. It would take two world wars before we became clearly aware that national States had to respond to an international community with laws that protected the fundamental rights of all, as well as institutions capable of guaranteeing the exercise of those rights to individuals and of sanctioning States that violated them.

1.3.3 The Glorious Revolution and the Bill of Rights *of 1689: The Enshrinement of Parliamentarism as an Instrument of Political Power Limitation*

If States emerged in the sixteenth century, the seventeenth century saw their consolidation and, where appropriate, their absolutisation. The State tended to identify itself with an institution, the monarchy ("the State is me", Louis XIV would come to say), [85] which had been accumulating power since its creation until the beginning of the Modern Age (fifteenth and sixteenth centuries).[86] Indeed, royal power ended up enjoying an absolute sovereignty that, residing in the person of the monarch—or monarchical institution—, seemed to have no limits. Modern absolutism, which

---

[85] *L'État, c'est moi* in its French version, or *Der Staat bin ich* in its German version.

[86] A synthesis of the emergence of the modern state and the notion of sovereignty in the modern period up to the French Revolution can be found in García de Enterría (1994), pp. 97 ff; on the notion of sovereignty in the Anglo-Saxon legal tradition, see Loughlin (2003), pp. 72–98.

went so far as to deny the theoretical existence of limits to political power, was incompatible with the recognition and protection of fundamental right.[87] Indeed, the absolute State, regardless of its form of government (monarchy, republic, democracy), is not compatible with the safeguarding of fundamental rights. Hence the history of human rights is closely linked to the limits placed on political power over time.[88] The European liberal revolutions precisely had the purpose of establishing limits to political power. This is what the French Revolution (1789) did, in that case even replacing the monarchical form of government with a republican one.

A century earlier, England, without going so far as to reject the monarchy, had its own revolution, the 'Glorious Revolution' (1688), whose final result was the limitation of political power by establishing parliamentary supremacy over the monarchy. [89] In England, monarchical power, following the trend of other countries, was increased and consolidated throughout the Tudor period (1485–1603) first, and then the Stuart period (1603–1714). It was precisely from the struggle between the monarchy and the English parliament, between the Stuart monarchs—especially James I and Charles I—and the House of Commons, that the recognition of the rights of the English arose, thanks to the approval of two important documents: the Petition of Rights (1628) and—in the context of the aforementioned Revolution—the Bill of Rights (1689).

The main objective of the Bill of Rights was to restore and strengthen various parliamentary powers which, after the absolutist reigns of Charles II and James II, had disappeared or had been greatly diminished. In the context of the Glorious Revolution, James II was deposed and replaced by his daughter Mary (1662–1694)—and her husband William III of Orange—(February 1689), on condition that they recognised the Bill of Rights and the constitutional or moderate

[87] It should be recognised that a certain germ of absolutism can be found in the medieval doctrine of the *absolute potestas* of the prince, which resulted from his right to *plenitudo potestatis*, and that the theoretical limits of this power were not always respected in practice. Hence Vázquez de Menchaca's attacks on this *potestas absoluta*, which indicates that it was sometimes practised outside the theoretical limits in the government of the Church and of the lay Power; however, it should be borne in mind that the marked limits (of theological, philosophical-moral, political and legal origin) of royal power proper to the Middle Ages began to disappear even in the theoretical sphere from the sixteenth century onwards; in this respect, see, for example, the study by Carpintero (1977), pp. 158–172.

[88] On the historical evolution of the limits of political power, see Masferrer and Obarrio (2012); as is well known, monarchical absolutism was the result of a slow and gradual process to which Jean Bodin (1530–1596) contributed decisively in the sixteenth century, who came to uphold royal sovereignty in the following terms: "Maiestas est summa in cives ac subditos legibus soluta potestas" (*Six libres de la république*, book I, chap. VIII). This is the classic text of the modern theory of sovereignty. Indeed, this definition of *souveraineté* or *summa potestas* as *in cives ac subditos legibus soluta potestas* ('power over citizens and subjects not subject to laws'), constitutes the theoretical basis of the sovereign power of the State as a supreme, permanent, indivisible and, in principle, legally irresponsible power. However, it is important not to lose sight of the fact that Jean Bodin never conceived of an unlimited notion of sovereignty, given that it could not transgress divine laws, natural laws and *ius Gentium*.

[89] Dorado (2001); Skinner (2008); on this subject, see also the classic study by Dicey (1885).

monarchy. This marked the beginning of a new era in which monarchs were accountable to Parliament for the exercise of their power. Parliament was strengthened, establishing a moderate monarchy that would never experience the monarchical absolutisms of eighteenth-century Europe. This was undoubtedly helped by the drafting—at Parliament's initiative—and approval—with royal sanction—of the Bill of Rights, a document setting out the respective duties and obligations of the King and Parliament. According to this Declaration, the King could not create or remove laws or taxes without the approval of Parliament; he could not collect money for his personal use without the approval of Parliament; he could not raise or maintain an army in times of peace without the approval of Parliament; elections of members of Parliament had to be free; Parliament had to meet frequently; the words of Parliament could not be obstructed or rejected anywhere; and so on.

The most important English precedent for the Bill of Rights (1689) had taken place more than half a century earlier, with the Petition of Rights, a petition drawn up in 1628 by the English Parliament and sent to Charles I as a declaration of civil liberties. This Declaration originated as Parliament's response—of refusal—to the monarch's request to finance his foreign policy, which led to the demand for forced loans, with the consequent quartering of troops in the homes of subjects who refused to pay. The monarch also arbitrarily arrested and imprisoned those who opposed his policies. These measures provoked great hostility in Parliament towards Charles I and the first Duke of Buckingham (George Villiers) and were the origin of the 'Petition of Rights'. This document, drafted by the distinguished jurist Sir Edward Coke, enshrined—on the basis of earlier statutes and official documents—four principles: (1) Prohibition of levying any tax without the consent of Parliament, (2) Prohibition of imprisoning any subject without a proven cause (reaffirming the right of *habeas corpus*, from the Latin, 'let you have the body', which marked a time limit to resolve in case of arrest), (3) Prohibition of quartering soldiers with citizens, and (4) Prohibition of martial law in times of peace.[90]

It should be borne in mind that these documents to confront the abuses of the monarchy do not recognise human rights, understood as universal and abstract, coming from a sphere other than that of existing law, but refer to the rights and liberties of the English, whose ownership corresponded to them by birth or by other titles (various forms of franchise or property), and guaranteed by grants of liberties ('Charters of liberties') or laws guaranteeing due process ('statutes of due process'). One example was, as will be seen, the Magna Carta of John Landless (1215), some chapters of which were taken up in both the 'Petition of Rights' (1628) and the 'Bill of Rights' (1689). The notion of 'rights of mankind' would not appear in English legal sources until a century later, in the reign of George II.

[90] As is well known, 'martial law' refers to temporary rule by military authorities in time of emergency when civilian authorities are deemed unable to function. The legal effects of such a declaration vary from State to State, but usually involve the suspension of civil rights, as well as the extension of summary military justice or military law to the civilian population. Although in theory temporary in nature, in practice a state of martial law can be of considerable and sometimes indefinite duration.

Authors such as Thomas Hobbes (1588–1679) and John Locke (1632–1704) contributed notably, as will be seen, to resolving the controversy over royal power and its limits, as well as the controversy over which political system could best guarantee the peace and security of the community and the rights of its individuals. While Hobbes (*Leviathan*, 1651), following—in part—Jean Bodin's thesis, opted for a doctrine that granted absolute power to the monarchy, because—according to him—only that absolute power could guarantee the peace and security of the community and its individuals, Locke—with his *Two Treatises on Civil Government* (1689)—defended the existence of rights (life, liberty and property) which, being prior to political power (that is, pre-political in nature), constituted the raison d'être of the State and marked, at the same time, an insurmountable limit to political power.[91]

In this sense, Locke defended—like Jean Bodin—the existence of limits that Hobbes omitted. Jean Bodin, in defending the absolute power of the monarch, pointed out that the latter could not infringe upon divine laws, natural laws, the law of nations, the private property of the family, as well as those customs and covenants or conventions that formed the basis of a political community. Locke, following this line, by sustaining the pre-political nature of some rights, established natural law (or human nature) and natural rights as a limit to the power of the state. Locke's theses would exert a great influence in the eighteenth century and would become the main intellectual nectar or source of the modern Declarations of Rights of that century (Declaration of Virginia, 1776; Declaration of Independence of the United States, 1776; Declaration of the Rights of Man and of the Citizen, 1789), and even of the twentieth century (Universal Declaration of Human Rights, 1948).

In any case, it should be noted that the relationship between natural law and natural or human rights was not only in the continental or European tradition, but also in the Anglo-Saxon tradition, starting with the English *common law*.[92]

1.4 Medieval Precedents of Human Rights (Eleventh to Fifteenth Centuries)

As we have seen, the recognition of the existence of certain rights that correspond to the members of a social community requires the existence of a political power and the experience of an abuse of that power to which we want to remedy. History hardly offers examples of communities which, without organisation or *potestas* (or *auctoritas*, at least), have enjoyed peace and stability. It is a fact, then, that

[91] Although it should be noted that Locke claimed, above all, individual private property, it can be inferred from the reading of his work that personal liberty was a reality "postulated" in view of freedom in the traffic of property. Thus, for example, when he speaks of "The Fundamental Law of Society", he refers only to property.

[92] In this regard, see Helmholz (2005), pp. 1–22.

every community requires a minimum political power that promotes, with greater or lesser success, order and social peace. On the other hand, that necessary political power could infringe on the rights and freedoms of the people who are part of that community. Thus, the lack of peace and social stability is usually related to political power, which, either by defect—or non-existence—or by excess, leaves the members of the community exposed to abuses, either by the most powerful individuals or by an absolute and all-embracing political power whose tentacles completely invade social and personal life.

After an early medieval period (eighth to tenth centuries) in which political power was conspicuous by its absence or was scarce—and therefore unable to guarantee a minimum of peace and social stability—, the monarchy emerged in the eleventh, twelfth and thirteenth centuries. The emergence of royal power was due to various factors, related to the reconquest and repopulation of Muslim territories, to the emergence of a medieval municipality whose incipient and progressive commercial activity was due to the new social class of the bourgeoisie, to the birth of the courts or parliament—when the representatives of the municipalities joined the old extraordinary *curiae*—, with the discovery and reception of the Justinian Compilation of classical Roman Law (*Corpus iuris civilis*), and with the creation of the universities that contributed, among other things, to the study and development of a legal science (*ius commune*) that came to legitimise and justify the power of the monarch (in the absence of the Emperor), to whom the power to create Law was attributed.

Thus began a new political stage in which the Emperor and the monarchs, were convinced that they had a monopoly on the creation of law. They fought zealously to exercise the full extent of this power (*plenitudo potestas*), against those powers that could impede the exercise of this privilege. Although monarchies became absolute from the sixteenth and seventeenth centuries onwards, the seed of absolutism was present from their origins, because the Roman Law that legitimised and justified their existence granted them absolute power, the same power enjoyed by the Roman Emperors in their period of maximum splendour and plenitude, that is, in the period of the Principate (from Octavian Augustus—27 B.C.—to Diocletianus—284 A. D.—, with whom the period of the Dominate, of decadence, would begin).

What were the institutions that succeeded in limiting the full power that supposedly belonged to the emperor or monarch? Although the only institution that, strictly speaking, became the main rival of the Emperor's *plenitudo potestas* was the Pope, there were other forces or powers capable of limiting the monarch's monopoly in the legislative power. The most relevant was the parliament or, if you prefer, the medieval courts or legislative assemblies, an institution that the monarch created and used until he wanted, getting rid of it as soon as he could, sometimes thanks to the title of conquest that brought him the victory in wars. This would be the case of Philip V with the Aragonese, Catalan and Valencian courts after the War of Succession (1700–1714). Of giving out a different sign would be the result of the Civil War provoked by the despotism of James II in England, where what finally prevailed—as we have seen—was the supremacy of the Parliament against the monarchy. In this sense, England was an exception in that modern context (seventeenth century), but it was neither the only nor the first territory to establish limits to royal power, as will be seen.

1.4.1 The Freedom of the Church from Secular Power: Libertas ecclesiae

The expression 'freedom' is the one that best expresses the action of 'freeing' oneself from a power that subjugates a person or institution, preventing it from the autonomy that is proper to it or corresponds to it. This is precisely what happened to the Church and its Pontificate in the tenth century (also called the 'Dark Century' or 'Iron Century'), when it was imprisoned by the feudal powers of an Empire (the Carolingian) in the process of decomposition. In this context, the intrusions of secular power into the Church, which came to a head under Emperor Charles Martel—son of Ludovico Pio and grandson of Charlemagne—left the Holy See in the hands of the feudal factions that dominated the city of Rome and thus exercised full control over the election of Popes in particular and the government of the Church in general. This unfortunate period in the history of the Church ended with the rise of a new Empire—considered the basic political form of Christendom—the Holy Roman Empire, initiated by the German Emperor Otto I (936–973), who was crowned by the Pope in St. Peter's on February 2, 962. This coronation signified the renewal of the Empire ('renovatio Imperii') and the transfer of the Empire from the Frankish (or Carolingian) kings to its new holders, the kings of Germany ('translatio Imperii'). However, the interference of the secular powers in ecclesiastical affairs in general, and in the pontifical election in particular, did not cease.

The Church wanted to free itself from this yoke and was anxious to create the conditions that would allow it to enjoy the autonomy it was entitled to.[93] Only in this way could it remedy the three great evils that afflicted it: simony (acquisition of ecclesiastical offices at a price), 'Nicolaism' (incontinence of the clergy) and lay investiture (the provision of ecclesiastical offices by the secular powers), which was the root and origin of the other two, since this form of provision lent itself to simoniac abuses in appointments, while explaining the low moral stature of those who unfortunately came to occupy those offices.[94]

The longed-for '*libertas ecclesiae*' was the work of the Gregorian Popes and, more specifically, of Gregory VII, who carried out a far-reaching reform in only

---

[93] At times, the pretensions of the Church went even further, and the Popes, rather than freeing themselves from this yoke, wanted to extend their power. It is a complex subject which it is not possible to treat it as it deserves to be treated. The great defender of the purity of the Church was, in the fifteenth century, John of Gerson, who demanded a council from the Pope, and in view of his refusals, reminded the Emperor that he also had *jurisdictio* to convoke such a council. That council came with Trent (1545–1563), but very late and urged on by the Holy See, prompted by the success of the Reformers.

[94] On this subject, see Orlandis (2006), pp. 281–282.

12 years (1073–1085). The fundamental principles of the Gregorian Reform were synthesised in his *Dictatus Papae* (1075), a document in which Gregory VII collected 27 propositions defending the supremacy of spiritual power over temporal power. Although they were not new, their formulation was novel by collecting the dispersed original texts and presenting them as an ideology. The *Dictatus* proclaimed that the supremacy of Christianity belonged to the Roman Pontiff, who represented spiritual power in the world. To him, therefore, belonged the direction of the *societas christiana*, and under his authority were both the emperor and the secular kings or princes. More particularly, the pope was attributed with the power to depose the emperor, or to release his subjects from the oath of allegiance sworn to unrighteous princes, powers which bring about remarkable political and religious consequences.

Alongside the supremacy of the Papacy in medieval Christendom, founded on the principle of the superiority of spiritual over temporal power, there was another reason of a historical nature, namely the 'Donation of Constantine', whose authenticity was hardly doubted by anyone at the time (until the humanist Lorenzo Valla proved it to be false in 1440). According to the *Dictatus Papae*, the Pope could use the imperial insignia thanks to the supposed cession of imperial sovereignty that Constantine had made to Pope Sylvester over the Western Roman Empire. This title was used by Gregory VII to claim sovereignty over the territories reconquered from Muslim rule, and remained in force for centuries, extending its scope of application, and affecting lands that were never conquered by the Muslims. Thus, for example, we have already seen how the Catholic Monarchs, after the discovery of America, hastened to ask the Pope for bulls or titles that legitimised or justified the occupation of non-Christian lands, since, according to the political conception of medieval Christianity, the lands of the infidels (non-faithful or non-Christians) belonged to the Pope, and only he could authorise their occupation if it was for the evangelisation of their peoples.

1.4.2 Medieval Parliamentarism

Alongside the Church, the parliamentary assemblies, which emerged in the twelfth and thirteenth centuries, ended up constituting a threat to the political and legislative monopoly to which the monarchs had already aspired in those medieval centuries. The courts, whose precise nature has been the subject of debate, succeeded in placing limits on the exercise of royal power. Regardless of their nature and theoretical functions, what is certain is that, in practice, not infrequently the monarch was obliged—sometimes, due to particularly difficult or adverse circumstances—to reach agreements and make concessions whose content may well be considered as a precedent of modern rights and liberties.

1.4.2.1 Was the Magna Carta (John I of England, 1215) the First?

In this sense, it is well known for the Magna Carta (London, 15.VI.1215), John I of England (known as John without Land), who, found himself in a delicate situation (due to social problems and serious difficulties in foreign policy), was skilfully compelled to sign a document that, while establishing limits to the exercise of feudal power, enshrined a set of legal and procedural guarantees.[95] The text is known as *Magna charta libertatum* (*Magna Carta of liberties*) because it makes, as Clause I states, a concession of liberties:

> TO ALL FREE MEN OF OUR KINGDOM we have also granted, for us and our heirs for ever, all the liberties written out below, to have and to keep for them and their heirs, of us and our heirs.

Although the text states that it is addressed to all the free people of the kingdom, it is well known that the assembly was only attended by the aristocrats (the barons), and the 63 clauses of which the document is composed ensured the feudal rights of the aristocracy (the barons) against the royal power. In addition to establishing that the monarch could not—with few exceptions—demand the scutage (tribute or payment made to the king for the expenses of war) or the aid (monetary amount) without general consent (Clause 12), for which purpose the nobles would have to be summoned ('the archbishops, bishops, abbots, earls and greater barons', Clause 14), it was established that the city of London 'shall enjoy all its ancient liberties and free customs both by land and by sea. We also will and grant that all other cities, boroughs, towns, and ports shall enjoy all their liberties and free customs' (Clause 13).

The most notable aspect of this text, however, was the establishment of legal and procedural guarantees in Clauses 39 and 40, which enshrined the right to due process and the right to judicial protection, respectively:

> No free man shall be seized or imprisoned, or stripped of his rights or possessions, or outlawed or exiled, or deprived of his standing in any way, nor will we proceed with force against him, or send others to do so, except by the lawful judgment of his equals or by the law of the land (Clause 39).
>
> To no one will we sell, to no one deny or delay right or justice (Clause 40).

Although historiography—beginning with English one—has mythologised this text, the fact is that its content, both the idea of granting liberties and the establishment of the aforementioned guarantees, was not something new or novel at the beginning of the thirteenth century. Indeed, in the second half of the twelfth century, processes of a similar nature had taken place in other European territories, giving rise to texts with very similar content.

---

[95] The literature on the Magna Carta is notably extensive; the most recent one is, most probably, by Baker (2023); see also other relatively recent works by Loengard (2010), Vincent (2014, 2015), Carpenter (2015), Church (2015), Holt (2015), Baker (2017).

1.4.2.2 The Golden Bull (Andrew II of Hungary, 1222)

Other text of a similar nature, adopted after the Magna Carta, was the 'Golden Bull' (1222), promulgated by King Andrew II of Hungary, under pressure from increasingly powerful feudal lords. The document, called 'Aranybulla' in Hungarian, consisted of 31 chapters and remained in force until the Bulgarian revolution of 1848, when it was partially suppressed. The first two chapters may serve to give an idea of its nature and content:

> Let no nobleman be arrested (unjustly), nor oppressed by the desire of any power (Ch. I).
>
> The Noblemen are declared to be exempt from the payment of taxes, nor will money be collected from their treasuries. Neither will their residences be occupied, nor their villages, and these may only be visited by those who have been invited. No taxes will be levied on the Church. (Chapter III)
> (Source: Wikipedia).

Some argue that, as per the text, if the Hungarian king could not maintain the guarantees contained therein, it was considered lawful to rise against the monarch. Notably, the text affected the nobility, not the freemen living in the emerging medieval cities. The Golden Bull was one of the first European documents to give evidence of the medieval tendency toward limiting royal power.

The year 2022 was the 800th Anniversary of the approval of the Golden Bull by Andrew II of Hungary (1222),[96] regarded as one the first European documents that notably limited royal power. The king would not have limited his power if he was not under pressure from powerful, feudal lords. According to current interpretations, however, the Golden Bull codified the policies of the king comprising concessions made to the nobility that supported him in the internal political struggles and pursuit of his reform agenda. Practically, the basis of royal powers was rearranged, which may seem paradoxical, as limiting royal power was also a way to strengthen it. The case was similar to that of the *Decreta*, as we will see now.

1.4.2.3 The Spanish Origins of Western Parliamentarism and the Rule of Law in the Medieval Western World: The *Cortes* of León and Their *Decreta* (1188)

Although historiography, beginning with the English one, has mythologised the *Magna charta libertatum*, its content in the idea of granting liberties and establishing the aforementioned guarantees, was not novel at the beginning of the thirteenth century. However, it can be perceived in the more general context of political and economic transformations that occurred in Western Europe and some Central European states like Hungary, as seen. Thus, from similar processes emerged texts with similar content.

[96] *De Bulla Aurea. Andraea II Regis Hungarie, 1222*, Verona: Edizioni Valdonega, 1999; see also some chapters in their English version in pp. 181–247, and the bibliography in pp. 249–254.

This section intends to provide evidence of this historical truth. First, I will highlight the challenge of being immune to a biased observation and analysis of legal traditions when political and ideological ("national") interests are at stake and why the tendency of limiting royal power emerged and spread in medieval Europe. Then, I will argue for why the *Decreta* of the Cortes of León (1188) was a pioneering document, giving evidence of a tendency present in many European territories. Note the assumption that other documents, potentially older than the *Decreta* of León from different European territories, might be discovered in the future, for which a revision and recognition of which document is the first in Europe would be in order. Otherwise, the *Decreta* of the Cortes de León assumes the pioneering position.

In the Cortes of Cádiz (1812) context, Francisco Martínez Marina defended the thesis that there was a historical continuity between the nineteenth-century Cortes and the medieval ones, particularly those celebrated in Castile and León.[97] Decades later, Joaquín Francisco Pacheco maintained the contrary thesis concerning the substantive criminal law contained in the Criminal Code of 1848, arguing that nothing from the past had been kept because everything was useless and unfit for modern times.[98]

These two examples show the temptation to mix scholarship with politics or legal science with ideology, which I learned from my colleague, J.M. Scholz, as I began work as a research fellow at the *Max-Planck-Institut für europäische Rechtsgeschichte* in summer 2000. He warned me of the incompatibility between doing research and political devotion.[99] Some of my research projects affirmed that Scholz was right. Controversies or rivalries between scholars from different schools of thought, nations, or traditions also affirm this truth. In the codification movement context, how "Codiphobia" poisoned the debate about the convenience to resort to the technique of codification to undertake legal reform in nineteenth-century England[100] or how passions overshadowed the discussion about whether to codify the private law of New York are notable.[101]

Accordingly, the title of this section may seem quite provocative from an ideological or nationalistic perspective. Are the origins of limiting royal power in the Middle Ages really "Spanish"[102]? Is it not possible that the emergence of the first documents and institutions limiting royal power could have arisen in other European territories rather than the Iberian Peninsula? Perhaps, it is; however, current evidence

[97] Martínez Marina (1813); see Masferrer (2018a), pp. 276–292.

[98] See Masferrer (2018a, b), pp. 193–242.

[99] I remember he used the expression "*Mitmachen*", meaning to participate, contribute, play along with, or get involved in something in to transform the social reality.

[100] Amos (1856), pp. xvi, xix; see also Masferrer (2019b), pp. 1–31, particularly, pp. 11–22.

[101] Reimann (1989); on this matter, see also my works: Masferrer (2008, 2010, pp. 355–430).

[102] The expression "Spanish" is only applicable from the reign of the Catholic monarchs (1479–1504), particularly, from Charles V (1516–1556), onward, a period where the political unity of the Spanish monarchy was compatible with the legal diversity. Thus, the different kingdoms and territories of the crown of Castile and Aragon had their political and legal institutions; Masferrer (2009), Ch. 10.

points to the *Decreta* of León of 1188 as the first document, whose content regarding limiting royal power is, as will be seen, similar to that of the famous Magna Carta (1215) of John, King of England. I am quite convinced that other European territories might have had similar texts or practices before 1188. In Spain, for example, from the Fueros of Sobrarbe that appeared in the middle of the ninth century emerged the "Antes leyes que reyes" ("First laws and only afterward kings") principle.[103]

In thirteenth-century Europe, places such as England, France, the Holy German Empire, Italy, Poland, Hungary, and Spain limited royal power. That century witnessed the origins of two relevant political and legal institutions: the rule of law or principle of legality (connected to the recognition of rights, though not in the modern sense, and concession of privileges), and parliamentarism (connected to the idea of an agreement or pact among those affected by decisions: "*Quod omnes tangit, ab omnibus debet approbari*").[104]

Unsurprisingly, the thirteenth century witnessed the emergence of royal power and the approval of charters and legal institutions to limit such power, which explains why most medieval institutions were particularly studied, praised, and idealised in sixteenth-century Europe. In England, particularly in the seventeenth century, royal absolutism threatened the status quo of social states, especially the nobility privileges and the natural rights of freemen. As kings did not enjoy much political power in many European territories in the eleventh and twelfth centuries, there was no reason to limit royal power. However, the emergence of royal power in the thirteenth century, given various historical factors (e.g., social, economic, military, cultural, political, and legal), furnished the need for limiting royal power. Similarly, the emergence of royal absolutism in the sixteenth and seventeenth centuries, also given various factors, induced some lawyers to focus on medieval institutions that had emerged precisely to limit royal power. Examples include the interest of Aragón's lawyers in the *Fuero of Sobrarbe* in the sixteenth century or that of English lawyers in the *Magna Carta* in the seventeenth century.

Spain in the thirteenth century comprised various autonomous kingdoms or territories: Castile, León, Aragón, Catalonia, Navarre, Basque provinces (Álava, Guipúzcoa y Vizcaya), Valencia, and Majorca (the Catalan territory was called *Principatus* or Principality).[105] Except for the Balearic islands and Basque provinces, all Spanish territories had their parliaments (or *Cortes*, as they were called in the sources), attended by the three social states: the ecclesiastical nobility, secular

[103] See footnote n. 11.

[104] Condorelli (2013); see also Merello Arecco (2005).

[105] While Castile and León were definitely united by Ferdinand III in 1230, Aragon and Catalonia were also united in 1137 from the marriage of Ramon Berenguer and Petronila of Aragón; later, the kingdom of Aragón comprised united Valencia, Majorca, Menorca, and the Italian territories of Sicily, Corsica, Sardinia, and Naples. Hence, most territories of the Basque provinces were united to Castile at the beginning of the thirteenth century. The marriage of Ferdinand of Aragon and Isabelle of Castile politically united both kingdoms, from which the Spanish monarchy under the Catholic kings emerged (1469). In 1512, Navarre was incorporated to Castile.

nobility, and common people or representatives of the cities. Evidence suggests that the attendance of common people started in Castile and Aragón-Catalonia in 1214 and León in 1188.

Parliaments did not emerge from the royal awareness of the benefits of limiting royal power but from a royal dire need for various reasons (personal or familiar, political, economic, or military). In Spain, kings began to resort to assemblies in the Early Middle Ages when their power did not guarantee peace and security. Accordingly, particularly relevant were, for example, the assemblies of peace and truce of God.[106] Other institutions of assemblies somehow revealed the weakness of royal power: *curia regis* and councils (where kings were supported by secular and ecclesiastic nobility) and charters of the population (where nobility and freemen supported military undertakings by occupying new territories reconquered from Muslims). Such assemblies did not appear to limit royal power, given that, at that time, the king, was a *primum inter pares* or looked for support to remedy his weakness.

The Arabic invasion of the Iberian Peninsula created a peculiar situation that encouraged or "forced" the common people to sometimes defend themselves, even in regions without any political or royal initiative or support. It induced the emergence of a popular legal culture characterised by the existence of laws without a king, giving rise to the abovementioned principle in Aragón and Navarre, "*Antes leyes que reyes*" ("Laws first and kings afterward"), as it would be presented in the early modern age.[107] This principle might have appeared in the *Fueros de Sobrarbe*, a charter allegedly enacted in the Pyrenean valley of Sobrarbe in the middle of the ninth century, according to a falsified version of the *Fuero de Tudela* (postdated to 1117). As per legend, the *Fuero de Sobrarbe* contained some liberties, including the following: laws may not be impaired, a mediator judge shall watch, and it shall be lawful to appeal to the king should anyone be injured.

In the late Middle Ages, even though royal power was strengthened for various reasons (e.g., the emergence of cities and merchants and their incorporation in parliaments, the creation of universities, and the prestige of Roman law that supported kings as main legislators), kings were not adequately strong to address political turmoil without being compelled to make concessions. Thus, the *Privilegio de la Unión* granted to Aragón in 1287 was quite similar to the English *Magna Carta*, as the nobility took advantage of the challenging situation of Alphons III of Aragón to obtain prerogatives that were confirmed in the Cortes of Zaragoza (1347) but derogated a year later by Pedro IV because of the Battle of Épila. Like the *Magna Carta*, the *Privilegio de la Unión* affected the nobility, not the freemen. The *Privilegio General* granted in 1283 by Pedro III in the context of the military intervention in Sicily and its consequences (economic, political, religious, and social) affected the cities of Aragón.[108]

---

[106] Hoffmann (1964); Head and Landes (1992); Kosto (2003); Masferrer (2014), pp. 31–39.

[107] García Pérez (2008).

[108] Danvila (1881); González (1975); Lalinde (1980); Sarasa (1979, 1984).

Notably, both Privileges of Aragón—*Privilegio General* (1283) and *Privilegio de la Unión* (1287–1348)—were linked to ninth-century *Fuero de Sobrarbe*. Moreover, the Fuero de Sobrarbe was somehow present in the cities of Aragón (through the *Fueros of Aragón*, 1283) and Navarre (through the *Fueros de Navarra*, 1238).

In Catalonia, another political turmoil led Jaume I to summon the representatives of the cities in the Cortes of Lleida in 1214. For some historians, the first Cortes of Castile were also celebrated in 1214.[109] There is no doubt that the first Cortes of León, convoked and presided over by Alphons IX, occurred in 1188, followed by the Cortes of 1202 and 1208.[110] Irrespective of whether these meetings of León should be called "Cortes" or *Curia extraordinaria*[111] or whether Cortes *stricto sensu* started in the thirteenth century,[112] it seems clear that they were attended by citizens.[113] Thus, they might be regarded as "Cortes."[114]

The document that justifies the title of this section is the first Cortes of León, particularly their *Decreta*. Unlike the *Fueros de Sobrarbe*, which belong to the ninth century but whose historical basis is not entirely certain or consistent, there is evidence that (1) these Cortes were celebrated in 1188, (2) Alphons IX invited citizens from different cities to attend and participate (as he would do it again in 1202 and 1208), and (3) two bodies of laws were enacted (some constitutions against violence and thieves and the *Decreta*, the original of which has not been found, though there are many original and cartulary copies). The text of the *Decreta*, originally drafted and approved in Latin,[115] has since been translated into Spanish[116] and English[117] and, recently, Hungarian,[118] comprises 17 chapters.

These *Decreta* are relevant from a historical perspective because (1) they reflect a strategy to strengthen royal power by obtaining institutional support rather than weakening the monarch's power, and (2) they show how adopting a wider representative assembly or a parliamentary system strengthened royal power. That is, the outcome of the Cortes of León of 1188 was twofold: (a) maintaining justice and ensuring peace in the kingdom by resorting to the rule of law or legality principle, and (b) enhancing the joint participation of common people in discussing matters

[109] See Procter (1980); O'Callaghan (1989).

[110] Colmeiro (1861), Ch. IX; Cavero (2009); some historians discussed whether the first Cortes of Castile and León were celebrated in Burgos (1187), in San Esteban de Gormaz (1187), or in León (1188); or whether the first Cortes of the Iberian Peninsula occurred in Portugal in 1143; see Martín (2003); See also the works by Fernando Arvizu Galagarra: Arvizu (1988); Arvizu (1994); Arvizu (2002).

[111] See, for example, Estepa (2002), pp. 183–184; De Ayala (1996); Mitre (1989); Procter (1980), pp. 67 ss.

[112] Nieto (2011), pp. 197–241.

[113] Fernández (1988).

[114] For this view, see González and González (2018).

[115] González (1944), pp. 23–26.

[116] Fernández (1993), pp. 93–117.

[117] Seijas (2016); see this version—with some minor corrections—in the Appendix of the book.

[118] Mezey (2022).

that affected them. What happened in León in 1188 would spread and become common in other European jurisdictions some years later: German Diet (1232), English parliament (1265), and French General States (1302).

While the *Privilegio General* (1283) and *Privilegio de la Unión* (1287) are relevant texts in introducing the principle of the rule of law and some judicial guarantees, the *Decreta* of León (1188) were approved almost a century earlier. Though Aragón's *Fuero de Sobrarbe* is much older than the *Decreta*, no documentary evidence dispels the tradition surrounding this legal source. Hence, the *Decreta* of León in the Iberian Peninsula are the earliest document comparable to the *Magna Carta*, where the king committed himself before the social estates, including the citizens, to respect the law and guarantee a set of procedural rules (which is today called the "right to due process").

What were the circumstances surrounding these Cortes of León, considered to be the first in the history of Western European parliamentarism? The economic needs of Alfonso IX of León from the rising prices after a tax increase to cope with the break of the reconquest and the need for income to cope with the war with Portugal and Castile led the monarch to convene an extraordinary *curia regia*, where, for the first time in Europe, discounting the Icelandic case (with its legislative assembly, the "Althing"), the representatives of the city (with voice and vote) were invited. The king, realising the need for strengthening his social and political legitimacy, made the wise decision to submit a set of decrees for approval. Such *Decreta* included the recognition of a set of rights and liberties, such as the inviolability of home and mail, the obligation of the monarch to convoke Cortes and make war or declare peace, and the guarantee of various individual and collective rights.

Leaving aside the importance of the Cortes of León from a parliamentary perspective, their *Decreta* are perfectly comparable to the English Magna Carta in defending some principles connected to the rule of law and judicial guarantees. Below are brief references to some chapters containing these principles.[119]

Chapter I contains a royal commitment to observe and contribute to compliance with the customs established by Alphons IX's antecessors, establishing and confirming under oath that he would "respect the good customs (...) established by my predecessors" (Ch. I).[120]

Chapters II and III contain a royal commitment that only accurate, well-founded evidence would amount to an accusation, where the royal curia acts as the highest court of appeal. In Chapter II, Alfonso IX promised not to deny justice to anyone "if anyone should make or present a denunciation of anyone to me," threatening the informer who could not prove his accusation with "the punishment that the accused would have suffered if the accusation had been proven" (Ch. II). Moreover, given the

---

[119]See the English version of the *Decreta* of León 1188 in the Appendix, reproducing the translation by Seijas (2016), from the Spanish version by Fernández (1993), pp. 93–117.

[120]Such customs included the *Fuero de León* approved in 1017; see *Fueros locales del Reino de León (910–1230). Antología*, Madrid: Boletín Oficial del Estado, 2018 (available at https://www.boe.es/biblioteca_juridica/publicacion.php?id=PUB-LH-2018-61).

denunciation, the king promised to treat the denounced person following the law, since "I will never cause him harm or damage to his person or properties until he is subpoenaed in writing to respond to justice in my curia in the manner that my curia determined" (Ch. III). The content of both chapters (II and III) was indeed quite similar to what would later be drafted in Chapter 39 of the *Magna Carta*.[121] Moreover, as will be seen, Chapter IX punished those *justicias* [judges] who do not administer justice according to the prescribed legal procedure.

In Chapter IV, the king promised that he would make neither peace nor war, nor would he make agreements without the advice of bishops, nobles, and good men. He pledges neither to "wage war nor make peace or make any agreement without the counsel of the bishops, nobles, and good men, by whose advice I must abide" (Ch. IV).

Chapters V and VII sought the protection of property (houses, lands, and trees). It goes beyond private vengeance by committing to protect property, as long as the offended party "presents the complaint to me or to the lord of the land or to the justices appointed by me or by the bishop or by the lord of the land," while also protecting the alleged offender (or accused) "so he will not suffer any harm," and who is allowed to "present a guarantor or give a guarantee according to the ancient law [*fuero*]" (Ch. V).

Beyond prohibiting riots (tumult disturbing the public peace) (Ch. VI), it prohibits the theft of things (movable or immovable) that are in the possession of others, whether done with (Ch. VII) or without (Ch. VIII) violence. Chapter VIII discouraged and punished private revenge, calling offices to enforce the laws of towns and villages. It also provides that no one may be seized by another person "but through the justices or mayors designated by me; and they and the landlords do faithfully enforce the law in the cities and in the boroughs [*alfores*] for those who seek it" (Ch. VIII).

Chapter IX addresses those in charge of adjudicating and enforcing the law, establishing punishments for judges who do not enforce the law, ignore the plaintiff, or administer justice when damages or offenses have been caused or committed. It lays down the obligation to do justice following a legal procedure, with a 3-day term for the *justicias* to admit the demand, foreseeing the consequences of a supposed refusal on their part:

> I also decreed that if one of the justices denied justice to the plaintiff or delayed it maliciously or did not recognise his right by the third day, he should present witnesses before one of the aforementioned 'justicias' by whose testimony stating the truth of the matter and compel the justice to pay the plaintiff twice as much of his demand and the costs. And if all the justices of that land deny justice to the plaintiff, he should take witnesses from good men by whom it is proven and give pledge without responsibility instead of the justices and mayors, as much

[121] *Magna Carta*, Ch. 39: "No free man shall be arrested or imprisoned or deprived of his rights or property, nor put outlawed or banished or otherwise deprived of his rank, nor shall we use force against him or send others to do so, except by virtue of judicial sentence of his peers or by law of the realm."

> for the demand as for the costs, so that the justices would satisfy twice and also concerning the damage, that would ensure whom guarantees, the justices would pay double (Ch. IX).

Chapter X prescribes that judicial decisions and judges must be followed and respected.

Chapter XIII punishes, in general terms, the offended party who, rejecting the legally established procedures to do justice and compensate for the offense, chooses to take justice into his own hands by causing some damage to the offender, in which case "he should pay double, and if also he should kill him, he should be declared a treacherous" (Ch. XIII).

The justices were sanctioned if they refused to do justice or did not arrest "immediately and without delay" anyone who "wander[ed] by chance from one city to another (...) and someone with seal should come from justices to the justices (...) they should not hesitate in detaining him and doing justice" (Ch. XIV).

Beyond the obligations and duties required of the justices, the monarch also came to their defense, stating "that no one should appeal the justices nor grab the pledges when he did not want to comply with the justice; and if he should do this, he should repay twice the damage, the demand, and the costs and also pay the justices 60 *sueldos* [wages]" (Ch. X). The end of that same chapter contains the following general clause of protection for the *justicias* in charge of administering justice:

> And if any of the justices suffered any harm in carrying out the justice, all the men of that land will reimburse him for all the damage, in case he who did him harm should not have means to pay him; and if it happens, that one in addition may kill him, he would be taken as a traitor and a treacherous (Ch. X).

Sanctions were also provided for those who did not appear before the justices when summoned by them in accordance with the law (Ch. XI).

Another decree established the inviolability of the home, imposing heavy financial penalties and exonerating the homeowners of a possible homicide committed in self-defense (Ch. XII).

Chapter XVI addresses the rule of law. It prescribes that nobody shall be accused or tried by either royal or city court unless established by law. Prescribing that no one should go to trial before the royal curia or the court of León "unless for those causes for which he should go according to their own ancient laws [*fueros*]" (Ch. XVI) was the logical consequence of the royal commitment to respect "the good customs" established by his predecessors (Ch. I) to proceed "according to the ancient law [fuero]" (Ch. V) and act in conformity with the privilege and ancient customs of his land (Ch. VIII). Indeed, such commitment to the rule of law was quite similar to what would later be drafted in Chapters 39 and 40 of the *Magna Carta*.[122]

Further, to this royal recognition of rights and liberties, those attending the Cortes of 1188 (bishops, knights, and citizens) responded by committing themselves to be

[122] *Magna Carta*, Ch. 39: "No free man shall be arrested or imprisoned or deprived of his rights or property, nor put outlawed or banished or otherwise deprived of his rank, nor shall we use force against him or send others to do so, except by virtue of judicial sentence of his peers or by law of the realm"; Ch. 40: "We will not sell, deny or delay to anyone his right or justice."

faithful to the king in his counsel "to maintain justice and keep the peace in my kingdom" (Ch. XVII). Hence, Chapter XVII establishes that all participants of the Cortes shall swear faithfulness to the king to keep justice and peace and ensure public order throughout the kingdom.

The agreement of the *Decreta* in the Cortes of 1188 notably contributed to legitimising the social and political power of Alphons IX. Moreover, considering the content of its provisions, it is more than reasonable that such decrees have been called the "*Magna Carta Leonesa.*" However, it would be a mistake, to think all the precepts were new. Some had already been enacted. Accordingly, Alfonso IX confirmed the Fueros de León (1017, by Alphons V). Provisions such as those prohibiting attacks on the property of others, ordering the resolution of disputes before the courts, or preventing the King from entering into war without general consent were well known during the reign of Alfonso VII of León (1135). New decrees were added to these precepts in 1188 concerning, for example, cases of violence on (movable and immovable) things, recourse to justice in such cases, and other guarantees of a procedural nature. A few years later, in Galicia, "constitutions" (1194) would develop some of these precepts of 1188.

The *Decreta* insists on the idea that offenses or damages must be repaired or remedied through the enforcement of the law (mainly, the Fuero of León, 1017) and in court (rather than resorting to private revenge), calling for the respect of the judicial procedure and right conduct of judicial proceedings.

Thus, the Cortes of León and their *Decreta* are considered the oldest preserved written records of the parliamentary tradition in the Western world and, by extension, of modern parliamentary democracy. Unlike the *Magna Carta*, these *Decreta* were never abolished up until the nineteenth century when modern codes replaced older laws approved by Alphons the Wise (the *Fuero Juzgo*—containing the *Decreta*—the *Fuero Real*, the *Siete Partidas*, and the *Espéculo*).

On the 19th of June 2013, the UNESCO recognised the Cortes of León as the "Cradle of parliamentarism," and the *Decreta* was declared "Memory of the World" for being "the oldest written document of the parliamentary system in Europe."[123] Perhaps, more importantly, the Cortes of León and their *Decreta* reflect how a king, for the first time, "put the power of law above his own power, and not vice versa."[124]

Hence, for now, the first documented precedent of the rule of law and representative democracy in the Western world can be found in 1188 in León, a city that had enacted its law (Fuero de León) in a council presided by Alphons V in 1017. Thus, the people of León already appreciated what the law was about.

The possibility of Spanish influences regarding the Hungarian Golden Bull might not be excluded because there are certain ties between the Kingdoms of Aragón and Hungary in the analysed period. The brother of King Andrew II of Hungary, King Emeric (who reigned between the 1196–1204 period) married, perhaps in 1196, Constance, the daughter of King Alfonso II of Aragón (Constance, after the death of

[123] International Memory of the World Register (2013)

[124] Suárez (1976) (this quotation is from López González (2015), p. 8).

her husband, became the wife of Frederick II, Holy Roman Emperor). The queen was accompanied to her new home by a court and clerical entourage: the latter may have been a bearer of political ideas. Iberian influences are certainly documented, for example, in the heraldic motifs. After Emeric's death (1204), Constance and their child, the child King Ladislaus III, fled to Vienna, but there, Ladislaus died at the age of approximately 5, and Andrew, later the signatory of the Hungarian Golden Bull, was crowned king. The dynastical relations between the Árpád dynasty of Hungary and the Kingdom of Aragón continued: the daughter of Andrew II of Hungary, Violant of Hungary, was the wife of King James I of Aragón (the Conqueror). Their marriage occurred in 1235, more than a decade later than the issuance of the Hungarian Golden Bull, and some years before King James I of Aragón liberated Valencia (1238). After this battle, King James I rewarded several Hungarian knights who took part in the fighting and arrived on the Iberian Peninsula alongside queen Violant.

Affirming that the *Decreta* of León (1188) constitutes a relevant historical precedent of the rule of law and representative democracy in the Western world neither means ignoring the radical differences between two social, cultural, political, and legal contexts (the twelfth-century medieval and the nineteenth-century liberal and constitutional-legal orders) nor denying the mythological character of some historical texts, such as the *Fueros de Sobrarbe*, *Cortes de León*, and *Carta Magna*.[125] It does rather mean that such documents show how medieval Europe started to be aware of the convenience of limiting political power through law, using the law as a safeguard against the abusive and arbitrary exercise of political power.[126]

Many notions, categories, and principles radically changed throughout time but do not preclude the possibility to reconstruct their historical development. Sovereignty, notably, changed in the Middle Ages, then in the early modern age (with the rise of royal absolutism), and, eventually, in the late modern age (with the emergence of liberal and constitutional systems after the French and American revolutions). However, such changes should not prevent legal historians from trying to describe and analyse such development.

Nobody will deny that the Second World War context from which the legal notion of "human rights" emerged was radically different from that of the rise of "fundamental rights" in the eighteenth and nineteenth centuries) and "natural rights" in the sixteenth century. However, it should not preclude the possibility of connecting such notions that are indeed connected.[127]

Can the expressions "rights" and "liberties" be used in the medieval context, as some scholars use them?[128] Arguably, yes; however, clarification is needed: though such expressions might appear in the sources, their meaning and scope might not

---

[125] Lorente (2016).

[126] Masferrer and Obarrio (2012).

[127] Haakonsen (1991); see also Masferrer (2019c).

[128] See footnote n. 12.

extend to expectations of contemporary reading. However, it seems less appropriate to use the expressions "individual freedoms"[129] or "fundamental rights"[130] in the medieval context.

1.4.2.4 Its Legal Standing: *quod omnes tangit ab omnibus approbari debet*

Once the Courts arose, the medieval doctrine of *ius commune* would be in charge of looking for a way to justify or legitimise them legally. This was achieved by resorting to a precept of the Code of Justinian, in which, dealing with a question of private law related to the term of the guardianship in case of plurality of guardians, the following statement appears:

> For then, whether they were testamentary, or whether appointed by virtue of information, or whether legitimate, or whether simply appointed, it is necessary that all give their consent, so that ***what concerns all equally may be approved by all***. All of these is to be observed in the same way also with regard to curators (CI. 5, 59, 5. 2) (the text in italics and bold is ours).

Law follows reality. This is the norm and this is what happened in this case. First the Courts came into being and then a legal principle was sought that would allow them to be legitimised. To do so, they searched throughout the *Corpus iuris civilis*, and it mattered little to them to find it in the heart of a legal institution (tutela) far removed from the Courts. For them, that was secondary: the important thing was that Roman law contained a principle that could well be applied to the case in question.

1.4.3 Municipal Freedom and Autonomy: Charta libertatis

As we have seen, it was precisely the incorporation of the representatives of the cities into the ancient extraordinary curiae that gave rise to medieval assemblies that made it possible to place limits on royal power, and within which a set of rights and liberties was enshrined that constitute an important precedent of modern constitutionalism or, if one prefers, of modern rights and liberties.

However, it is worth noting the importance, in this respect, of the medieval municipality, an institution whose origin was—as has been said—prior to the medieval Cortes, and which can be considered as the precedent of the modern State. It should be remembered that both the Cortes of León (1188) and the Magna Carta (1215) contained a precept confirming the rights and liberties already granted to both the city of León and the city of London. In fact, the emergence of the medieval municipality was due to the granting—by the king or the lord and nobles—of a set of rights, liberties, immunities, and freedoms that were completely new at

[129] Cited in the footnote n. 12.

[130] Dávila (2017).

that time, since it meant the creation of an alternative legal-public regime to the existing one, that is, to the manorial one, in which its inhabitants—mostly peasants—were subject to the power or jurisdiction of a lord, whose exercise could easily fall into abuses and arbitrariness.

The notion of freedom became so closely associated with the medieval municipality that in Germany the saying "stadtluft macht frei", i.e., 'the air of the city makes free' (whoever lives in it) became popular.

It could be asked why this regime of liberties was granted, and how it was carried out, questions whose complete development would exceed the limits of the present text, but which should be dealt with and related succinctly. Various factors explain the emergence of the municipality, as well as the will of the monarch to promote its creation and development by granting it a privileged legal status of autonomy, thanks to which its inhabitants could govern themselves, administer justice, create legal norms, etc.

In the Iberian Peninsula, the reconquest and repopulation of lands that had been occupied by the Muslims was probably the most important factor, but it was not the only one. This is how José María Font Rius summarised the set of factors that led to the emergence of the medieval municipality:

> Campaigns of territorial reconquest in the face of Islamic domination (...); the constitution of settlements and agrarian colonisations as the natural culmination of this enterprise and the basis of its economic and civil organisation; the impulse of mercantile development and, especially, the promotion of the urban and rural classes within the centre of population; the struggle of royalty against feudalism, with the repercussions of this in the confrontation of the people affected by feudal ties, etc.[131]

Along with the reconquest enterprise, the economic growth and the emergence of a new merchant class dedicated to trade, to the development of a business that generated more income than those who were dedicated to the exploitation of the land, changed the social landscape of the time. Moreover, these merchants, by settling outside the walls of the old towns—or 'burghs', hence the name of the new class as 'bourgeois'—, changed the social and geographical physiognomy of cities that, in a short time, experienced a remarkable growth. Demography in Europe also experienced a remarkable increase: between the eleventh and fourteenth centuries, the European population tripled. The cities—both urban and rural—not only contributed to this demographic growth, but also, in part, made it possible, viable and sustainable, creating wealth and promoting a growing commercial and agricultural activity that would end up involving a greater number of people.

From the beginning, the monarchy looked favourably on this transformation. Monarchs were in charge of supporting the creation and development of the cities, and being fully aware of their contribution to the growth and development of their territories. For that to be possible, monarchs needed a bourgeois class to provide with an income that the nobles could not give them, and it was also highly convenient for them to be able to rely on a new social class when negotiating agreements with the

[131] Font (1983), p. 50.

nobles (hence, the latter became—in the Cortes—the 'royal arm'). Moreover, the same Roman Law that had contributed so much to confirm the royal power (by subrogating the king in the position of the emperor), was also useful to regulate the new relationships that arose within a municipality that, however much it had grown, would hardly reach the complexity and sophistication of ancient Rome. Note that in Rome originated and developed the *ius civile*, that classical Roman Law that, being later on collected in the Justinian Compilation (528–533), was discovered and recovered from the eleventh century onwards, studied at the then emerging universities and received throughout Europe.

How did the monarchy contribute to the creation of the municipality? Its contribution was fundamental, because it provided the regime with what it needed for its development, through the concession of privileges, liberties, immunities and franchises that were unknown in the scope of the existing manorial regime at that time. And he did this through the granting of a document that constituted the legal basis for the creation of the medieval municipality: the brief charters or charters of population and franchise, so well researched by some authors, both legal historians and medievalists.

These documents—called *carta franchitatis*, *carta libertatis et franchitatis*, *francheza et securitatis*, *libertas et securitas*, or even *constitutio libertatis*—were "real particular laws intended to regulate the relations of the inhabitants with the public power and, therefore, with exclusive reference to public law."[132] Without prejudice to their broad content, they were aimed at the social, economic and political progress of an urban or rural nucleus. With regard to the political sphere, which is the one that interests us here, these charters or charters satisfied the "aspirations or demands of the population", while contributing to "consolidate popular support for the granting authority."[133]

What did these aspirations or demands of the inhabitants of these urban or rural areas consist of? In that the authority—the monarch or the lord—, by granting these charters, acknowledged the existence of rights and duties between him and his inhabitants. In other words, obtaining such a *carta libertatis* meant "the formal, written determination of rights and duties between the inhabitants of a place and their sovereign or lord, as opposed to the traditional vagueness or indeterminacy of customary law that provided a wider margin of arbitrariness on the part of the latter."[134]

More specifically, such *constitutiones libertatis* entailed, in the first place, the free possession of land and other public-legal guarantees such as the protection and security of persons, their own bodily integrity or indemnity, the peaceful possession of goods (which prevented any coercive action outside justice), the free circulation of goods and merchandise (free from 'marks' or arbitrary seizures), the protection of the market, as well as of the access roads to the locality. In addition to these

---

[132]Font (1983), p. 53.

[133]Font (1983), p. 59.

[134]Font (1983), p. 218.

guarantees, there were also procedural ones, which expressed the commitment of the public authorities to administer justice in an upright manner.[135] From the eleventh century onwards, charters were granted which, in addition to establishing exemptions from any census and service, offered security to people and goods by prohibiting any arbitrary coercive action (Barcelona, 1025; Vall de Lord, 1068; Vilafranca de Conflent, 1090; Tàrrega, 1116; Barcelona, 1162; among others).[136]

> On 16 November 1118, Alfonso VII, on granting Toledo its privileges, stipulated that all disputes should be resolved in accordance with the Fuero Juzgo "in front of the very noble and very wise men who are always with the mayor of the city to adjudicate the disputes of the towns."[137]

Another important area of these *letters libertatis* was that relating to the civil liberty of the inhabitants of towns and villages. The granting of these letters meant the recognition and enjoyment of full legal capacity to its inhabitants, who were no longer subject to the *bad* manorial customs that restricted their personal and domicile freedom, the free disposal of their goods *inter-vivos* and *mortis-causa*, as well as the personal servitudes of the manorial regime. An important complement to this civil freedom, thanks to which the inhabitants were 'freed' from the *bad* manorial *usages* and servitudes, was the freedom of economic activity, by which the citizens could carry out, "without any restriction, certain industrial and mercantile operations or use certain services that normally—or at least originally—were of exclusive or preferential exercise or exploitation by the dominical or jurisdictional lords."[138]

From the twelfth century onwards, several charters contain such civil liberties. In Toledo, Alfonso VI granted the Mozarabs, on 19 March 1101, a charter of security with several express references to the new regime of freedom (Ricardo Izquierdo Benito, *Privilegios reales otorgados a Toledo durante la Edad Media (1101-1494)*, Toledo, 1990, pp. 90–91). Charters of similar content can be found in the Catalan Principality from the middle of the twelfth century (Vall d'Osor, 1144; Espluga de Francolí, 1171; Verdú, 1184; Solsona, 1195; Vilanova de la Barca, 1212; Igualada, 1235; among others).[139]

[135] Font (1983), pp. 218–219.

[136] On some population charters with obvious political overtones, see Font (1983), pp. 222–223.

[137] Izquierdo (1990), p. 95.

[138] Font (1983), pp. 219–220.

[139] On the lifting of restrictions on civil rights, see Font (1983), pp. 226–228.

1.5 Other More Distant Precedents in the History of Human Rights

Are there precedents for human rights in Greece and Rome, and are there precedents even more remote in origin than those of antiquity? The answer to both statements is yes. Any precept that, by limiting political power, has established and protected a sphere of freedom for the subjects that make up a political community, constitutes a precedent or link in the chain of formation and development of human rights.

The more developed the political power is, the greater the risk of violating this sphere of personal freedom, although this experience is the best context for rectifying and straightening the course through the establishment of guarantees. As will be seen, Roman law, thanks to the influence of Stoic philosophy, made a notable advance in this field.

It would be more complex to venture which was the first normative text in the history of human rights. Some argue that the 'Cyrus Cylinder', drafted in 539 BC by Cyrus the Great of the Achaemenid Empire of Persia (formerly Iran) after the conquest of Babylon, may be the first human rights document. This text, with which the monarch tried to win over the population, freed the slaves, declared that all people had the right to choose their own religion and established racial equality.

Although Roman law texts are not usually cited as a precedent for human rights, this omission does not do justice to the historical truth. As will be seen in the following section, the notion of subjective right, which would be the object of notable development by canon law and doctrine, was present in several precepts of Roman law.

In the Arab sphere, the 'Pact of the Virtuous' ('Hilf-al-fudûl') was agreed upon by tribes around 590 A.D. This was a pact of honour and justice that committed the tribes beyond tribal alliances based on political or commercial interests. By virtue of this pact of honour and chivalry, chiefs and members of numerous tribes obliged themselves to intervene in conflicts and to take the side of the oppressed against the oppressors, regardless of who they were, and regardless of the pacts they might have with other tribes. This covenant thus placed respect for the principles of justice and support for the oppressed above all other considerations of kinship or power.[140]

1.6 Nature, Natural Law and Natural Rights

Although the expressions 'nature', 'natural law' and 'natural rights' have appeared on occasion throughout these pages, we have preferred that the main idea or guiding thread of this brief history of human rights be another, namely that of the limitation of political power. In fact, the common element of the different precedents or

[140] Ramadan (2009), pp. 40–43.

episodes that mark this history has been the establishment of limits to political power—sometimes self-imposed—in order to guarantee a space of freedom and autonomy for the members of the community subject to its rulers.

We have seen how modern constitutionalism consisted precisely in the recognition of a space of freedom, with its fundamental rights and liberties, whose protection constituted the raison d'être of the State, and in which the public power was forbidden any kind of interference or intrusion. This same idea of limitation is found in the Spanish colonisation of America (a context in which the universal nature of natural rights was defended), in the wars of religion and their consequent peace treaties (with which the path towards religious tolerance and freedom began), in the civil wars provoked by the struggle between the crown and the parliament (which contributed to the consecration of parliamentarism as an instrument to limit political power), as well as in the medieval context, in which the Church managed to free itself from the yoke of secular power (*libertas ecclesiae*), the estates (ecclesiastical, secular and citizen) managed to consecrate—through agreement—a set of limits and guarantees against the power of the monarch (Cortes of León, 1188; Magna Carta, 1215; Golden Bull, 1222), just as families and entire communities managed to 'free themselves' from the subjection of the feudal regime thanks to the concession of privileges and liberties (*Charta libertatis*) that constituted the legal basis of a new regime, the municipal regime, in which the creation of law and the administration of justice, no longer depending on the arbitrary will of the lord, was largely the responsibility of the inhabitants of each municipality (*stadtluft macht frei*).

It is useful now, however, to briefly describe the evolution of the idea of human rights from a more ius-philosophical or philosophical-political perspective than a merely political (*Realpolitik*) or constitutional one. Without such a perspective, this history would be incomplete because it would lack the idea or concept-basis on which the need to establish limits to political power was justified or legitimised. Otherwise, it could be thought—wrongly—that the establishment of such limits arose for a merely empirical reason, that is, because of the sad experience of the abuses committed by political power, when, in fact, both the convenience of those limits and the idea that gave them substance had been the object of study and development since Antiquity.

In this sense, the notion of 'natural rights', so important in North American Independence and in the French Revolution, was not an invention of Enlightenment thought, but the result of a multi-secular development. We have already seen how this idea was very present in the convulsive England of the seventeenth century, as well as in the Spanish colonisation of America during the sixteenth century. But these 'natural rights' were not a creation of the Second Scholasticism (Francisco de Vitoria, Domingo de Soto, Francisco Suárez, etc.) either, but came from the doctrine of authors such as John Duns Scotus (1266–1308) and, above all, William of Ockham (1288–1347), who in turn started from the doctrine of Thomas Aquinas (1225–1274), among others. All these authors tried to establish a clear connection between 'natural law' and 'natural rights', arguing that the latter derived from the former. Moreover, medieval canon law contributed to this evolution by developing the idea of 'subjective law', which attributed to the subject a set of faculties or powers, a notion quite different from the—until then known—'objective law'. This contribution of medieval canon law was not entirely original either, since Roman Law already had texts, whose content was closer to the notion of 'subjective right' than to that of 'objective right'. On the other hand, the concepts of 'nature' and 'natural law', from which would emerge 'natural rights' (fourteenth to eighteenth centuries) that would later become 'fundamental rights' (nineteenth century) and 'human rights' (twentieth century), are very ancient, and, of course, predate the Christian era.

Although the historical development of this evolution would completely exceed the limits of these pages, it is worth summarising its main milestones in order to understand to what extent natural law has been the basis and the lifeblood that has given origin and life to human rights throughout their history, from Antiquity until the mid-twentieth century, where, when the UDHR (1948) was drafted, it was decided to avoid mentioning it due to lack of unanimity.[141]

1.6.1 Antiquity

Readily in Antiquity, Aristotle (384–322 B.C.) distinguished between 'natural justice' and 'legal justice' (or justice of law). According to him, while the former was the same everywhere, the latter could be different from one place to another, depending on the opinion of different people and peoples. In any case, Aristotle was referring only to the Hellenic sphere, and considered the barbarians as slaves, incapable of forming just societies.

1.6.1.1 Stoicism

It was the Stoics who had the broadest conception of natural law. According to them, the whole cosmos showed the existence of a divine intelligence that governed all things according to a universal natural law. Men, being endowed with reason-which is a part of the aforementioned divine intelligence that governs everything—were, by nature, free and equal. The prominence that the Stoics gave to reason, however, left little room for the free exercise of the will, leading to a somewhat deterministic system, in which only by choosing what was in conformity with nature could the desired state of serenity be attained in the midst of the vicissitudes of life, in health or in sickness, in wealth or in poverty.

[141] For the part I follow Tierney (2008); López Hernández (1998); Carpintero (2000, 2013); Hervada (1987).

1.6.1.2 Cicero

The influence of Stoic philosophy was felt in authors such as Cicero. Cicero, in his *De republica*, made a forceful defence of natural law by pointing out that true law is the right reason in conformity with nature, which, being universal, permanent and invariable, neither the senate nor the people can detach the ties that bind us to it. In *De legibus* he pointed out that justice is based on right, and that right is the supreme reason inscribed in nature and in human reason, prescribing what is to be done and forbidding its opposite. Cicero further pointed out that since all human beings are endowed with the same reason and the same sense of justice, they are all part of the same community. He went so far as to affirm that reason is a gift that conferred on man a likeness to God, distinguishing him from all other creatures.

1.6.1.3 Roman sources

Stoic philosophy and Cicero's theses found their way into Roman law, both in legal sources and in the writings of the great jurists. In this sense, the tripartite division of natural law made by Ulpian is well known: (1) animal natural law (what nature has taught to all animals, including procreation and the breeding of offspring); (2) human natural law; and (3) *ius gentium*, the concept of which is not unambiguous in the sources. While in some it is identified with natural law, in others it seems to consist of a set of human covenants or conventions that would replace—at least in part—human natural law. In this respect, for example, Ulpian pointed out that while all men are born free—in conformity with human natural law—slavery had arisen from the *ius gentium*. In any case, Roman jurists treated natural law as an abstract or philosophical concept, and never considered, for example, whether natural law could prevail over existing law if the two conflicted. What is certain is that Roman law left many texts that contradicted each other and the solution to these contradictions would be taken care of by the jurists of the *ius commune from the* eleventh and twelfth centuries onwards.

1.6.1.4 Christian Sources

Christianity took up much of the legacy of Stoicism and authors such as Cicero. St. Paul, for example, referring to the pagans, affirms that they have the law written in their hearts (Romans 2:14–15). In short, he was referring to the Ten Commandments, which, besides being known—first by the chosen people and then by Christians—because they were written on the tablets of the law, were also accessible to the pagans because they were inscribed in the hearts of all men. This idea would be reiterated by the early Fathers of the Church such as St. Irenaeus, who affirmed that God, before leaving the commandments of the law written on stone, inscribed these natural precepts in the hearts of men. St. Augustine pointed out that the natural law of man had its source in the eternal divine law, which was the divine reason and will prescribing the preservation of the natural order. Augustine of Hippo defined divine providence as the natural law inscribed in the rational soul. In this sense, just as the natural order of the universe was governed by divine reason or intelligence, so the natural order proper to the human soul was to be governed by a reason that was to overcome the force of the passions. Moreover, man, unlike the animals, has a free will, which allows him to act contrary to the dictates of reason. Augustine stressed the sinful condition of man as the cause of natural disorder, with the consequent loss of the natural order of freedom and innocence established by God. According to him, servitude and government are due only to the human proclivity for sin.

1.6.2 Middle Ages

1.6.2.1 The Canonist Doctrine

Already in the twelfth century, the contribution of canon law to the development of natural law was remarkable. The Decree of Gratian (1140) contained a definition of natural law that is considered to be the golden rule of the Bible: 'natural law is what is contained in Holy Scripture, whereby one is obliged to do to another that which one would wish for oneself, and is forbidden to do to another that which one would not wish to be done to oneself' (*Decretum Magistri Gratiani, dictum ante Dist.*, I, C. I). Although this was undoubtedly a good way of defining natural law, it is true that even the canonical texts had contradictory elements. Thus, for example, Gratian himself pointed out that, by natural law, all things were common to all, and that the right to property was introduced by custom and Roman law.[142] However, further on, he pointed out that any custom or law contrary to natural law was null and void. What, then, should be the consequence of this principle with regard to the right of property? He said nothing about it. Apart from these paradoxes that remained unresolved in the canonical texts, the main contributions of canon law to the connection between natural law and the history of human rights, or natural rights, were twofold: (a) the treatment of natural law as a permissive or optional right, and (b) the notion of natural law in a subjective sense, that is, as an inherent or corresponding attribute of the human being. Let us see them now in a succinct way.[143]

(a) *Natural law as a permissive or optional right*: some authors have denied the possible connection between natural law and natural rights because, according to

[142]This doctrine constituted the "*Communis omnium possessio*" which St. Isidore of Seville had specified as part of natural law. The other great part was the "*Omnium una libertas*". Gratian, trained in early medieval sources, was necessarily familiar with the "Etymologies" of St. Isidore, which used to be the textbook in the various schools before the medieval university.

[143]In this regard, see Carpintero (1981).

them, the content of the former constrains human conduct, obliging us to do or not to do something, while natural rights confer a margin for freedom or free will. Nothing could be further from the truth. Such a view loses sight of the fact that, from the twelfth century onwards, natural law acquired a new sense or a new meaning, according to which a human sphere of free choice was established. Canonists realised that this interpretation resolved some of the apparent contradictions raised by the canonical texts. Thus, for example, the contradiction of the right to property was resolved if the principle of common or non-private property was understood as an optional or permissive norm, which did not impose any kind of obligation, leaving the option or path of private property open. Some canonists even found in a Pauline text (I Cor. 6:12) the authority that allowed them to justify or legitimise this recent doctrine. 'All things are lawful for me, but not all things are expedient,' said St. Paul. And St. Ambrose, referring to this 'all things are lawful for me', added 'by natural right' ('*lege naturae*'). From the twelfth century onwards, therefore, by natural law we could also understand what was permitted or approved, and not only what was subject to obligation or prohibition. From then on—and until the eighteenth century—optional or permissive law became an important part of natural law, and formed the basis of natural rights.

(b) *Natural law in a subjective sense*: As we have already seen, Cicero had already considered natural law as an innate force inscribed in man. The canonists also tended to define it as an inner force of man, connected to reason and will. Varying the Ciceronian notion, they also began to define *ius naturale* as a power, faculty or capacity inherent in the human being. This subjective notion of *ius naturale* as a power or faculty, initially referring only to the ability to distinguish between good and evil, between right and wrong, when associated with the idea of reason and free will, ended up being understood or identified with the natural rights that every human being could exercise, acting freely or claiming something that corresponds to him or is due to him. The first example of this natural right developed by the canonist doctrine was that of the poor to be supported by the wealth of the rich. From there, many thinkers would develop this notion over several centuries (William of Ockham, John Gerson, Francisco de Vitoria, Domingo de Soto, Francisco Suárez, Hugo Grotius, Samuel Pufendorf, Christian Wolf, Christian Thomasius, etc.), using the expressions 'the right of the poor to be supported by the wealth of the rich' and 'the right of the rich to be supported by the wealth of the rich', using the expressions 'power', 'faculty' or 'capacity' when defining right ('*ius*' in Latin, or 'law' in English) as subjective right. As Brian Tierney points out, although the canonists did not develop a coherent theory of 'natural rights', they did create the language (with its concept and terminology) that would later enable the development of that theory.

Together with this linguistic contribution of Canon Law to the development of natural rights, we should add the existence of some legal-canonical precepts whose objective consisted in the protection of rights (or 'legal rights' in English), among which we should highlight the right not to incriminate oneself and to remain silent in criminal proceedings, the right to marry freely, or the right to participate in elections, among others.[144]

1.6.2.2 Thomas Aquinas

Thomas Aquinas was the medieval author who contributed the most to the development of the notion of natural law. After defining law in general as 'the ordering of reason for the common good promulgated by the one entrusted with the duty of care to the community' (Summa Theologica I, 2ae.90.4), he distinguished between eternal law, natural law, human law and divine law. Following Augustine, Thomas Aquinas defined eternal law as the divine plan of the universe that was existing in the mind of God, that rule of divine wisdom which moves all things to their proper end. Insofar as all other laws derive from this divine law, irrational creatures tend to reach their own end in a deterministic way, while human beings, endowed with understanding and free will, have the capacity to discern (with reason) and adhere (with will) to the principles of the eternal law in general, and those concerning human beings in particular (human-natural law), since, according to Aquinas, natural law is nothing other than the participation of the eternal law in the rational creature. In analysing the content of this natural law, Thomas Aquinas affirmed that its first principle consists of 'doing good and avoiding evil', and that the other principles derive from it, although their concreteness is not immediate, requiring reflection on the inclinations of the human being. Among these natural inclinations, the first is the inclination to self-preservation (or survival), which humans share with all the beings of creation; the second is the inclination to procreation and the raising of offspring, which humans share with other animals; and thirdly all the inclinations that are proper and exclusive to man (such as not treating badly or insulting those with whom one must coexist).

In dealing with human laws, Thomas Aquinas was aware that man is subject to inclinations, both good and evil, and that human reason has the capacity to distinguish one from the other, although it is true that it can be affected by concupiscence or other passion, as well as by vices. Hence the need for coercive laws in order to ensure the application of the principles of natural law, the observance of which is essential for peaceful human coexistence (for example, laws penalising murder, theft, etc.). Moreover, human laws are necessary because natural law contains only general principles, without specifying their application in particular circumstances (natural law compels, for example, criminalising theft, but does not specify the sentence, which may vary in different geographical-temporal contexts). According to him, human laws can be related to natural law in two different ways, either as conclusions derived from its principles, or as a specific concretisation of a sphere that natural law has left undetermined. It is here, then, that this notion of natural law as a

[144]On this question, see, for example, Helmholz (2010).

permissive right or sphere appears once again. However, Thomas Aquinas did not make explicit or develop the idea of 'natural rights'.

1.6.2.3 John Duns Scotus and William of Ockham

Those who did, a few years later, and within the framework of scholastic philosophy, were the Franciscans John Duns Scotus and William of Ockham. The former, responding to the criticism addressed to Aquinas that the excessive emphasis placed on divine reason implied a certain limit or restriction to divine omnipotence, affirmed that the will is not necessarily determined by reason.[145]

For Scotus, the moral order and the natural precepts that could be deduced by reason were limited, while the rest, the greater part of reality, was the product of the divine will and its knowledge depended fundamentally on revelation, even though they may present flashes of reasonableness. This has its consequences in the field of natural law because, for Scotus, only the first two commandments were entirely natural law in the strict sense; the rest—the third, occupying an intermediate position—were so only in a broad sense, falling more within the field of freedom and the will of God (knowable thanks to revelation) than in a strictly rational consistency, even though they may maintain a certain moral reasonableness. Hence God can, if he sees fit, dispense with their fulfillment or even command the contrary, as he did when he ordered Abraham to sacrifice his son Isaac. As can be seen, Scotus "thus departs from the harmonious conception of faith and reason carved out by St. Thomas and produces a crack in philosophical-theological intellectualism."[146] Moreover, by advocating the reality of the individual, he also initiated a transformation of metaphysical knowledge, leading it towards the particular and sensible, "a step prior to the appearance of later nominalism and the gestation of modern science." [147]

In short, Scotus initiated the crisis of the classical conception of natural law, formulated by Thomas Aquinas, a rupture that had two axes: (1) to separate the order of being, reserving its knowledge to the realm of the theoretical sciences (metaphysics), and that of acting—or morality—to the practical sciences (moral theology); and (2) to root the moral order and its foundation in the divine will, apart from intelligence. Consequently, "the natural law, therefore, does not derive from the order of being, from the nature of things and, in the last analysis, from human nature, but from divine freedom and omnipotence."[148]

Ockham went further by arguing that the whole universe, including the moral world, existed in this way for the simple reason that God had willed it so, so that if he

[145] On Duns Scotus, see López Hernández (1998), p. 207–213; Hervada (1987), pp. 183–185; Carpintero (2013), pp. 105–116.

[146] López Hernández (1998), p. 208.

[147] López Hernández (1998), p. 208.

[148] López Hernández (1998), p. 213.

had intended it, he could have done things differently, even to the point of considering conduct such as theft or adultery as virtuous.[149] This voluntarist conception of the moral and legal order—including the proper sphere of natural law—led him to defend "a practically absolute moral contingentism" by which he "understands the dictates of natural reason as a mere expression of the will of God."[150] Or, in other words, with this voluntarist conception, "the dictates of natural reason are not considered as reflections of the demands of human nature, but as reflections of the divine will (voluntarism) or as manifestations of the subjective conscience of each man (moral subjectivism)." [151]

The second backbone of Ockham's thought was nominalism, a philosophical current that understood that only the entity or singular being is real, not the universal concepts, which are either mere mental generalisations (conceptualism), or simple names only useful to designate a multiplicity of singular beings (nominalism *stricto sensu*). With nominalism, the essence and nature of beings—man among them—cease to have real consistency, and metaphysics loses its relation with the moral and legal order, being relegated to the theological sphere.[152]

For Ockham, natural law is actually a divine command, the result of God's 'unconditioned will'. In short, things are good because He commands them or bad because He forbids them. In fact, God's 'unconditioned will' could have willed the opposite, commanding that He be hated and forbidding that He be loved. However, Ockham's voluntarism went largely unnoticed in Second Spanish Scholasticism. Carpintero only found, in legal doctrine, a few citations to his work in the *Controversias ilustres* (1560), by Fernando Vázquez, who picked up Ockham's confused idea that "God can order us whatever He wills, because the divine will is not subject to any order of being."[153] This would explain how Samuel Pufendorf, in provoking in the seventeenth century the controversy about intellectualism or divine voluntarism, quoted Vázquez and not Ockham.[154]

In any case, the voluntarist conception led Ockham to hold that the whole content of the Decalogue is contingent, including also the first three commandments, considered necessary and immutable by Scotus. Therefore, for him, the moral natural law is "entirely a divine law, born of the will of God", ceasing to be "a law of the divine intellect accessible for that very reason to human reason through evidence."[155] In any case, Ockham, while recognising that God could perfectly well

[149] According to Brian Tierney, some have misinterpreted Ockham's thesis. This does not seem to be the opinion of other authors after analysing the work of William of Ockham: López Hernández (1998), pp. 214–223; Hervada (1987), pp. 189–191; Carpintero (2013), pp. 116–121; on Ockham, see the classic work by Villey (1969a), pp. 116–121.

[150] Hervada (1987), p. 189.

[151] Hervada (1987), p. 189.

[152] Carpintero (2013), p. 118, argues that "Ockham did not fully propose a nominalist philosophy: the first nominalist system was that of Thomas Hobbes".

[153] Carpintero (2013), p. 118.

[154] Carpintero (2013), p.118.

[155] López Hernández (1998), p. 216.

change the natural law after having created it, understood that "as long as the present order subsists, men are bound by God to guide their moral conduct according to right reason. Revelation helps man in the way of salvation, but in temporal things, before and after revelation, men also have the help of natural reason."[156] And, in this line, he adds: "As long as the natural order continues, there will be no perfectly virtuous act that is not in conformity with the right reason inherent in [man] at the present time."[157] From there, in dealing with moral action, he reproduces—in a certain way, not without some contradiction—God's approach in man: for a moral act to be in conformity with the natural law, two requirements must be met: (1) unconditional freedom ("it must be a completely free action, in which the human will is not determined by any cause, not even by reason"),[158] and (2) the act "must also be in conformity with the dictates of right reason about its object." The law of nature, being the work of the will of God, can contain any commandment except that which violates the principle of non-contradiction.[159]

It is surprising how Ockhamist thought tried to combine a voluntarist conception of natural law, devoid of any reason outside the mere—unconditional and even capricious—will of God, with a remarkable prominence given to right reason or natural reason "as long as the present order subsists". In this sense, Tierley argues that Ockham gave three definitions of the term natural right, all of them related to reason:

1. Immutable moral precepts (in conformity with natural reason), such as those contained in the Ten Commandments
2. The right existing in the state of innocence, the validity of which is maintained so long as man lives in accordance with the dictates of reason
3. The natural law that comes from natural reason on the basis of human experience; it is a law ('suppositious law') that presupposes the real—not ideal—situation of man, after his nature has been wounded—but not fallen or corrupted—by original sin[160]

I do not quite share Tierley's view in this regard. In my opinion, this threefold conceptual order of Natural Law does not really fit with Ockham's thought. He, and the nominalists, spoke of the following rights: (1) an original right prior to the Natural Law, because it came from *Ex prima justitia Dei*; (2) an evangelical right; (3) a natural law, to which neither Scotus nor he place importance because the natural law has no relevance in the properly moral and supernatural life. For Ockham, the right which 'reason' *naturally* shows to man is just another part of

[156] López Hernández (1998), pp. 216–217.

[157] William of Ockham, Comment. Sent., III, q. 12, CCC (collected by López Hernández (1998), p. 217).

[158] William of Ockham, Comment. Sent., I, 1, 6, P, R (collected by López Hernández (1998), p. 217).

[159] López Hernández (1998), p. 217.

[160] On this question, see—in addition to the above study by Tierney (2008), and Offler (1977).

nature, adiaphoric to moral duty; (4) a right of human origin, which is based solely on the consensus of the community; and (5) a doctrinal or jurisprudential right, which is rather an '*ars iniquitatis*'. Some nominalists of the following century introduced still require further distinctions of 'law'.

In this sense, the following three modes of natural law seem to us to be more in accord with Ockham's thought:

(a) In a first way, what is called natural right is that which is in conformity with natural reason, which in no case errs, e.g., do not adulterate, do not lie, etc.
(b) in a second way, natural law is that which must be observed by those who are governed by natural equity alone, without any natural law (state of nature)
(c) finally, natural law is called the law of nations or that which derives from any other human fact for obvious reasons[161]

Of course, Ockham was not "a systematic or even an ordained thinker,"[162] nor was he a systematic or even an ordained thinker when it came to natural law, especially when it came to questions of political order, a context in which he chose to use the term "natural law". It was here, in the context of a dispute between Pope John XXII and the leaders of the Franciscan Order, that Ockham made his main contribution to the development of natural rights,[163] elaborating a theory of rights based on reason and Scripture.[164] The Franciscans held that they could make a de facto lawful use of things *without* any property right over them. John XXII responded that such de facto use would only be lawful if it was based on some *right.* The Franciscans then turned to natural law, according to which all things are common, and that it was positive law that introduced the right of ownership. For this, they relied on the thesis of Pope Nicholas III, who had defended this thesis in his Decree *Exiit.* This led Ockham to write his *Opus nonaginta dierum*, where he collected the following subjective notion of right (*ius*):

> In a general sense, law is to be understood as any lawful power, and [therefore] law may be called license.[165]

And later on, Ockham further specifies the two characteristic features of this subjective right when he deals with the right of use:

> a) It is a *faculty* or power ('*potestas*'), therefore, a quality of the subject, attributed to his will, insofar as with this faculty man can perform actions, either to use or dispose of a thing, or to

---

[161] Ockham, Dialogus, pars III, tract. II, lib. III, cap. IV (we quote the translation of Hervada (1987), p. 190, the Latin text of which appears in footnote n. 407.

[162] Carpintero (2013), p. 118.

[163] In this respect, see Carpintero (2003), pp. 35–287, in particular pp. 71 ff; Guzmán (2003); Guzmán (2009), pp. 21 ff; Guzmán (2013); Brett (1997); Folgado (1960).

[164] On this subject, see López Hernández (1998), pp. 217–222; Carpintero (2003), pp. 69–71; (2013), pp. 116–121.

[165] Ockham, Opus nonaginta dierum, 61, 2 (collected by López Hernández (1998), p. 219).

> defend or vindicate that thing in court; b) It is licit, that is, it is a faculty of action based on a just (reasonable) cause and exempt from guilt.[166]

Moreover, since this power or faculty could be conferred in three ways that correspond to the three forms of objective right understood as law or norm (by natural law, by positive law—human or divine—, and by an act authorised by a law—e.g., contract), there is a correspondence between *ius* as objective right and *ius* as subjective right.[167]

On the other hand, after pointing out that subjective right is that power or faculty in accordance with reason, by resorting to biblical sources, he relied on texts that refer to 'Christian right' as a 'right of freedom.'[168] Christian liberty, then, requires that the Pope's power have its limits in the 'natural rights' of his subjects. This thesis appeared in a more developed form in his work against tyranny, entitled *Breviloquium*, which asserted that papal tyranny would infringe on 'the rights and liberties granted by God and nature', and that to infringe such rights would constitute a vice.

In addressing natural rights, Ockham sought to defend the idea that all earthly power (including the papal one) and the right of property came from natural law, not from the pope, while also recognising a sphere of man's moral autonomy in which everyone should be able to act freely. Thus, for example, taking a vow of virginity or being ordained a priest, being good actions in themselves, could not be commanded by the Pope. Such choices, Ockham pointed out, were 'liberties' which God and nature had granted to mortals and could not be taken away by any authority (civil or ecclesiastical).

However, his basis of argument was alien or contrary to law. In fact, "he cannot argue in legal terms because what he defends is, legally, an absurdity."[169] Carpintero refers to the absurdity of sustaining the possible existence of a *usus* that does not constitute an *ius utendi*, or of a license to use a thing that does not imply an *ius utendi*. To defend that there could be a *usus* devoid of juridical foundation, he resorted to the distinction between '*jus fori*' (human right) and '*jus poli*' (divine right), but in reality, this *usus* is not only opposed to positive law but also to divine law because it refers to a '*prima bonitas moralis*' whose content and scope is much greater than divine law. Let us read the following statement of Ockham:

> I grant that we use right, but not 'jus fori', but 'jus poli', for everything we do rightly outside human right is 'jus poli'. Thus, to act rightly is nothing other than to act in a morally right way, and rightful use is morally right use, so that we can say that there is a right to possess, and a morally proper possession (...). 'Jus poli' is [in reality] that 'natural equity' which has

[166] Ockham, Opus nonaginta dierum, 6, 4 (collected by López Hernández (1998), p. 219).

[167] López Hernández (1998), p. 219.

[168] "Lex evangelica est lex libertatis", he states in his work Magistri Guilhelmi de Ockham super potestate de summi pontificis octo quaestionum decisiones, Lyon, 1496, q. 1, Ch. 6 (collected by Carpintero (2003), p. 79, footnote n. 183).

[169] Carpintero (2003), p. 78.

> been revealed to us by God, which accords with right reason, and which exists without a purely positive human or divine constitution.[170]

And in another passage Ockham draws some consequences from this approach:

> ...whatever benefits me and does you no harm, is immutably suited to equity, even in the absence of a positive law that expressly permits it; and human laws cannot state otherwise, for then it would be an iniquitous law that proceeds against charity.[171]

For Carpintero, the consequence is clear: "Every man appears as a *potentia libera*, with lawful and enforceable possibilities of action that are prior to any right."[172] And Paolo Grossi, glossing the Decree *Exiit* of Pope Nicholas III, highlights another aspect related to the same consequence: "...the separation between law and facts made law lose its objective dimension to assume the dimension 'di un atto di volizione' ('an act of the will')."[173]

The defence of these natural faculties or qualities, prior to law, was intentionally brought up to combat the Pope's theory of *plenitudo potestatis*, as well as to argue in favour of evangelical poverty in its Franciscan conception. Hence his thesis, already referred to, of the "*Lex evangelica*" as "*lex libertatis*."[174] The corollary of this defence of liberty had a clear message: the Pope has no power to destroy the rights and liberties of the Christian people, because his power has been conferred on him "for the edification and not for the destruction of the liberty given to us by God and nature."[175]

It has been described above how the Church tried to protect its own space of freedom against the interference of the secular power in the ecclesiastical sphere (*libertas ecclesiae*), although at other times it also tried to interfere in secular affairs. In the fourteenth century, as we have just observed, something different happened. Within the Church, a theological current demanded a freedom outside canon law, giving rise to "an idea of freedom prior to any order, especially juridical", to an idea of "dominative freedom" understood as "*dominativa facultas ipsius voluntatis*", that is, a freedom that, understood as its own dominion and antithesis of slavery, consists in the independence and autonomy of each man.[176]

---

[170] Ockham, Opus nonaginta, Ch. 65, pp. 574, 577 (collected by Carpintero (2003), pp. 78–79, footnotes nn. 179–180).

[171] Ockham, Opus nonaginta, Ch. 66, p. 581 (collected by Carpintero (2003), p. 79, footnote n. 179).

[172] Carpintero (2003), p. 79.

[173] Grossi (1972), p. 303 (collected by Carpintero (2003), p. 79, footnote n. 182).

[174] See footnote n. 132 as well as the corresponding main text.

[175] Ockham, Magistri Guilhelmi de Ockham..., q. 3, Ch. 4 (taken up by Carpintero (2003), p. 80, footnote n. 184); Carpintero then notes how the source of this freedom is twofold, God and nature, a faithful reflection of the *puris naturalibus* theory, which defended an independence of the natural order (nature) from the supernatural order (God), so that man has two distinct ends, human fullness (natural) and the life of grace (supernatural), as if man could attain fullness and happiness apart from God.

[176] Grossi (1972), pp. 310–311 (collected by Carpintero (2003), pp. 80–81).

This vision of freedom, which is at the basis of the modern subjective notion of right, was born in the theology of the fourteenth century and became generalised in the sixteenth century. According to Solari's thesis, the Church, by pursuing its supernatural ends and thus opposing political power (civil or secular), helped to lead the individual towards the interior and spiritual, so that, in the face of the struggles between civil and ecclesiastical power, the individual ended up emancipating himself from both powers.[177]

1.6.2.4 John of Gerson and Konrad Summenhart

A few years later, the French philosopher—and theologian—John of Gerson (1363–1429) developed Ockham's thesis.[178] Following Ockham in defining subjective right as a power or faculty that is based on reason, he added that insofar as all creatures were directed by divine reason, one could recognise the right of each creature to make its own decisions, and this makes it complete in itself. This thesis, although it would be discussed by theologians, was rarely accepted.

His main contribution to the development of law as a faculty or *potestas* was particularly relevant because he was the first who, when considering *jus* in that sense, offered a justifying theory or doctrine. And he provided it in trying to resolve the scandalous crisis of schism, which led him to try to determine who has the power in the Church, the pope or the council. Believing that it was the council, the expression *jus* allowed him to "affirm a superiority of law of the council over the pope and removed the doubts in a bare dispute of powers."[179]

In defending a double meaning of *jus*, he distinguished between that which refers to the law and that which refers to "immediate power or authority, which is proper to someone according to the opinion based on right reason."[180] Following this line of thought, he even goes so far as to maintain that every positive entity, as much as it has of entity and goodness, has as much of law:

> Let us declare, then, that every positive entity, as much as it has of entity and, consequently, of goodness, has as much of right, thus defined in general. Thus the sky has a right to water, the sun to light, the fire to heat, the swallow to nest, and absolutely every creature to whatever it can do good by natural faculty, the evident reason being that such things all suit them according to the dictates of right divine reason; otherwise they would never persist; so man, even the sinner, has a right to many things, as do other creatures left to their natures.[181]

[177] Solari (1911), p. 5 (collected by Carpintero (2003), p. 80, footnote n. 190).

[178] On this point, see Carpintero (2000, pp. 118–120; 2003, pp. 82–85; 2013, pp. 121–123); Guzmán (2003), Part II (El derecho-facultad en la Edad Media), 2; Guzmán (2009), pp. 17–22; Guzmán (2013), pp. 82–83; Folgado (1960), pp. 153–154.

[179] Guzmán (2013), p. 81.

[180] Gerson (1987) (collected by Guzmán (2013), pp. 81–82).

[181] Gerson, Liber de vita spirituali animae: "Dicamus igitur, quod omne ens positivum quantum habet de entitate et ex consequenti, de bonitate, tantumdem habet de iure sic generaliter definito. In

According to Guzmán Brito's opinion, as the faculty or power is a quality and this is not exclusive of the human being, the consequence that animals and inanimate things also have rights is far reaching. In effect, once the idea of faculty or power has been adopted as qualities to define the right, as these are not exclusive of the human being, it was possible to extend the rights to non-human beings because, "the right-faculty depends on the entity; and hence Gerson has sentenced that every positive entity, as much as it has of entity, so much it has of right"[182] or, in other words, "in general, any creature has the right to everything that it can do well by natural faculty, because that which it can do well by natural faculty is its faculty or power, or right."[183]

It was a disciple of Gerson, Konrad Summenhart (1450/1462–1501/1502), who, commenting on his master's definition, transmitted it to Francisco de Vitoria, who in turn bequeathed it to the most important jurists and theologians of the sixteenth century.[184] The contribution of Gerson's disciple was twofold.[185] First, he incorporated the idea of moral lawfulness, hence his preference for *facultas*, not *potestas*, because while the latter indicates the capacity to do something, both lawful and unlawful (*potestas agendi sive licita sive illicita*), faculty comes from *fas*, a term that denotes lawfulness and, consequently, means the capacity to do something morally lawful (*facultas* as a *potestas agendi licita*). For Summenhart, 'power' is the genus, of which 'faculty' is the species, although the former is to be understood as the capacity or "the power of someone to act freely."[186]

In the second place, he introduced the variant in his master's foundation: "as much right, or dominion, someone has towards a certain thing, as much action is allowed"[187] or, as Guzmán Brito summarises, "as much right as possible action"[188]; and this is so because Summenhart considered the power in which the right consists as a relation, a relation between the power and the action to which it is directed;

hunc modum, caelum ius habet ad influendum, sol ad illuminandum, ignis ad calefaciendum, hirundo ad nidificandum, immo et quaelibet creatura in omni eo quod bene agere naturali potest facultate: cuius ratio perspicua est, quoniam omnia omnia talia convenient eis secundum dictamen rectae rationis divinae, alioquin nunquam persisterent; sic homo etiam peccator ius habet ad multa, sicut et aliae creaturae naturis suis derelictae"; collected by Guzmán (2013), p. 82; by the same author, see also Guzmán (2009), pp. 18–19, footnote n. 13.

[182] Guzmán (2013), p. 83.

[183] Guzmán (2009), p. 20.

[184] Guzmán (2013), pp. 22–27; Carpintero (2003), pp. 85–90.

[185] On Conrad of Summenhart, see Tierney (1997), pp. 242–252; Varkemaa (2005, 2006); Guzmán (2007).

[186] Summenhart, De contractibus licitis atque illicitus tractatus, Treatise I, q. 1 (taken up by Carpintero (2003), p. 89, footnote n. 245).

[187] Summenhart, De contractibus licitis atque illicitus tractatus, Treatise I, q. 1, p. 4, 1st col (collected by Guzmán (2009), p. 26, footnote n. 28).

[188] Guzmán (2009), p. 26, who points out, in footnote n. 29, that "the expression 'acción posible' abbreviates the original 'acción que le es permitido ejercer', because it is not about the action actually executed".

hence, "the measure of the right is not so much the power itself, as an absolute, as the act or action to which it is oriented."[189]

As can be seen, for Summenhart, every right or dominion is a *habitudo seu relatio* that does not end in the thing itself, but comprises the acts and actions that the holder exercises with it or over it.[190] Following Gerson, he understood right as dominion, hence he defined it as "the power or faculty adequate to oneself which is proper to each according to the orders of first justice... or according to the orders of right reason."[191] Logically, every dominion, faculty or right must come from some prior law; not in vain because the word "faculty" refers to the possibility of doing something according to a law that already exists. However, the quality (*qualitas*) refers to a human reality that exists by itself, apart from a pre-existing law.[192] In this context, it is worth noting another original contribution of Summenhart, when he defends the existence of an "intrinsic law of rational nature" apart from divine law:

> Every dominion belongs to someone according to a law, either the law founded intrinsically in rational nature, which is the law of reason, or an extrinsic law, which may be a divine or human law.[193]

However, as Carpintero rightly observes, Summenhart did not explore "the possibility of a law based exclusively on human reason, apart from divine law, and he points to the *dominium beatificum*, which belongs first and foremost to God, as the source of all faculties". The Ockhamist influence, as well as the aforementioned theory *in puris naturalibus*, are undeniable.[194]

In any case, it is possible that Summenhart's doctrine is "the first—and if not the first, then the most complete—doctrinal exposition of the natural right of every person to freedom". Following Gerson, Summenhart holds that "the original dominion corresponds to the *dominium libertatis*, which is a free faculty proceeding from a gratuitous gift of God, by which He gives us to act with our rational soul in producing our voluntary acts, or suspending them, with the aim of obtaining perfect happiness."[195] And Carpintero adds:

> Moreover, freedom itself is a certain kind of right, and the free man has the right over himself to do what he wills. Thus, the Instituta explains that freedom is the natural faculty of one who

---

[189] Guzmán (2009), p. 26.

[190] Summenhart, De contractibus licitis atque illicitus tractatus, Treatise I, q. 1 (collected by Carpintero (2003), p. 87, footnote n. 223).

[191] Summenhart, De contractibus licitis atque illicitus tractatus, Treatise I, q. 1, p. 1 (collected by Carpintero (2003), p. 87, footnote n. 227).

[192] Megías (1992); quoted by Carpintero (2003), p. 88, footnote n. 228.

[193] Summenhart, De contractibus licitis atque illicitus tractatus, Treatise I, q. 5, p. 22 (taken up by Carpintero (2003), p. 88, footnote n. 229).

[194] Carpintero (2003), p. 88.

[195] Summenhart, De contractibus licitis atque illicitus tractatus, Treatise I, q. 1, p. 1 (collected by Carpintero (2003), pp. 89–90, footnote n. 246).

can do what he wills, except what is forbidden to him by violence or right. Thus, the free man always has a right over his person.[196]

1.6.3 Sixteenth and Seventeenth Centuries

After the medieval contributions of Scotus and Ockham, those of Gerson and Summenhart constituted the bridge between the Middle Ages and Modernity,[197] a period in which, although natural rights would continue to be the object of study and development, they were related to two other important themes, of very ancient origin, namely, the origin and limits of political power. While the former refers to the contractualist thesis of political power, the latter has to do with natural law and natural rights, although these were not the only limits to the exercise of public power.

It would be a mistake to think that the idea of the social contract as the original title of political power is incompatible with natural law or the recognition of natural rights, although this statement is true in the doctrine of some authors, as we shall see. In any case, it is important not to confuse the rule with the exception. And, from the sixteenth to the eighteenth century, the thesis of a social contract incompatible with natural law and with the pre-political or pre-contractual character of fundamental rights was, of course, the exception, and not the general rule.

On the other hand, it should be emphasised—as has already been said—that both questions, the origin of political power and its limits, were not new, but rather quite old. Once again, it was the political, social and cultural circumstances of the modern period that led to the further studies and doctrinal development of them. While the question of the limits of political power was the subject of a remarkable development since Antiquity,[198] the question of its origin developed in a particular way from the thirteenth century onwards, in line with the process of the consolidation of royal power.

As will be seen, there were two main theses on the origin of political power: those who maintained that the proximate cause of political power was the political community itself or historical circumstances—war, alliance between peoples, etc.—(Thomas Aquinas, Francisco de Vitoria, etc.); and those who referred both the remote and proximate origin of political power to God.[199]

---

[196] Carpintero (2003), p. 90.

[197] Other authors prior to the modern authors should be mentioned, such as Iohannes Maior, Iohannes Driedo, as well as Jacobo Almain, Gabriel Biel and Juan Mayor, among others; for the first two, see Guzmán (2009), pp. 26–28; for the others, see Carpintero (2003), pp. 90 ff.

[198] On the limits of political power, see Masferrer and Obarrio (2012, 2014).

[199] To refer directly, or in the near future, to God was an English and Reformed thing. Hence the Defence of the Catholic Faith against the Errors of the Anglican Sect (1613), by Francisco Suarez. This was a doctrine very expressly condemned by the Catholic Church, which only held that political power was necessary by natural right. The appointment of princes was the task of legitimacy in hereditary succession, or of the election of subjects.

Although it may seem paradoxical, the truth is that the latter thesis acquired greater predicament in the modern context than in the medieval one, in the midst of civil wars and doctrinal-religious disputes. Hence the paradigmatic example of this thesis is found, for example, in the work *True Law of Free Monarchies* (1598), in which the English monarch James I considered the king as 'God's lieutenant', thus being able to demand the passive obedience of his subjects and the safeguarding of order and peace. But this was not the only English exponent, nor was England the only territory where the seed of absolute political power or monarchical absolutism germinated, as we shall see.

Let us now consider, from this broader perspective—relating natural law and natural rights to the origin and limits of political power—the theses of some of the main thinkers of the sixteenth and eighteenth centuries.

As we have seen, in the context of Spanish colonisation in America, several authors such as Francisco de Vitoria, Fernando Vázquez de Menchaca and Domingo de Soto, among others, defended the 'natural rights' of the indigenous people. In particular, we have already paid special attention to the theses of Bartolomé de las Casas, Francisco de Vitoria and—to a lesser extent—Hugo Grotius. As was said, their theses were not novel, nor were they the ones who created the notion of 'natural rights'. Now, after the historical journey that has been made, this statement is much better understood.

1.6.3.1 Francisco de Vitoria and Domingo de Soto

Francisco de Vitoria (1483–1546) argued that the origin of political power and government should be based on consensus, because, insofar as all have a right to self-defence, he saw no reason why some should rule over others. However, he also argued that once political power was constituted, the ruler held political power directly from God, and not by a concession from the community. Vitoria thus fell somewhere in between, arriving at a somewhat contradictory point: he defended, on the one hand, that the origin of political power rested on the consensus of the community, but he maintained, on the other hand, that this power, once instituted, came from God and not from the community.[200]

With regard to his contribution to natural rights, we will add little to what we have already seen, limiting ourselves only to that which allows us to follow our guiding thread.[201] Vitoria modified the Thomistic definition of *ius*. First of all, he did not share the Thomistic idea that Law is the object of Justice. And this is so because, in his opinion, it is "unheard of that an object (*ius*) assumes a name from its potency (the virtue of *iustitia* in this case), and that the opposite is more regular; thus, for

[200] de Vitoria (1934), p. 64: "ius est potestas vel facultas conveniens alicui secundum leges" (quoted by Guzmán (2013), p. 83, footnote n. 22).

[201] For an extensive and rigorous description, see Guzmán (2009), pp. 33–109; Carpintero (2003), pp. 205–207.

example, the word 'odour' ('*odor*'), with which the object of smell or olfactory potency is designated, is not derived from 'olfato' ('*olfactus*'), but the other way round, because smell is prior to the olfactory potency."[202] In order to reconcile this difference with Thomas Aquinas, he pointed out that the term *ius* has three meanings: the just, the science of the just, and 'the law itself'. In adding this third meaning, he departed "drastically from his source, for not only had Thomas not included the idea of law as a meaning of the word *ius*, but, on the contrary, he had said positively and unequivocally that 'law, properly speaking, is not law itself, but a certain reason of law.'"[203]

It was when dealing with dominion that Vitoria introduced the notion of right-faculty, which, in spite of coming from Gerson and Summenhart, has a style of its own:

> The right is the power or authority that is proper to someone according to the laws, that is, the power given to me, for example, by the law to do whatever is necessary.[204]

It does not seem that Vitoria's definition of right and dominion as faculties, non-existent in Thomas Aquinas and well known to Vitoria from his studies in Paris—where Jean de Gerson and his disciple Konrad Summenhart were well known—was aimed at defending the natural rights of the Indians. In Guzmán Brito's opinion, apart from the indisputable prestige of Gerson and Summenhart, the main function of this notion is to be found in the Vitorian model of private law based on the domain.[205] Vitoria rejected Gerson's thesis that things and animals had rights[206] . Although the question is complex and susceptible to numerous nuances, it could be affirmed that Vitoria "took up, instead of discarding, this low medieval legacy of Franciscan roots [being a Dominican], and gave it a first organisation under legal categories, which had to prepare the more definitive organisation that would operate the rationalist Natural Law of the seventeenth and eighteenth centuries."[207]

Domingo de Soto (1495–1560), who also studied in Paris and was a close collaborator of Francisco de Vitoria after joining the University of Salamanca, did not go so far.[208] On the one hand, he did not accept the third meaning of *ius* as law, as Vitoria did. On the other hand, "he adopted the notion of faculty or power, but within narrower limits than Vitoria."[209] In fact, Soto did not admit a meaning of law as faculty or power, which distanced him from his colleague Vitoria. The notion of *facultas* only appears directly when dealing with dominion: for Soto, only

[202] Guzmán (2009), pp. 35–36.

[203] Guzmán (2009), p. 37, taking up the Thomist source in Suma Teológica 2ª 2, Cuesti. 57ªart. 1°, solut. 2ª: "lex non est ipsa ius, proprie loquendo, sed aliquis ratio iuris".

[204] de Vitoria (1934), cuest. 62ª, art. 1, no. 5 (collected by Guzmán (2009), p. 89, footnote 195).

[205] In this regard, see Guzmán (2009), pp. 62–91.

[206] Guzmán (2013), p. 83.

[207] Guzmán (2009), p. 92.

[208] In this regard, see Guzmán (2009), pp. 112–141.

[209] Guzmán (2009), p. 111.

dominion—not, right—can be defined as faculty, and moreover with a limitation, being '*facultas et ius*' and not only '*facultas*'. He rejects Summenhart's identification of dominion and right, understanding dominion as a special *ius*, as a species within the (wider) genus right; hence he considers dominion as *facultas et ius*, and not only as *facultas*. Following this line of thought, he defines dominion as "the faculty proper to each one and the right in anything, which he can employ for his own benefit, for any use permitted by law."[210] Consequently, Soto circumscribed the dominion, to the discussion of the aspects that Vitoria and his predecessors dealt with in the field of the right-faculty, as a general idea.[211] Finally, he did not admit that animals and inanimate beings have any dominion over things; however, while Vitoria rejected that possibility because only men could suffer injury, Soto affirmed that "dominion is proper only to those who enjoy understanding and free will; and therefore to them alone also the dominion of things is proper."[212]

1.6.3.2 Luis de Molina and Francisco Suárez

Luis de Molina (1535–1600),[213] a Jesuit who did not belong to the school of Salamanca, returned to Vitoria's triple meaning of law: what is just, the laws (natural and positive) and the art or expertise with which what is just is known (that is, legal science). From the last meaning Molina makes other meanings emanate, such as the one that defines right as "faculty and power that a man has to something."[214] He raised again, as Vitoria did, the notion of *facultas* or *potestas* to a general meaning of law. Moreover, in his opinion, he understands that the best way to define the right in this sense is the following: "the power to do or to obtain something, or to insist on it, or to have it in some other way, which, if contravened without a legitimate cause, does an injury to the one who has it."[215] This recourse to injuria seems to come from Vitoria.

Francisco Suárez (1548–1617) went further by introducing the notion of right-faculty in the first of the two meanings of law, that which refers to justice.[216] In his view, *ius* means that which is *iustum et aequum*, which is the object of justice. But justice has two senses, that which refers to all kinds of virtue, and that of the

---

[210] Domingo de Soto, De iustitia et iure, p. 281 (collected by Guzmán (2009), p. 117, footnote n. 246).

[211] Guzmán (2009), p. 127.

[212] Domingo de Soto, De iustitia et iure, II, p. 284 (text translated and collected by Guzmán (2009), p. 122, footnote n. 258).

[213] On this, see Guzmán (2009), pp. 143–188; for the abundant literature on Suárez, see a part of it collected in pp. 189–190, footnote n. 386.

[214] Luis de Molina, De iustitia et iure opera omnia tractatibus quinque, trat. I, disput. 1ª, núm. 4 (text collected by Guzmán (2009), pp. 146–147, footnote n. 299).

[215] Luis de Molina, De iustitia et iure opera omnia tractatibus quinque, trat. II, disput. 1ª, princ. and no. 1 (text collected by Guzmán (2009), p. 148, footnote n. 301).

[216] In this regard, see Guzmán (2009), pp. 189–230.

particular virtue that grants to each one what is his, a distinction that came from the distinction (Aristotelian and Thomistic) between general justice and particular justice. Although *ius* refers to both meanings of justice, Suárez understood that the second was more in use and more appropriate.[217] In short, the more proper meaning of *ius* lies in the notion of right faculty, which he defines as follows: "a certain moral faculty, which each one has, either to a thing that is his own, or to a thing that is due to him."[218] As can be seen, Suárez indirectly attributed the character of 'strict' to the notion of right-faculty, "since if the strict meaning of *ius* is *iustum*, and *iustum* is defined as faculty, it follows without further ado that the strict meaning of *ius* is its definition as faculty."[219] A conclusion in accordance with the following text of Suárez: "Therefore, that action or moral faculty, which each one has to a thing of his own, or to something in some way belonging to him, is called 'right' and this properly seems to be the object of justice."[220]

To the expression '*facultas*' (Vitoria had used '*potestad vel facultas*'), Suárez added the adjective '*moralis*', which is in fact his genuine contribution to the doctrine of right-faculty, accepted by Grotius and later by the modern School of Natural Law. In this way, he solved the difficult question of how law can be a power or faculty without being at the same time dependent on the entity. Let me explain. If the animal has the right to do whatever its physical capacity allows it to do, if the thief has the same physical power to take the thing as its owner has, in both cases the power or faculty depended at the same time on the entity of the actor, that is, on the physical capacity of the entity (animal or thief). This problem, not solved in Summenhart, Vitoria and Molina, found a solution in Suárez, who "distinguished two types of faculties, the physical and the moral, and used the second as the next genus of the definition of right (-faculty). With this, the faculties of animals and inanimate beings, alien to morality, and the physical faculties of human beings, in themselves considered, which, when judged in their exercise or in their action, are approved [legitimised or legitimate] (if they are not indifferent) as long as they are precisely the exercise or de facto development of a moral faculty, although the latter adds nothing physical or material in itself to the condition of its holder."[221]

On the other hand, Suárez denied, from the outset, the divine origin of the right of kings, a thesis that was widespread in England at that time. According to Suarez, the remote origin of political power is to be found in God, because God has inscribed in

---

[217] Francisco Suárez, *De legibus ac Deo legislatore* (collected by Guzmán (2009), p. 191, footnote n. 388).

[218] Francisco Suárez, De legibus..., lib. I, cap. 2, no. 4: "facultas quedam moralis, quam unusquisque habet, vel circa rem suam, vel ad rem sibi debitam" (collected by Guzmán (2009), p. 192, footnote n. 390); for Guzmán Brito, the distinction between ius in re and ius ad rem, as well as the notion of moral faculty, constituted the two great contributions of Suárez to the doctrine of right-faculty (pp. 228–230).

[219] Guzmán (2009), p. 192.

[220] Francisco Suárez, De legibus..., lib. I, Ch. 2, no. 4 (collected by Guzmán (2009), p. 193, footnote n. 393).

[221] Guzmán (2009), pp. 222–223.

man, a social being, the capacity to create political communities that have the capacity to institute political power or governments 'by the force of natural law alone' (*De legibus ac Deo legislatore*, 1612, 3.2.4). Once the political society was formed, since the authority of political power was not of divine but human origin, the form of government could be chosen by the community itself, just as the ruler was granted legislative power. This granting of power allowed the community to take it back, as well as the defence and rebellion against the ruler who did not fulfil his obligations, although it did not admit the death of the sovereign, however tyrannical he might be. Regarding the medieval controversy as to whether natural law was obligatory because it was commanded by God or because of the capacity of human reason to discern good from evil, Suárez admitted the capacity of reason, although he added that reason itself was a sign of the divine will for men.

1.6.3.3 Jean Bodin

Jean Bodin (1530–1596) defended—in *Les six livres de la République* (1576)—the absolute character of royal sovereignty, but established clear and insurmountable limits. Indeed, Bodin went so far as to uphold the absolute character of royal sovereignty as a 'power over citizens and subjects not subject to laws'. This conception formed the theoretical basis of the sovereign power of the state as a supreme, permanent, indivisible and, in principle, legally irresponsible power. However, it should be emphasised that he never conceived—as has been said—an unlimited notion of sovereignty, since it could not transgress divine laws, natural laws, the law of nations (*ius gentium*), the private property of the family, as well as those customs and covenants or conventions that formed the basis of a political community.[222]

1.6.3.4 Hugo Grotius

Hugo Grotius (1583–1645) drew from the sources of Francisco Suárez and other authors of the Second Scholasticism or the School of Salamanca.[223] Guzmán Brito has analysed to what extent the Grotian doctrine of right-faculty is indebted to the great Spanish neo-scholastics.[224] In this sense, Grotius recognised the existence of three meanings of *ius*: that which is just (or, rather, that which is not unjust), *qualitas moralis* and *lex*. Although it is true that Spanish authors derived the notion of *ius-facultas* (law-faculty or law-power) from *iustum*, Grotius also accepted this derivation. On the other hand, while Suárez used the expression '*facultas moralis*', Grotius

[222] See the classical work by Franklin (1973); see also Masferrer and Obarrio (2012), pp. 41–44.
[223] Guzmán (2009), pp. 231–232, in particular the bibliography in footnote n. 471.
[224] Guzmán (2009), pp. 231–251.

opted for '*qualitas moralis*'. However, this difference only refers to the different level of generality and, in reality, one presupposes the other and vice versa.[225]

With regard to the importance of nature and natural law as the basis of an international law that would protect the rights of all human beings equally, it is worth adding something else here. Although, in his view—following Suárez—the moral judgments of human reason sufficiently showed the divine will, Grotius held that the principles and rules of natural law stemmed from the social character of human beings, and that these rules alone—without the need to refer them expressly to God—could rule or govern social and political life.

In Brian Tierney's opinion, Grotius' 'impious hypothesis' (referring to the formula—already analysed—'etsi Deus non daretur'), contributed to the growth of secular doctrines of natural law, in which, instead of starting from the eternal law to finally arrive at the natural law, cognisable by human reason (as Thomas Aquinas or Francisco Suárez himself did), later authors—mostly Protestants, and, sometimes, atheists—would go the other way around, that is, from the bottom up, starting from an indistinct human nature existing in a 'state of nature', and trying to explain from there the emergence of political power and legal institutions by means of contracts or pacts freely entered between the individuals of a community. From this new perspective, the first moral principle 'do good and avoid evil' would be replaced by another, namely, 'contracts must be fulfilled'.

From then on, the content of this primordial 'state of nature', prior to the covenants that would allow the creation of a community and its political power, would be determined—or notably conditioned—by reasons of a theological-doctrinal nature (depending on whether it was held that human nature had been left corrupted after original sin—Protestant thesis—or only wounded although healed—Catholic view), or for political reasons, conferring on the 'state of nature' those features that would best serve to legitimise a certain form of government (for example, monarchy or, rather, monarchical absolutism).

1.6.3.5 Thomas Hobbes

This is undoubtedly the key to understanding the doctrine of Thomas Hobbes (1588–1679), who, in the convulsive context of a civil war, developed—in his work *Leviathan* (1651)—a philosophical-political theory that defended monarchical absolutism, granting absolute power to the king. With this aim, he presented a

[225] Guzmán (2009), pp. 239–240: "Grotius places *qualitas moralis* as the next genre of his definition while Suárez resorts to the genre of *facultas moralis*. But the difference lies only in the choice of a different level of generality. *Facultas*, in fact, is one of the species of the predicate of *qualitas*; so Grotius is only more generic than Suárez; which means that Suárez also sets out a *qualitas* when he speaks of *facultas*, just as Grotius sets out a *facultas* when he speaks of *qualitas*"; see also Guzmán Brito, "Historia de la denominación del derecho-facultad como 'subjetivo'", III, 4 *in fine*: "Thus, in speaking of *qualitas*, Grotius was going back to the remote genus, where the earlier authors, and still much of the later ones, remained in the proximate genus."

primordial 'state of nature' with tragic overtones, in which all individuals were at war with each other. In this context he popularised the expression '*homo homini lupus*', borrowing it from the Latin comedian Plautus (254–184 B.C.) in his play *Asinaria*. According to him, in that tremendous 'state' every man enjoyed the absolute right to protect his own life. Thus, he suggested that the best way to achieve security over one's own life would be a regime of peace, the preservation of which should be the goal of every social and political community. To this end, he developed a set of rules of natural law aimed at safeguarding peace. However—and, apart from these rules—, in the end he ended up pointing out that it was the laws, understood as mandates of the superior, which can guarantee peace. The solution to the situation of anarchy, typical of the 'state of nature', was not to rely on God and the aforementioned rules of natural law, but on the creation of a sovereign power (a kind of 'mortal god'). To institute this power, all men had to make a pact by which they submitted their own wills to a sovereign elected by a majority. The power of that sovereign was to be absolute, because the pact implied the authorisation of all acts which the sovereign might wish to carry out in order to safeguard the peace and security of his subjects. It was, therefore, a peculiar pact, since it did not generate reciprocal obligations between the ruler and the community, but a mere transmission of power to the ruler. With Hobbes, then, the idea of sovereign power reached its peak, given that the sovereign was granted a power that had no limits, despite the fact that 75 years earlier Jean Bodin had set theoretically insurmountable limits.

Hobbes also picked up the notion of the right-faculty in his work Leviathan:

> The Right of Nature, which Writers commonly call *Jus naturale*, is the Liberty each man hath, to use his own power, as he will himself, for the preservation of his own Nature; that is to say, of his own Life; and consequently, of doing anything, which in his own Judgement, and Reason, he shall conceive to be the aptest means thereunto.[226]

A similar definition was given in another of his well-known works:

> By the term 'right' is meant nothing else than the freedom of everyone to use his natural faculties according to right reason.[227]

1.6.3.6 Samuel Pufendorf

The idea of a double agreement, one to constitute the community or civil society and the other to institute political power, was not new. A few years before Locke, Samuel Pufendorf (1632–1694) had already employed it in his work *De iure naturae et gentium* (1672), the first published work with an express mention of 'natural law' in the same title. Although Pufendorf admitted the right of resistance against the arbitrary exercise of political power, he feared social turbulence more than the

[226] Hobbes (1968), pp. 183–192.

[227] Hobbes (1642), Ch. 1, para. 7 (collected by Guzmán (2003), III, 3); on the concept of subjective right in Hobbes, see Villey (1969a, b), pp. 179 ff.

excesses of the rulers, and therefore accepted absolute political power when it was exercised for the good of the community, and not to dispose capriciously of the lives of the subjects (*De iure naturae et gentium*, I, 7.8.3 and 7.8.7).

While Pufendorf's ideas would be used to justify German enlightened despotism, Locke's ideas helped to shape the republican thinking of the founding fathers of the United States, leaving a notable mark in their *Declaration of Independence* (1776), as well as in their Constitution (1781) and Bill of Rights (1791). In France, the ideas of liberty and equality, which were part of the legacy of natural law, acquired unusual status in the framework of the French Revolution, being enshrined in the *Declaration of the Rights of Man and of the Citizen* (1789), as well as in its first Constitutions (1791, 1793, 1795, etc.).

Pufendorf took up the legacy of the doctrine of right-faith with the following definition: "that moral quality by which we rightly rule over persons or possess a thing or by virtue of which something is due to us."[228]

1.6.3.7 John Locke

The doctrine of John Locke (1632–1704), who lived in a different context to that of Hobbes, pursued another objective: to confront the despotic or tyrannical exercise of royal power. And the historical context was very specific and had a very precise name, James II of England, who would provoke a convulsive decade (1680) that would lead to the 'Glorious Revolution' (1688) and the approval of the 'Bill of Rights' (1689) to which we have already referred. This context explains, to a large extent, John Locke's theses, as well as his distancing from those of Thomas Hobbes. That is why he was not interested in presenting—in his *Two Treatises on Government* (1689)—a Hobbesian 'state of nature', but a less tremendous and more humane one, in which everyone was free and equal, and governed by the natural law accessible and knowable by human reason itself. In this 'state', every man already enjoyed freedom 'within the framework permitted by natural law', which prescribed the preservation of one's own life and forbade any aggression or injury to others. If in Hobbes the fundamental rule of natural law consisted in the defence of one's own life, for Locke it was the preservation of mankind (*Two Treatises on Government*, II, 2, 9).

The 'state of nature' described by Locke needed a defect that would justify the consequent pact for the constitution of political power, and that was—according to him—the lack of impartiality of those who had to enforce the laws, especially when it was up to each individual to punish the transgressors. To avoid the chaos that such a situation would generate, a political power had to be constituted whose primary

[228] Samuel Pufendorf, *De jure naturae et gentium* (1672, Francofurti - Lipsiae, 1759), lib. I, Ch. 1, para. 20 (collected by Guzmán (2003), III, 3); on the subjective law, see Denzer (1972), pp. 129–134; on the presence of this definition of faculty right in other Central European authors in the seventeenth century (Christian Thomasius, Nikolaus Grundling, Gottfried W. Leibnitz) and first half of the eighteenth century (Christian Wolf), see Guzmán (2003), III, 3.

objective was the preservation of the lives, liberties and properties of all. The first step was 'incorporation', whereby individuals agreed to surrender their executive powers to the community; political power was then constituted by a second agreement made, in this case, between the community (already existing by virtue of the first agreement) and the rulers. On that second agreement it would depend on the form of government to be chosen, excluding beforehand the arbitrary absolute sovereignty that would include powers over the life and death of the subjects.[229] And the reason for that exclusion clause was quite clear: if men lack that arbitrary and absolute power over their own lives, they could never transfer that power to the ruler. For Locke, the basis of this second agreement is to be found in the trust that the community places in the rulers, who are presumed to conduct themselves for the common good and to govern according to existing laws. If that trust is betrayed by an abuse of this power, the community has the power to withdraw that trust, to rebel and to depose the rulers, thus requiring a new agreement between the community and the future rulers (*Two Treatises on Government*, II, 19).

1.6.4 Eighteenth and Nineteenth Centuries

In the eighteenth century, several schools of thought emerged that denied natural law, including empiricism (David Hume) and utilitarianism (Jeremy Bentham).

1.6.4.1 David Hume

According to the Scottish philosopher David Hume (1711–1776), it is not possible to extract or deduce moral judgments from natural empirical realities—including nature. The absolute separation between the material and the moral world, which came from René Descartes (1596–1650)—with the so-called Cartesian dualism by dividing reality into *res cogitans* & *res extensa*[230]—, meant denying the existence of a natural morality common to all men, which was incompatible with the defence of natural rights of a pre-political nature, that is, prior to political power. In his *Treatise on Human Nature* (1739)—some of whose ideas he would later take up in his

[229] It is the old, medieval distinction between the '*pactum societatis*' and the '*pactum subjectionis*'.

[230] Although this Cartesian distinction had fundamentally different scope, more in the field of delimitation of the search field of Mechanics, its possible influence in this respect cannot be ruled out; see Masferrer (2020). Moreover, it is worth remembering that the separation—beyond the simple distinction—between the Natural and the Human is very medieval: Duns Scotus, William of Ockham, and was taken up by John of Gerson, Konrad Summenhart or Gabriel Biel, who transmitted it to the Spaniards and to the Modern Age. The great difference between the medieval nominalists and the modern ones lies in the fact that the former relied on God—the *Prima justitia Dei*—, while the modern ones dispensed with God. However, their vision of nature was the same, which has been erroneously attributed only to the Modern Age.

Inquiry into the Principles of Morals (1751)—he denied the possibility of a rational foundation of ethics. Consequently, the object of morality lost its correlation with the true and the false. As reason lost its status as the source of value judgement (or as the judge of moral conduct), it had to be sought in sentiment, of a spontaneous and fluctuating origin and character, and at the same time easily exposed to merely circumstantial interests and alien to a good (or moral truth) which, if it existed, was now unavailable to human understanding.

When the correlation between nature or natural law and an ethics or morality cognisable to reason was lost, another basis or foundation of morality was found in 'utility'. Hence the close connection between empiricism and utilitarianism, an expression coined by Francis Hutcheson (1694–1746)—as well as his definition 'the greatest happiness for the greatest number'—, and later developed by Jeremy Bentham (1748–1832). It is not surprising that Bentham found reading Hume's work particularly inspiring.

It has been claimed that Hume was a moral sentimentalist. In arguing that it is not possible to justify moral principles intellectually, he replaced reason with feelings and emotions. According to him, some principles may simply seem better than others; and the reason why utilitarian principles seem better to us is that they may be in our interests and in the interests of others with whom we sympathise. In this sense, he argued that human beings are remarkably predisposed to endorse rules that promote the public utility of society. Hume used this idea to explain how we value a wide range of phenomena, from social and political institutions to personality traits. Hume's doctrine undoubtedly already contained the seeds of utilitarianism.[231]

1.6.4.2 Jeremy Bentham

It was, undoubtedly, Jeremy Bentham who developed the utilitarianism in his *Introduction to the Principles of Morals and Legislation* (1780; 1789 in the earliest Spanish translation). According to him, the fundamental criterion of morality is utility, understood as the attainment of pleasure. For him, 'seek pleasure and avoid suffering' should replace the old maxim 'do good and avoid evil'. This criterion of utility would apply to human acts as well as to law and to social, political, legal, and economic institutions. He therefore defended a new ethics, based on the enjoyment of life, considering sacrifice and suffering as pitfalls to be avoided in order to achieve a full and happy moral life, to achieve 'the greatest happiness for the greatest number'. Bentham identified, then, the good with the useful, with that which can increase pleasure and diminish pain. In this sense, his well-known affirmation is very expressive and surprising:

> Nature has placed mankind under the governance of two sovereign masters: pain and pleasure. It is for them alone to point out what we ought to do.

[231] In this regard, see the study by Baggolini (1966), which is still being published today.

Expressive, because it clearly reflects and synthesises the connection between morality, utility and pleasure, placing the latter at the centre of human morality. And surprising, because Bentham here uses the term nature in a sense that he himself rejects, although he does not stop using it to refer to a 'human nature' whose characteristic feature is the capacity to experience pleasure and pain (*Introduction to the Principles of Morals and Legislation*, chap. V), thus calling into question the distinction between the human and the animal condition. Indeed, if the dignity of man derives from his perception of pleasure and pain, the same could be said of animals, whose sensory experiences are similar to those of human beings. Hence, according to him, non-human animals should also be included in the realm of morality:

> Is there any reason why we should be allowed to torture animals? I see none.... There have been times when the greater part of the human race, under the denomination of slaves, have been treated in the same way .... as the inferior races of animals are now still treated. Perhaps the day will come when the rest of the animals will acquire the rights of which they could never be deprived except by the hand of tyranny. The French have already discovered that blackness of skin is no reason to abandon a human being to the whim of his torturer. Perhaps the day will come when it will be recognised that the number of legs, the hairiness of the skin, or the termination of the sacral bone are equally insufficient reasons for abandoning a sentient being to the same fate.... An adult horse or a dog can reason and communicate better than an infant of a day or a week or even a month old. But the question is not can they reason, or can they talk, but can they suffer? (...)
>
> If a being suffers, there can be no moral justification for refusing to take that suffering into consideration. No matter the nature of the being, the principle of equality requires that its suffering be considered equal to the similar suffering of any other (...)
>
> The day will come when the rest of the animal creation will be able to acquire those rights which could never be taken away from them except by the hand of tyranny (*Introduction to the Principles of Morals and Legislation*, chap. XVII).

With Bentham, then, ethics loses any substratum or objective referent. The expression 'nature' is usually used in its most physical-natural sense and not as a reality whose constitution determines moral principles accessible to reason. As we have seen, his notion of 'human nature' does not point to its rational character nor to its free will, remaining with feelings that pursue pleasurable experiences and avoid painful ones. By denying human nature, Bentham rejects natural law, not only because it is inaccessible to reason but also because he does not believe in its existence, nor does it seem relevant to human happiness.

1.6.4.3 John Stuart Mill

The utilitarianism found its main continuator in John Stuart Mill (1806–1873), in spite of the criticism addressed to Bentham in his work *Utilitarianism* (1863). Daughters of the utilitarian doctrine are 'consequentialism', which presents morality as a matter of calculating consequences (G.E.M. Anscombe, 1919–2001), and 'speciesism', which promotes the rights of animals—even giving them primacy over those of men (Peter Singer).

In his work *On Liberty* (1859), John Stuart Mill pointed out that social liberty consisted in placing limits on the power of the ruler, in order to prevent him from exercising it for his own interests, making decisions that could harm or damage society. He argued that the people should have the power to participate in government decisions. According to him, social liberty is "the nature and limit of the power that can be legitimately exercised by society over the individual". He advocated two ways of safeguarding that social liberty: (1) the recognition of certain immunities, called political rights or liberties; and (2) the establishment of a system of constitutional 'checks' or guarantees. Two years later, in his *Considerations on Representative Government* (1861), he called representative government the ideal form of government. Mill, as a disciple of Bentham, rejected the notions of nature and natural law. According to him, the expressions 'nature' and 'natural' were a source of 'false taste, false philosophy, false morality, and even bad law'.

1.6.4.4 Legal Positivism

In addition to the utilitarianism, John Stuart Mill also delved into positivism, a doctrine that he himself developed, together with Auguste Comte (1798–1857) and J.N.A. Terry (1795–1856), and that would prevail in the nineteenth century. In fact, the two main nineteenth-century legal school of thoughts, namely the School of Exegesis (French) and the Historical School of Law (German), in spite of starting from antagonistic philosophies (the former rationalism, the latter historicism) and presenting very different visions of Law (either as a product of reason or as a product of culture or history), had a common element, that is, legal positivism, completely rejecting natural law. Natural law was strongly attacked in the German nineteenth century. The great positivists of the nineteenth century were Ludwig Knapp, Rudolph von Jhering and Carl Bergbohm.[232] Since there is no natural law, there are no natural rights either, but only positive rights, that is to say, those rights that are effectively recognised by the laws. It is not that the laws protect or safeguard some rights because of their pre-political character, that is, because they are inherent to the dignity of the person, but for other reasons (utilitarian, historical, etc.), all of them circumstantial, because positivism does not recognise more reality than what is susceptible of being known and studied according to the empirical methodology,

[232] In relation to the rejection of natural law in nineteenth-century German science, two observations should be made: the first is that the positivists revolted above all against modern natural law (ius naturalism), which spoke only of states of nature and social contracts; they reacted against this excessive individualism, and hence the 'organicist' theories that appeared in the nineteenth century (Otto von Gierke, for example). At the same time, they pigeonholed the states of nature and all conception, in general, of natural law (regarding the antipathy against the states of nature, see the study by Francisco Carpintero (1989); the second is that Germany was politically too fragmented; the Germans wanted a strong, single "state" with only one set of laws, those dictated by the state (on this subject, see Carpintero (1993)).

typical of the natural sciences, in which its object is visible, measurable, countable and quantifiable.

1.6.4.5 Marxism and Other Totalitarian Political Systems

The primacy of the material and physical over the immaterial or spiritual, reflected in the application of the empirical methodology of mathematics and natural sciences, proper to the material and physical world (the Cartesian realm of res extensa), to the immaterial or spiritual realities, led to a new stream of thought that directly despised or denied the spiritual part of reality: Marxism, a doctrine that emerged in the second half of the nineteenth century and remained strong until the end of the last century. It should be noted, however, that materialism did not emerge in 1848, the year in which Marx "showed himself to be a Marxist", but already existed before that, when he presented himself as a liberal-atheist philosopher.[233]

Although some authors such as John Stuart Mill tried to establish limits to the State so that it would not abuse its power, and others defended a notion of popular sovereignty that would replace monarchical absolutism (Rosseaux) and thus

---

[233] The following text by Fichte, published in 1813, is eloquent in this sense:

"The State is an organisation of property owners, and the power of the State is only the servant of these owners, who is paid by them to render this service. The owners of property are the original citizens and the founders of the State, and those who come after them have their rights determined by what they decide; in their zeal for liberty there is hidden nothing but the eagerness for the lack of regulation, of law, in their acquisitions. With the affirmation that the church, school, trade corporations, guilds, and in general everything that does not refer to legislation, are not part of the State but are organisations for private persons, they only pretend that the State does not take charge of them and that consequently, they are not economically burdensome; therefore, they understand that the State would disappear if there were no more thieves.

From all this the following follows. In the first place, Humanity is divided into two great branches: that of the proprietors and that of the non-proprietors. The former does not, properly speaking, constitute the State, for they are prior to the State; rather it is they who maintain the State, just as a lord maintains his servants, so that they are his servants. He who can afford a servant does not work, and this—since the State is only a servant of the owners—explains why only non-owners become members of the State, for he who has his own property does not lower himself to serve: the servant serves because he has nothing, seeking a salary, like the soldier.

The State is (for the owner) a necessary evil because it costs money; consequently, it is a matter of making that evil as small as possible.

All war destroys property, and therefore peace is the first civic obligation. To be a citizen means to be an owner and to exercise an industry, as opposed to a wage earner. The prolongation of war destroys property, the supreme good of man together with life, and threatens life and health, the supreme goods. For this reason, it is necessary, by every means, to shorten the war.

Prejudices of barbarian times, such as the divine origin of kings, the sanctity of oaths, or national honour, are nothing to those who are clear about this simple rule: life comes first, money second, and the nation third. That is why the owners lose nothing when, after the war is over, they pay a new lord and remain secure; it is simply a relationship of dependence, which changes. What is important is that the victor actually secures the property of the one who has been disarmed, that he does not allow his soldiers to pillage, that he leaves trade free and does not introduce customs barriers" Fichte (1920), pp. 40–45 (text translated into Spanish and collected by Carpintero (1989), pp. 141–142).

guarantee the freedom of individuals, the truth is that, in reality, in the nineteenth century fundamental rights lacked consistency. And the fact is that, fleeing from monarchical absolutism, the various doctrinal streams of thought sowed a seed that did not take long to germinate, totalitarianism, which placed the State before the individual, a State that, already described as Leviathan in the seventeenth century (Hobbes), now became 'the great whole' (Rousseau) or 'totality' (Hegel and Marx). It is no coincidence, then, that the twentieth century saw the rise of totalitarian political regimes (National Socialism, Fascism, Marxism, Leninism, etc.) which, in addition to denying freedom and individual rights, ignore the dignity of the human person. The tragic consequences of the Second World War clearly reflect the extent to which legal positivism, heir to the empiricist and utilitarianism, can justify or legitimise laws and governmental acts that constitute a serious attack on the dignity of the person, trampling on his most basic freedoms and fundamental rights.

1.6.4.6 The Triumph of the Denomination of the Right-Faith as a 'Subjective Right'

Having traced the evolution of *ius-facultas* (law-faculty) from the medieval period to the eighteenth century, it is now necessary to describe how it emerged and triumphed as 'subjective law', as it is known today.[234] As it is well known, the expression 'subjective right' emerged in the German doctrine of the nineteenth century ('*subjectives Recht*'), and from there it was definitively imposed, becoming generalised in Europe and America. Now, how did this denomination enter German doctrine after Kant?[235]

The emergence of the expression 'subjective right' ('*subjectives Recht*') is due to a disciple of Christian Wolf, Georg Darjes (1714–1791), who distinguished between 'subjectively considered right' and 'objectively considered right' (*ius subiective sumto–ius obiective sumto*).[236] The same distinction was taken up by another

[234]We follow here the synthetic description of Guzmán (2003), V, 1–4.

[235]As Guzmán Brito points out, Kant (1724–1804) still used the scholastic means of expression, although already in German, to refer to the figure. He would say: '*Der Rechte als (moralische) Vermögen*' ('Right as moral power') (Kant (1785), B, 2, p. 237); or: '*Recht, als Befugnis (facultas moralis generatim)*' ('Right as faculty—as moral faculty in general' (Kant (1785), II, *Einleutung*, II, p. 383 (p. 222)).

[236]Darjes (1745), p. 12, para. 12: "...it follows that the system there composed is, truly and properly conceived, a natural law, which is called a system of natural law or law of nature objectively considered, which can be distinguished from natural law subjectively considered"; by the same author, Darjes (1751), observat. I, para. 6: "The word 'law' is taken grammatically or technically (...) Technically it is taken subjectively or objectively. Subjectively taken to mean a certain quality of the person, which is a faculty (...) If looked at objectively, it either means the same as 'law' (...) or it is taken systematically, as a science..."; translation by Guzmán (2003), footnote n. 59.

disciple of Wolf, Daniel Nettelbladt (1719–1791),[237] and by Gottfried Achenwall (1719–1772).[238]

Between 1803 (the year in which he published his *System des Pandektenrechts* of 1803) and 1840 (the year in which Savigny began to edit his *System des heutigen römischen Rechts*), "the more traditional periphrastic form ("law in the subjective–objective sense") and the newer substantive-adjectival form ("subjective–objective law") coexisted, although both forms appeared to be used with some reluctance."[239] This hesitant and reticent situation hardly changed after 1840,[240] the case of Bernhard Windscheid (1817–1892) being an interesting example.[241] Consequently, "the German treatises of the nineteenth century did not manage to fix the name of law as a faculty in '*Recht in subjectives Sinn*' or in '*subjectives Recht*'. The authors,

[237] Nettelbladt (1767), para. 229: "The faculty to act, that is, the possibility to act, is called moral if it comes from the law. But the moral faculty to act is called 'right' when it is subjectively considered, to which objectively considered right is opposed"); translation by Guzmán (2003), footnote n. 60.

[238] Achenwall (1750), para. 23: "The physical faculty of man, insofar as it is not impeded by any moral law, is a moral faculty and, in a word, (moral) right, taken broadly and subjectively, i.e. as an affection of the person"; translation by Guzmán (2003), footnote n. 61; on this point, see also Carpintero (1987), p. 491, footnote n. 44.

[239] Guzmán (2003), V, 2; and develops it as follows: "Kierulff (1806–1894), for example, spoke of "*s. (o) g.(enannte) Recht im subjectiven Sinn*" (the "so-called right in the subjective sense"); and Savigny himself, after expressing himself in the more traditional terms of "*Recht im subjetiven (-objektiven) Sinn*", added: "according to the linguistic usage of some moderns" *("nach dem Sprachgebrauch mancher Neueren")*. In the latter author also uses the expression "*subjektives Recht*", as opposed to "*objecktives Recht*"; but after resorting to this form of speech, Savigny feels obliged to add that it is according to a "known linguistic usage" *("nach einem bekannten Sprachgebrauch")*, or "according to some of the modern linguistic uses" *("nach dem Sprachgebrauch mancher Neueren")*. In fact, when Savigny first introduces the notion in his *System, he* prefers the even older, properly almost scholastic ("faculty") way: "*Diese Macht nennen wir ein Recht dieser Person, gleichbedeutend mit Befugnis*"; and only then does he add: "*Manche nennen es das Recht im subjectiven Sinn*". He does something similar with law as a rule: "*Diese Regel nennen wir das Recht schlechthin, oder das allgemeine Recht: manche nennen sie das Rechts im objectiven Sinn*"".

[240] Guzmán (2003), V, 3; and develops it as follows: "In 1843, Karl Adolph Vangerow (1808–1870), organises book I of his *Leitfaden für Pandekten-Vorlesungen* into a 1st chapter dealing: '*Von den Quellen des Rechts, oder dem Rechte im objectiven Sinne*'; and a 5th chapter, whose No. 1 is headed: '*Begriff der Rechts (im subjectiven Sinn)*'." The same duality is used by Karl Ludwig Arndts (1803–1878) in the Lehrbuch der Pandecten (1852). But in 1860, Leopold August Warnkönig (1794–1866) writes in his Institutiones iuris Romani privati (1819): "Iuris vocabulum hoc sensu intellectum [sc. as facultas] ius in senso subjectivo, i. (d) e.(st), subiective sumto insignire hodie dicunt".

[241] Guzmán (2003), V, 3: "In the first edition of his *Lehrbuch des Pandektenrechts* (1862) he had reluctantly referred to the "*s. (o) g.(enante) Recht im subjectiven Sinn*". But in the fifth edition (1879) he no longer refers to the two expressions in use and speaks of "*Rechts im objectiven Sinn, objectives Rechts*" and "*Recht in subjectives Sinn, subjectives Rechts*". However, the later Heinrich Dernburg (1829–1907), in his *Pandecten* (2nd ed., 1884), adheres to the older usage of "*Recht im objectiven–subjectiven Sinn*", while the no less late Ernst Immanuel Bekker (1827–1908), in his *System des heutigen Pandekten Rechts* of 1886, speaks of "*objective–subjective Rechts*"".

when they did not disregard both, oscillated between them, and sometimes (...) this happened in one and the same author."[242]

It was the monographic literature that picked up the terminology of "*subjective law*". It is probable that the *auctoritas* of Winscheid, who, from the 1878 edition of his *Lehrbuch* onwards, adopted this expression, may have contributed to this.[243] It could also have helped, according to Guzmán Brito's opinion, "the purely editorial and external fact that at the time of giving its title to a monographic work whose subject was law-faculty, it was very heavy or pedantic to include in its title a periphrastic expression such as '*Recht in subjectives Sinn*', *in* contrast with the other, more synthetic and compact one of '*subjectives Recht.*'"[244] Be that as it may, the fact is that at the end of the nineteenth century several works began to be published with the expression '*subjective law*' in their titles,[245] which was the key to the triumph of this expression in Germany and, shortly afterwards, its generalisation in Europe and America.

1.7 Final Considerations

Human rights can be based on different schools of philosophy. In fact, the protection of fundamental rights is currently defended and promoted from doctrines as diverse as Aristotelian, Kantian or utilitarian philosophies. This shows that such protection is absolutely indispensable for the peace of people and nations. But there is no peace without justice, and there is no justice without truth. Human rights that do not correspond to what man is, to his human dignity, could lead us to repeat regrettable historical episodes. We should learn from history, as Cicero pointed out. There are schools of philosophy whose basic assumptions do not seem to correspond to what man is, to his dignity. This is the case of utilitarianism and its doctrinal derivations (consequentialism, pragmatism, positivism, 'speciesism'—or the confusion between the human and the non-human—,[246] etc.), as history itself shows.

If, since Jean Bodin, the essence of sovereignty is the power to create Law,[247] and sovereignty consists fundamentally in the sovereignty of Law,[248] it is clear that limits should be placed on such sovereignty; otherwise, historical experience shows

[242] Guzmán (2003), V, 3 *in fine*.

[243] Winscheid (1862), p. 81, para. 37 (collected by Guzmán (2003), V, 4, footnote n. 82).

[244] Guzmán (2003), V, 4.

[245] August Thon, Rechtsnorm und subjektives Recht (1878), Carl Gustav Freudenstein, Die Rechtskraft nach der Reichscivilprocessordnung und ihre Wirkungen auf die subjectiven Rechte (Hanover, 1884), Georg Jellinek, System des subjectiven öffentlichen Rechte (1892) and Eduard Hölder, Ueber objectives und subjectives Recht (Leipzig, 1893).

[246] In this regard, see Ballesteros (2016).

[247] Arnaiz (1971), vol. II, p. 26.

[248] "Sovereign will is the antithesis of subjective will. And since the expression of this will takes the form of law, sovereignty in reality means the sovereignty of law" (Loughlin (2003), p. 87).

that the Law turns against human beings, denying them rights that they cannot assert because those who should recognise and protect them do not see beyond the strictly political-legal sphere, thus denying them a dignity that is rooted in their anthropological and social dimension of a pre-political nature.[249]

It is perhaps worth returning to the tradition of political thought, which goes from Cicero, defender of the *lex naturalis* and the *ius gentium*,[250] to the modern era, to recover the limits and the sense of moderation, where the people were understood as *consensus iuris et communitas utilitatis*,[251] and popular sovereignty, in the political sphere, enjoyed legitimacy as long as it was faithful to the Law and in accordance with the general interest. This conception could well serve as an adequate basis for the modern State, considering "Law as the defence of the individual and his inviolable prerogatives, as something that is above popular sovereignty itself."[252]

It is necessary to overcome the illusion of believing that democracy alone can guarantee freedom, an idea that European history itself, both ancient and more recent, clearly refutes. In fact, the last two centuries of history show that sovereignty without limits based on democracy alone cannot guarantee the freedom of the individual, but, on the contrary, can tend to undermine it. And this problem is still present today, even if it sometimes emerges in a less apparent or more subtle way.[253]

It is therefore necessary to return to the establishment of limits to the State that allow the safeguarding of individual rights and make it difficult for the public power, adopting a paternalistic attitude, to exercise an unrestrained power under the guise of

---

[249] Gearty (2010), who highlights the ongoing pernicious effects of Hobbesian thought: "But his [referring to Hobbes] well-known vision of the government of a state as the entity of absolute sovereignty, with the ability to exercise the power which could not be gained by those subject to it, was inevitably agreeable to those who, in subsequent generations, were to feel the need to act against a variety of perceived threats to the security of the state. Hobbes provides an important backdrop to the attacks on liberty in the name of security that have been such a feature of the democratic era, supplying that thread to the discussion which says security matters above all and (recalling our second point above) that security does not infringe liberty: that not only are those who do not notice repressive laws free, but so too are those coerced by fear into sullen obedience" (p. 10). And later, referring to the English sphere, he adds: "By the end of the 19th century, it is clear that Hobbes's security-state with a residual model of liberty, but without any strong notion of pre-political inalienable rights, is firmly in place" (p. 12).

[250] In this regard, see Obarrio (2011); see also Domingo (2010), pp. 6–8; on the relationship between *ius naturale* and *ius gentium*, see Waldron (2005, 2008).

[251] Cicero, *De re publica*, book 1, n. 25: "...an assemblage of the multitude associated by common consent, for reciprocal rights, and reciprocal usefulness" (I used the English version available at https://www.gutenberg.org/cache/epub/54161/pg54161-images.html); Ballesteros (2006), p. 113; see also Obarrio (2011).

[252] Ballesteros (2006), p. 114.

[253] Fried (2007), p. 165: "But that is my point. In modern, liberal, welfare-administrative democracies, the impositions on liberty are likely to be gentle, marginal. But we must be vigilant, recognise them for what they are, or we will lose our grip on what liberty is, coming to confuse it with comfort, a generalised decency, or just democracy itself-a confusion that lovers of the state would be glad to foist upon us. But liberty is not the same as democracy."

a democratic legitimacy that pretends to justify everything or almost everything. For this, it is necessary to recognise human rights that are prior to the State, and not mere 'creatures' of the State,[254] that is, natural rights—rather than pre-political rights[255]—over which no State should dispose,[256] nor legislate at will, thus avoiding conceiving the law as a formal passport that allows the State an excessive exercise, that is, without moderation or limits, of power.[257]

It is true that the establishment of limits on the exercise of State power and the creation of law may not solve all the dilemmas that the protection of fundamental rights brings with it, but it can offer valuable help in overcoming its excessively utilitarian approach, which, by focusing more on the *quantum* than the *quod*, ignores the pre-political dimension of human rights, thus trivialising—if not ignoring—the dignity and greatness of every human being, leaving them defenceless against the omnipotent power of the Leviathan.[258]

---

[254]Fried (2007), p. 72: "It is because our rights emanate from whom and what we are that we may form, re-form, or accept states in order to make our rights more certain and secure. So those who say that our rights depend on or are the creatures of the state have it the wrong way around". This raises, however, a problem that is not lost on Fried and he describes as follows: "What we cannot get to on our own, without laws and so without a state, is the content and detail of those rights. And rights without content are empty. Liberty means honouring our rights, and if the content of our rights is only what the state says it is, then while the *general idea* of rights, and the *general idea* of liberty may be secure against the state, the *substance* of each depends entirely on the state after all."

[255]I understand that here the expression 'natural' is preferable to 'pre-political', although the expression 'natural rights' can also pose the same problem depending on the meaning given to it. This terminology, 'pre-political', prior to the State, was that of the natural legal philosophers (iusnaturalists), who started from the *status naturae*, in which isolated individuals (not persons) live, bearers of 'natural rights' (hence the risk of also using this expression), who create political power by convention, in order to defend their rights in political society. Those of us who think that the figure of the isolated individual is a fiction, which has never existed and never will exist, do not use the expression 'pre-political'. Not in vain, Aristotle already affirmed that man is, *velis nolis*, a political animal. As the human being is born in the bosom of a society, of a political community, more or less civilised, there is in fact no pre-political right, in the same way that there are not or have not been pre-political men. Therefore, the adjective 'pre-political' should be reserved, *stricto sensu*, to refer to what is most immediately influenced by modern natural law (iusnaturalism), such as the American and French Bills of Rights, emphasising that this term comes from a group of very questionable theories, such as those of the modern natural legal philosophers (iusnaturalists). That said, since the expression 'natural rights' also carries a similar danger, one could use the expression 'pre-political rights' in the same sense as 'natural rights', that is, referring to the fact that the State does not create these rights, but recognises them, not emanating from the power of the State, but from the very dignity of each human being.

[256]Fried (2007), pp. 144–145: "If we have some rights, and therefore liberties, that are pre-political rights which the state is bound to recognise, rights that are there before the state gets down to the business of defining rights, then, like Archimedes with his lever, we have a place to stand, and liberty can move the world. To put it in more traditional language, unless we have natural law, pre-political rights, liberty is not secure"; on this, see also pp. 80, 84–85, 90–94 and 155.

[257]Gross (2003); see also the review of this study by Dyzenhaus (2008), xiv–xvi.

[258]One might think that this statement is excessively harsh, perhaps applicable *stricto sensu* only to some countries such as North Korea or, perhaps, Venezuela, but not to the USA or the countries of the European Union. However, in Western states there is more and more undue interference of

Some Cited Normative Sources and Declarations

Spain

Fueros locales del Reino de León (910–1230). Antología, Madrid: Boletín Oficial del Estado, 2018 (available at https://www.boe.es/biblioteca_juridica/publicacion.php?id=PUB-LH-2018-61).

*Leyes políticas españolas fundamentales (1808-1978) (*compiled and prologue by E. Tierno Galván). Madrid, Tecnos, 1984.

Las Constituciones de España (compilation and foreword by Jorge Esteban). Madrid, CEPC, 2000.

International

Barna Mezey (ed.), *Az Aranybulla a joghistóriában*, Mádl Ferenc Összehasonlító Jogi Intézet, Budapest, 2022

De Bulla Aurea. Andraea II Regis Hungarie, 1222, Verona: Edizioni Valdonega, 1999.

Textos básicos de la Historia constitucional comparada (ed. and prologue by J. Varela Suanzes). Madrid, CEPC, 1998.

Virginia Declaration of Rights (June 12, 1776).

Declaration of Independence of the United States (July 4, 1776)

Constitution of the United States of America (1787).

Declaration of the Rights of Man and of the Citizen (1789)

French Constitution of 1791.

Amendment to the American Constitution (December 15, 1791).

Charter of the United Nations (San Francisco, 26 June 1945).

American Declaration of the Rights and Duties of Man (May 2, 1948).

Universal Declaration of Human Rights (Paris, 10 December 1948).

References

Doctrinal and Bibliographical Sources

Achenwall G (1750) Ius naturae in usum auditorium. Sumptibus Victorini Bossigelii

---

political power in the lives of citizens, and even more so in the current global context, in which financial and media power is remaining in a few hands; on this subject, see Masferrer (2019a), pp. 11–20; Obarrio (2021a).

Amos A (1856) Ruins of time: Exemplified in Sir Mathew Hale's history of the pleas of the crown. Deighton Bell, Cambridge
Arendt H (1968) The origins of totalitarianism, 3rd edn, New York. https://www.scielo.cl/scielo.php?script=sci_arttext&pid=S0716-54552005000100008
Arnaiz A (1971) Soberanía y potestad: de la soberanía del pueblo, de la potestad del Estado. Universidad Nacional Autónoma de México, México
Arvizu F (1988) Las Cortes de León de 1188 y sus decretos. Un ensayo de crítica institucional. In: El Reino de León en la Alta Edad Media. I. Cortes, Concilios y Fueros. Centro de Estudios e Investigación San Isidoro, León, pp 13–141
Arvizu F (1994) Más sobre los Decretos de las Cortes de León de 1188. Anuario de Historia del Derecho español 63–64:1193–1238
Arvizu F (2002) Las primeras Cortes leonesas. In: Regnum: Corona y Cortes en Benavente (1202–2002). Ayuntamiento de Benavente, Benavente, pp 37–46
Baggolini L (1966) La simpatía nella morale en el diritto. Aspetti del pensiero di Adam Smith e orientamenti attuali. G. Giappichelli, Torino
Baker J (2023) Magna Carta. In: Balogh E (ed) Golden bulls and chartas: European medieval documents of liberties. Miskolc: Ferenc Mádl Institute of Comparative Law – Central European Academic Publishing, Budapest, pp 195–207
Ballesteros J (1974) Introduction. In: Cotta S (1974) Itinerarios humanos del Derecho. Ed. Eunsa, Pamplona
Ballesteros J (2006) Repensar la paz. EIUNSA, Madrid
Ballesteros J (2016) Tipos de deshumanismos: la confusión humano/no humano. In: Carbonell C, Flamarique L (eds) De simios, cyborgsy dioses. La naturalización del hombre a debate. Biblioteca-Nueva, Madrid, pp 175–194
Biel G (1574) Commentarii doctissimi in IIIIII Sententiarum libros. Brixiae
Böckenförde E-W (1987) Menschenrechte und Menschenwürde. Historische Voraussetzungen—säkulare Gestalt—christliches Verständnis. Klett-Cotta, Stuttgart
Böckenförde E-W (2002) Geschichte der Rechts- und Staatsphilosophie—Antike und Mittelalter. Mohr Siebeck, Tübingen
Böckenförde E-W (2007) Der säkularisierte Staat. Sein Charakter, seine Rechtfertigung und seine Probleme im 21. Jahrhundert. Themenband. München
Bonnett D (1992) Los protectores de naturales en la Audiencia de Quito: siglos XVII y XVIII. Flacso, Quito
Brett A-S (1997) Liberty, right and nature: individual rights in later scholastic thought. Cambridge University Press, Cambridge
Carl Gustav Freudenstein (1884) Die Rechtskraft nach der Reichscivilprocessordnung und ihre Wirkungen auf die subjectiven Rechte. Hanover
Carpenter D (2015) Magna Carta. Penguin Classics, London
Carpintero F (1977) Del Derecho natural medieval al Derecho natural moderno: Fernando Vázquez de Menchaca. University of Salamanca, Salamanca
Carpintero F (1981) El derecho natural laico en la Edad Media. Persona y Derecho VIII:33–100
Carpintero F (1987) La independencia y autonomía del individuo: los orígenes de la persona jurídica. Anuario de Filosofía del Derecho 4:477–522
Carpintero F (1989) La Cabeza de Jano. Servicio de Publicaciones de la Universidad de Cádiz, Cádiz
Carpintero F (1993) Los inicios del positivismo jurídico en Centroeuropa. Actas, Madrid
Carpintero F (2000) Historia breve del Derecho natural. Colex, Madrid
Carpintero F (2003) El desarrollo de la facultad individual en la Escolástica. In: Carpintero F et al (eds) El derecho subjetivo en su Historia. Servicio de Publicaciones de la Universidad de Cádiz, Cádiz
Carpintero F (2013) La ley natural. Una realidad aun por explicar. UNAM, México City
Carpintero F (2016a) El movimiento constitucional antes de la Revolución. Res Publica. Rivista di Studi Storio-Politici 15:35–58

Carpintero F (2016b) Human dignity in Thomas Aquinas. Person Law 74:97–116
Carpintero F (2017) Hugo Grocio visto por sus contemporáneos. Rivista Internazionale di Filosofia del Diritto 2(3):171–196
Carré de Malberg R (1931) La loi expression de la volonté générale. Etude sur le concept de la loi dans la Constitution de 1875. Sirey, Paris
Carré de Malberg R (1998) Teoría general del Estado, 2nd edn. Fondo de Cultura Económica, México
Cavero G (2009) Alfonso IX de León y el iter de su Corte (1188–1230). e-Spania. Revue interdisciplinaire d'etudes hispaniques medievales et modernes 8. http://e-spania.revues.org/18626?lang=en
Church S (2015) King John: England, Magna Carta and the making of a tyrant. Macmillan, London
Cicero De Officiis. Available at http://www.stoics.com/cicero_book.html
Cicero De re publica. Available at https://www.gutenberg.org/cache/epub/54161/pg54161-images.html
Colmeiro M (1861) Cortes de los antiguos reinos de León y de Castilla. Imp. y Estereotipia de M. Rivadeneyra, Madrid
Condorelli O (2013) 'Quod omnes tangit, debet ab omnibus approbari'. Note sull'origine e sull'utilizzazione del principio tra medio evo e prima età moderna. Ius Canonicum 53:101–127
Constant B (1988) De la libertad de los antiguos comparada con la de los modernos. In: Constant B (ed) Del Espíritu de Conquista. Tecnos, Madrid
Coronas S-M (1998) Las Leyes fundamentales del Antiguo Régimen. In: Coronas S-M (ed) Estudios de Historia del Derecho Público. Tirant lo Blanch, Valencia, pp 218–310
Cotta S (1963) Philosophie et politique dans l'oeuvre de Rousseau. Une esai d'interpretation. ARSP XLIX-2 3:171–189
Cotta S (1964) La position du probleme de la politique chez Rousseau. In: Etudes sur le Contrat Social de Jean-Jacques Rousseau. Belles Lettres, Paris, pp 177–190
Cotta S (1965) Theorie politique et theorie religeuse chez Rousseau. Annales de Philisophie politique 5. Rousseau et la philisophie politique 171–194
Cotta S (1974) Itinerarios humanos del Derecho. Ed. Eunsa, Pamplona
Cutter CR (1986) The Protector de Indios in Colonial New Mexico, 1659-1821. Historical Society of New Mexico & University of New Mexico Press, Albuquerque
Danvila M (1881) Las libertades de Aragón: ensayo histórico, jurídico y político. Imprenta de Fortanet, Madrid
Darjes JG (1745) Institutiones jurisprudentiae universalis. Apvd Christ. Henr. Cvno
Darjes JG (1751) Observationes iuris naturalis, socialis et gentium ad ordinem systematis sui selectae. Ienae
Dávila O (2017) La protección de los derechos fundamentales en la Alta Edad Media española. La Carta Magna de León. Revista Chilena de Historia del Derecho 25:203–211
De Ayala C (1996) Alfonso IX, último monarca del reino de León (1188–1230). In: Álvarez C (ed) Reyes de León: monarcas leoneses del 850 al 1230. Edilesa, León, pp 193–216
Denzer H (1972) Moralphilosophie und Naturrecht bei Samuel Pufendorf. Eine geistes- und wissenschaftgeschichtliche Untersuchung zur Geburt des Naturrechts aus der Praktischen Philosopie. Beck, München
de Sepúlveda J-G (1984) Demócrates Segundo o de las justas causas de la guerra contra los Indios, 2nd edn. Consejo Superior de Investigaciones Científicas. Instituto Francisco de Vitoria, Madrid
de Vitoria F (1934) De iustitia. Publicaciones de la Asociación Francisco de Vitoria, n.° 5, Madrid
de Vitoria F (1960) Relecciones teológicas. BAC, Madrid
Díaz E (1997) Libertad-igualdad en la Declaración de Derechos del Hombre y del Ciudadano de 1789. In: Filosofía y Derecho. Studies in honour of Professor José Corts Grau, vol I. University of Valencia, Valencia
Dicey A-V (1885) Introduction to the study of the Law of the Constitution. Macmillan, London
Domingo R (2010) The new global law. Cambridge University Press, Cambridge

Dorado J (2001) La lucha por la Constitución. Las teorías del Fundamental Law en la Inglaterra del siglo XVII. CEPC, Madrid
Duguit L (1913) Les transformations du droit public, Paris: Armand Colin, 1913 (I used the English version entitled Law in the Modern State, trans. Frida and Harold Laski). London, Allen & Unwin, p 1921
Duguit L (1922) Souveraineté et liberté, Paris (I used the Spanish version entitled Soberanía y libertad, Madrid, 1922).
Duguit L (1937) Manual de Derecho constitucional. Librería Española y Extranjera, Madrid
Dyzenhaus D (2008) Civil rights and security. Ashgate, Farnham
Escudero J-A (2011) Cortes y Constitución de Cádiz. 200 años. Fundación Rafael del Pino-Espasa, Madrid
Esteban J (2000) Las Constituciones de España. CEPC, Madrid
Estepa C (2002) Los orígenes de las Cortes. In: El reino de León en la época de las Cortes de Benavente. Jornadas de Estudios Históricos. Benavente, 7–17 mayo de 2002. Centro de Estudios Benaventanos "Ledo del Pozo", Salamanca, pp 181–190
Fazio M (2006) Historia de las ideas contemporáneas. Una lectura del proceso de secularización. RIALP, Madrid
Fernández J-M (1988) Cortes, concilios y fueros leoneses. El reino de León en la Alta Edad Media. Editorial Centro de Estudios e Investigación San Isidoro, León
Fernández J-M (1993) La curia regia de León de 1188 y sus "Decreta" y Constitución. Editorial Centro de Estudios e Investigación San Isidoro, León
Fichte JG (Vorträgen gehalten im Sommer 1813, publ. 1920) Die Staatslehre, oder über das Verhaltniss des Urstaates zum Vernunftreiche. Berlin
Figgis J-N (1998) Studies of political thought. From Gerson to Grotius, 1414-1625. Thoemmes, Bristol
Folgado A (1960) Evolución histórica del concepto del Derecho subjetivo. Estudio especial en los teólogo-juristas del siglo XVI. Biblioteca 'La Ciudad de Dios' Pax Iuris, San Lorenzo de El Escorial
Font J-M (1983) Cartas de Población y Franquicia de Cataluña. CSIC, Madrid
Franklin JH (1973) Jean Bodin and the rise of absolutist theory. Cambridge University Press, Cambridge
Fried C (2007) Modern liberty and the limits of the government. W.W. Norton, New York
García de Enterría E (1981) Revolución francesa y Administración contemporánea, 2nd edn. Taurus, Madrid
García de Enterría E (1994) La lengua de los derechos. La formación del Derecho Público europeo tras la Revolución Francesa. Civitas, Madrid
García Pérez RD (2008) Antes leyes que reyes. Cultura jurídica y constitución política en la Edad Moderna (Navarra, 1512–1808). Giuffrè, Milano
Gearty C-A (2010) Escaping Hobbes: liberty and security for our democratic (not anti-terrorist) age. LSE Legal Studies Working Paper 3. http://ssrn.com/abstract=1543121
Gerson I (repr. 1987) Liber de vita spirituali animae
González J (1944) Alfonso IX. In: Consejo Superior de Investigaciones Científicas (CSIC), Madrid
González L (1975) Las Uniones aragonesas y las Cortes del Reino (1283-1301). CSIC, Zaragoza
González E (dir), González E (coord) (2018) Las Cortes de León: cuna del parlamentarismo, Cortes Generales. Centro de Estudios Políticos y Constitucionales, Madrid
Goodale M (2011) On universality and the transnational validity of human rights. http://www.irmgard-coninx-stiftung.de/fileadmin/user_upload/pdf/archive/026%20Goodale.pdf
Grimm D (1973) Solidarität als Rechtsprinzip. Die Rechts- und Staatslehre Leon Duguits in ihrer Zeit. Athenäum, Frankfurt
Gross O (2003) Chaos and rules: should responses to violent crises always be constitutional. Yale Law J 112:1011–1134
Grossi P (1972) Usus facti. La nozione di proprietà nella inaugurazione dell'età nuova. Quaderni fiorentini per la storia del pensiero giuridico moderno 1(1):287–355

Grotius H (1625a) The rights of war and peace, 1901 edition. Paris. http://oll.libertyfund.org/titles/553#Grotius_0138_583-585
Grotius H (1625b) De jure belli ac pacis. Paris
Guzmán A (2003) Historia de la denominación del derecho-facultad como 'subjetivo'. Revista de Estudios Histórico-Jurídicos 25:407–443
Guzmán A (2007) In quaelibet re, tantumdem est de iure quantum de entitate. La concepción ontológica del derecho-facultad a fines de la Edad Media y en la Época Moderna. Revista de Estudios Histórico-Jurídicos 29:293–310
Guzmán A (2009) El derecho como facultad en la Neoescolástica española del siglo XVI. Iustel, Madrid
Guzmán A (2013) Breve relación histórica sobre la formación y el desarrollo de la noción de derecho definido como facultad o potestad ('derecho subjetivo'). Ars Iuris Salmanticensis. Studies 1(1):73–95
Haakonsen K (1991) From natural law to the rights of man: a European perspective on American debates. In: Haakonssen K, Lacey ML (eds) A culture of rights: the bill of rights in philosophy, politics, and law. CUP, Cambridge, pp 19–61
Hauriou M (2003) Principios de Derecho público y constitucional. Granada, Editorial Comares
Head T, Landes R (eds) (1992) The peace of god: social violence and religious response in France around the year 1000. Cornell University Press, Ithaca, NY
Helmholz R-H (2005) Natural law and human rights in English Law: From Bracton to Blackstone. Ave Maria Law Rev 1:1–22
Helmholz R-H (2010) Human rights in the canon law. In: Witte J, Alexander F-S (eds) Christianity and human rights: an introduction. Cambridge University Press, Cambridge, pp 99–112
Hervada J (1987) Historia de la ciencia del Derecho natural. Eunsa, Pamplona
Hobbes T (1642) De cive
Hobbes T (1968) Leviathan, 1968 edition. Penguin, Harmondsworth
Hoffmann H (1964) Gottesfriede und Treuga Die. Monumenta Germaniae Historica, Stuttgart
Hölder E (1893) Ueber objectives und subjectives Recht. Deichert, Leipzig
Holt JC (2015) Magna Carta (3rd ed. by G. Garnett and J. Hudson). Cambridge University Press, Cambridge
International Memory of the World Register (2013) The Decreta of León of 1188. The oldest documentary manifestation of the European Parliamentary System. https://en.unesco.org/memoryoftheworld/registry/251
Izquierdo R (1990) Privilegios reales otorgados a Toledo durante la Edad Media (1101-1494). Instituto Provincial de Investigaciones y Estudios Toledanos, Toledo
Jellinek G (1892) System des subjectiven öffentlichen Rechte. J. C. B. Mohr, Freiburg
Jiménez R (2001) El Constitucionalismo. IVAP, Oñati
Jiménez R (2003) Constitutionalism. Proceso de formación y fundamentos del Derecho constitucional. Marcial Pons, Madrid
Kant I (1785) Groundwork of the Metaphysics of Morals -Grundlegung zur Metaphysik der Sitten-
Kleinig J (1981) Cultural relativism and human rights. In: Erh-SoonTay A (ed) Teaching human rights. Australian National Commission for UNESCO, Canberra, pp 111–118
Kleinig J (2007) Does the language of human rights have traction in the 'war on terrorism'? Paper presented at the annual meeting of the American Political Science Association, Hyatt Regency Chicago and the Sheraton Chicago Hotel and Towers, Chicago, IL, Aug 30. http://www.allacademic.com/meta/p209183_index.html
Kosto A-J (2003) Reasons for assembly in Catalonia and Aragón, 900–1200. In: Barnwell P-S, Mostert M (eds) Political assemblies in the earlier in the middle ages. Brepols, Turnhout, pp 133–149
Kotzour M (2003) Sovereignty today. Palabras clave para un diálogo europeo-latinoamericano sobre un atributo del Estado constitucional moderno. In: Häberle P, Kotzour M (eds) De la soberanía al Derecho Constitucional común: palabras clave para un diálogo europeo-latinoamericano. Universidad Nacional Autónoma de México, México, pp 85–122

Kotzour M (2005) Universality—a principle of European and global constitutionalism. Electron J Const Hist 6:201–228
Kriegel B (1995) The state and the rule of law. Princeton University Press, Princeton, NJ
Lalinde J (1980) Los derechos individuales en el Privilegio General del Aragón. Anuario de Historia del Derecho Español 50:55–68
Loengard JS (ed) (2010) Magna Carta and the England of John. Boydell & Brewer, Woodbridge
Loewenstein K (1945) An international bill of human rights. Curr Hist 9(50):273–283
López González H (2015) The leones Parliament of 1188: the first parliament of the Western world (The Magna Carta of Alfonso IX). https://web.archive.org/web/20160304070224/http://www.interun.ru/ss/interun/u/files/charterv_e.pdf
López Hernández J (1998) Historia de la Filosofía del Derecho Clásica y Moderna. Tirant lo Blanch, Valencia
López Ulla J-M (1999) Orígenes constitucionales de control judicial de las leyes. Tecnos, Madrid
Lorente M (2016) La Carta Magna y otros mitos constitucionales. Almacén de Derecho January 27th. https://almacendederecho.org/la-carta-magna-y-otros-mitos-constitucionales
Loughlin M (2003) The idea of public law. Oxford University Press, Oxford
Loughlin M (2016) The erosion of sovereignty. Neth J Legal Philos 2:57–81
Maestre A (2004) 'Todas las gentes del mundo son hombres': El gran debate entre Fray Bartolomé de las Casas (1474-1566) y Juan Ginés de Sepúlveda (1490-1573). Anales del Seminario de Historia de la Filosofía 21:91–134
Martín J-L (2003) Las Cortes Medievales. In: Fuentes E, Martín J-L (dirs) De las Cortes históricas a los parlamentos democráticos. Castilla y León. Siglos XII-XXI. Actas del Congreso Científico, Benavente, 21–25 de octubre de 2002. VIII Centenario Cortes de Benavente. Dykinson, Madrid, pp 29–64
Martínez Marina F (1813) Teoría de las Cortes o grandes juntas nacionales de los reinos de León y Castilla. Fermín Villalpando, Madrid
Masferrer A (2005) El alcance de la prohibición de las penas inhumanas y degradantes en el constitucionalismo español y europeo. Una contribución histórico-comparada al contenido penal del constitucionalismo español y alemán. In: Presente y futuro de la Constitución española de 1978. Tirant lo Blanch - Facultad de Derecho (Univ. Valencia), Valencia, pp 515–544
Masferrer A (2008) The passionate discussion among common lawyers about postbellum American codification: an approach to its legal argumentation. Arizona State Law J 40(1):173–256
Masferrer A (2009) Spanish legal traditions. A comparative legal history outline, 2nd ed 2012. Dykinson, Madrid
Masferrer A (2010) Defense of the common law against postbellum American codification: reasonable and fallacious argumentation. Am J Legal Hist 50(4):355–430
Masferrer A (2011) La soberanía nacional en las Cortes gaditanas: su debate y aprobación. In: Escudero J-A (dir) Cortes y Constitución de Cádiz. 200 años, vol 2. Fundación Rafael del Pino-Espasa, Madrid, pp 639–672
Masferrer A (2014) Peace and liberty in the Catalan medieval legal tradition. A contribution to the interaction between religious law and secular law in the European Middle Ages. In: Sunde J-Ø (ed) Constitutionalism in Europe before 1789. Constitutional arrangements from the High Middle Ages to the French Revolution. Pax Forlag A/S, Oslo, pp 28–48
Masferrer A (2018a) Francisco Martínez Marina. In: Domingo R, Martínez-Torrón J (eds) Great Christian jurists in Spanish history. CUP & Center for the Study of Law and Religion at Emory University, Cambridge, pp 276–292
Masferrer A (2018b) The myth of French influence over Spanish codification. The general part of the criminal codes of 1822 and 1848. In: Masferrer A (ed) The Western codification of criminal law: the myth of its predominant French influence revisited. Springer, Dordrecht, pp 193–242
Masferrer A (2019a) Para una nueva cultura política. Catarata, Valencia
Masferrer A (2019b) The French codification and 'codiphobia' in common law traditions. Tulane Eur Civil Law Forum 34:1–31

Masferrer A (2019c) Human dignity in the early sixteenth century Spanish scholasticism: Francisco de Vitoria and Fray Bartolomé de las Casas. De rebus divinis et humanis. In: Dondorp H, Schermaier M, Sirks B (eds) Essays in honour of Jan Hallebeek Vandenhoeck & Ruprecht Verlage, Göttingen, pp 203–213
Masferrer A (2020) Criminal law and morality revisited: interdisciplinary perspectives. In: Masferrer A (ed) Criminal law and morality in the age of consent: interdisciplinary perspectives. Springer, Dordrecht, pp 1–27
Masferrer A, Obarrio J-A (2012) The state power and the limits of the principle of sovereignty: an historical approach. In: Masferrer A (ed) Post 9/11 and the state of permanent legal emergency. Springer, Dordrecht, pp 15–51
Masferrer A, Obarrio J-A (2014) El principio de soberanía: una aproximación histórica a sus límites. In: Historia y Derecho. Studies dedicated to Professor Santos Coronas, vol 2. KRK Ediciones- University of Oviedo, pp 987–1010
Megías J-J (1992) De la facultad moral a la cualidad moral. Anuario de Filosofía del Derecho 9: 325–349
Merello Arecco I (2005) La máxima 'Quod omnes tangit': Una aproximación al estado del tema. Revista de estudios histórico-jurídicos 27:163–175
Mezey B (ed) (2022) Az Aranybulla a joghistóriában. Mádl Ferenc Összehasonlító Jogi Intézet, Budapest
Morgan ES (2006) The invention of the people. In: El surgimiento de la soberanía popular en Inglaterra y Estados Unidos. Siglo veintiuno editores, Madrid
Mitre E (1989) A ochocientos años de las ¿primeras? Cortes hispánicas (León 1188): Mitos políticos y memoria histórica en la formación del parlamentarismo europeo. Mayurqa 22:415–426
Morsink J (1999) The universal declaration of human rights. Origins, drafting and intent. Origins, drafting and intent. University of Pennsylvania Press, Philadelphia
Moyn S (2018) Not enough: human rights in an unequal world. Harvard University Press, Cambridge, MA/London
Nettelbladt D (1749, 3rd ed. 1767) Systema elementare universae iurisprudentiae naturalis. Halae
Nieto J-M (2011) La expansión de las asambleas representativas en los reinos hispánicos: una aproximación comparativa. In: de Navarra G (ed) 1212–1214: El trienio que hizo a Europa. XXXVII Semana de Estudios Medievales. Estella, 19–23 julio de 2010. Fondo de Publicaciones del Gobierno de Navarra, Pamplona, pp 197–241
Novoa M (2016) The protectors of Indians in the royal audience of Lima. History, careers and legal culture, 1575-1775. Brill-Nijhoff, Leiden
Obarrio J-A (2011) Cicero and the limits of power. In: Masferrer A (ed) Rule of law and fundamental rights in the fight against terrorism. Una aproximación histórica y jurídico-comparada. Aranzadi-Thompson, Pamplona, pp 47–73
Obarrio J-A (2021a) 1984 (George Orwell). Diálogos entre el Derecho y la Literatura. Los Totalitarismos I. Dykinson, Madrid
Obarrio J-A (2021b) Cartas a un amigo alemán (Albert Camus). Diálogos entre el Derecho y la Literatura. Los Totalitarismos II. Dykinson, Madrid
O'Callaghan J-F (1989) The Cortes of Castile-León, 1188-1300. University of Pennsylvania Press, Philadelphia
Ockham W (1496) Magistri Guilhelmi de Ockham super potestate de summi pontificis octo quaestionum decisiones. Lyon
Offler H-S (1977) The three modes of natural law in Ockham. A revision of the text. Franciscan Stud 23:207–218
Orlandis J (2006) Historia de la Iglesia. I. La Iglesia Antigua y Medieval, 11th edn. Palabra, Madrid
Paine T (1962) Die Rechte des Menschen. Akademie, Berlin
Pardo J (1991) Notas sobre la historia del control de constitucionalidad en Francia hasta la aparición del Consejo Constitucional. Revista de Estudios Políticos 72:243–258
Procter E-S (1980) Curia and Cortes in León and Castile 1072–1295. Cambridge University Press, Cambridge
Ramadan T (2009) Muhammad: life and teachings of the Prophet of Islam. Kairós, Madrid

Reimann M (1989) The historical school against codification: Savigny, Carter, and the defeat of the New York Civil Code. Am J Comp Law 37:95–119

Renteln A-D (1985) The unanswered challenge of relativism and the consequences for human rights. Hum Rights Q 7(4):514–540

Rhonheimer M (2005) The political ethos of constitutional democracy and the place of natural law in public reason: Rawls's 'political liberalism' revisited. Am J Jurisprudence 50:1–70

Rousseau J-J (2007) The social contract or principles of political law, 5th edn. Tecnos, Madrid

Rousseau J-J (1964) Letters écrites de la Montagne, Lettre VIII. In: Rousseau J-J (ed) Ouvres complètes de la Bibliothèque de La Pléiade. Paris

Ruigómez C (1988) Una política indigenista de los Habsburgo: el protector de indios en el Perú. Ediciones de Cultura Hispánica, Madrid

Sarasa E (1979) Las Cortes de Aragón en la Edad Media. Guara, Zaragoza

Sarasa E (1984) El Privilegio General de Aragón. La defensa de las libertades aragonesas en la Edad Moderna. Cortes de Aragón, Zaragoza

Seijas M-E (2016) Origin of parliamentarism: an historical review from its crisis: León (Spain) as cradle of parliamentarism. Revista Acadêmica da Faculdade de Direito do Recife 88(2). https://periodicos.ufpe.br/revistas/ACADEMICA/article/view/12100

Skinner Q (2008) Hobbes and Republican liberty. Cambridge University Press, Cambridge

Solari G (1911) L'idea individuale e l'idea sociale nel diritto privato. Fratelli Bocca, Milano-Torino-Roma

Suárez L (1976) Historia de España Antigua y Media. Rialp, Madrid

Stuurman S (2017) The invention of humanity. Equality and cultural difference in world history. Harvard University Press, Cambridge, MA

Talmon JL (1956) Los orígenes de la democracia totalitaria (translated by M. Cardenal). Aguilar, Madrid

Thon A (1878) Rechtsnorm und subjektives Recht. Scientia, Aalen

Tierney B (2008) Natural law and natural rights. In: Witte J, Alexander F-S (eds) Christianity and law: an introduction. Cambridge University Press, Cambridge, pp 89–103

Tierney B (1997) The idea of natural rights. In: Studies on natural rights natural law and church law. Grands Rapids, Michigan, Cambridge, pp 1150–1625

Tierno E (ed) (1984) Leyes políticas españolas fundamentales (1808-1978). Tecnos, Madrid

Tomás y Valiente F (1980) Prólogo. In: Los inicios del constitucionalismo español: de las Cortes de Cádiz a la crisis de la Monarquía absoluta (1808-1833). University of Valencia, Valencia

Varela J (1998) Basic texts of comparative constitutional history. CEPC, Madrid

Varela J (2007) Derechos y libertades en la historia constitucional, con especial referencia a España. In: Varela J (ed) Política y Constitución en España (1808-1978). CEPC, Madrid, pp 109–119

Varkemaa J (2005) Justification through being: Conrad Summenhart on natural rights. In: Krave J, Saarinen R (eds) Moral philosophy on the threshold of modernity. Springer, Dordrecht, pp 181–193

Varkemaa J (2006) Summenhart's theory of rights: a culmination of the late medieval discourse on individual rights. In: Mäkinen V, Korkman P (eds) Transformation in medieval and early-moderns rights discourse. Springer, Dordrecht, pp 119–147

Villey M (1969a) Droit subjectif II: Le droit de l'individu chez Hobbes. In: Villey M (ed) Seize essais de philosophie du droit dont un sur la crise universitaire. Dalloz, Paris

Villey M (1969b) La genèse du droit subjectif chez Guillaume d'Occam. In: Villey M (ed) Seize essais de philosophie du droit dont un sur la crise universitaire. Dalloz, Paris, pp 140–178

Vincent N (2014) Magna Carta: the foundation of freedom 1215-2015. Third Millennium, London

Vincent N (2015) Magna Carta: origins and legacy. Bodleian Library, Oxford

Waldron J (2005) Foreign law and the modern Ius Gentium. Harv Law Rev 119(1):129–147. http://www.trinitinture.com/documents/waldron1.pdf

Waldron J (2008) Ius Gentium: a defense of Gentili's equation of the law of nations and the law of nature. NYU School of Law, Public Law Research Paper 08-34. http://ssrn.com/abstract=1280897

Winscheid B (1862) Lehrbuch des Pandektenrechts. Buddeus, Düsseldorf

Wyduckel C (1979) Princeps legibus solutus. Eine Untersuchung zur Frühmoderne Rechts-und Staatslehre. Duncker & Humblot, Berlin

Chapter 2
Looking Backwards on the Notion of Human Dignity: From the Spanish 1978 Constitution to the Discovery of America

2.1 Human Dignity in the Current Spanish Constitution

The expression 'human dignity' was included in the text of the Spanish Constitution of 197.[1] The introduction of human dignity in Spanish constitutionalism was late. No constitutional text prior to the current Constitution (1978) included it (1812, 1837, 1845, 1845, 1869, 1876, 1931). But it was done when approving the first Constitution of the second half of the twentieth century. And it was included in Title I ("Of the Fundamental Rights and Duties"), in its Article 10.1, stating the following:

> *The dignity of the person*, the inviolable rights inherent to him, the free development of the personality, respect for the law and the rights of others are the foundation of political order and social peace.[2]

According to the wording of the text itself, respect for the rights of others is a requirement of human dignity itself, which is also the foundation and fundamental value of the legal system,[3] together with the 'higher values' set out in Article 1 ("freedom, justice, equality and political pluralism").

All fundamental rights, contained in Section 1 of Chapter II ("Fundamental rights and public liberties"), derive from and find their basis in human dignity, as expressly stated in the aforementioned Article 10.1 ("the inviolable rights inherent to it").

---

[1] Spanish Constitution, 6 December 1978; in this respect, see Fernández (1995).

[2] Art. 10.1 Spanish Constitution 1978 (EC 1978; available at http://www.congreso.es/consti/constitucion/indice/titulos/articulos.jsp?ini=10&fin=55&tipo=2, date of consultation: 9 January 2017); followed by Art. 10.2 which states that "The rules relating to the fundamental rights and freedoms recognised by the Constitution shall be interpreted in accordance with the Universal Declaration of Human Rights and the international treaties and agreements on the same matters ratified by Spain".

[3] In this regard, see Fernández (1995); on whether human dignity is, in addition, a fundamental right, see Gómez (2005).

A. Masferrer, *The Making of Dignity and Human Rights in the Western Tradition*, Studies in the History of Law and Justice 29,
https://doi.org/10.1007/978-3-031-46667-0_2

2.2 Human Dignity in Comparative Constitutional Law

Since the first half of the last century,[4] in particular since the *Charter of the United Nations* (26 June 1945), most European and Latin American Constitutions have chosen to include this notion in their Magna Carta.[5]

Spain introduced early the express reference to human dignity in its constitutional text, in comparison with other States. As will be seen, the Mexican Constitution—unlike the Spanish and German constitutions—did not make "human dignity the 'cornerstone' of the entire Mexican legal system."[6] Most of the countries that approved a constitutional text after the Second World War opted to make an express mention to the notion of human dignity, a situation that did not occur in México since it already had a Constitution since 1917, a reformed text of 1857. Let us look, then, at the Mexican case, before dealing with that of other European countries.

2.2.1 *México*

The history of human dignity in Mexican Constitutionalism—unlike that of its fundamental rights—is relatively recent and brief.[7] The first Mexican Constitution, that of 1824, did not include this concept. Neither did that of 1857, nor that of 1917. It was seventy years ago when, in the context of the second reform of Article 3 (education) of the 1917 constitutional text, published on December 30, 1946, it was established that education...

> It will contribute to a better human coexistence, both by the elements that it provides, in order to strengthen in the student, together with the appreciation for the *dignity of the person* and the integrity of the family, the conviction of the general interest of society, and by the care that it takes to support the ideals of fraternity and equality of rights of all men, avoiding the privileges of races, sects, groups, sexes or individuals.[8]

---

[4]The first legal text—of which we are aware—in which the notion of 'dignity' (human) appears, expressly, was the Irish Constitution of 1937, whose preamble read as follows: "In the Name of the Most Holy Trinity, from Whom is all authority and to Whom, as our final end, all actions both of men and States must be referred, We, the people of Éire, Humbly acknowledging all our obligations to our Divine Lord, Jesus Christ, Who sustained our fathers through centuries of trial, Gratefully remembering their heroic and unremitting struggle to regain the rightful independence of our Nation, And seeking to promote the common good, with due observance of Prudence, Justice and Charity, so that the *dignity and freedom of the individual may be assured*, true social order attained, the unity of our country restored, and concord established with other nations, do hereby adopt, enact, and give to ourselves this Constitution"; italics added.

[5]For a history of human dignity, see Rosen (2012); Moyn (2010, 2014).

[6]García González (2008), main text between footnotes 68 and 69.

[7]In this regard, see Díaz (2008), López Sánchez (2009), Gonzalo (2016).

[8]Article 3°, section I, fr. c), Constitution of México, 1917 (CM 1917), which reforms that of February 5, 1857; the reproduced text includes the reform published on December 30, 1946 (available at http://www.diputados.gob.mx/bibliot/publica/inveyana/polint/cua2/evolucion.htm); I

The present text is of particular importance because it confers on México the honour of being the first country in the Western tradition to have introduced the expression 'dignity' in its state (or national) constitutional text.

A few years later, although this same section was partially modified in the third amendment to the same Article 3 on education, published on 28 January 1992, it retained the expression 'dignity':

> It will contribute to a better human coexistence, both by the elements it brings to strengthen in the student, together with the appreciation for the *dignity of the person* and the integrity of the family, the conviction of the general interest of society, and by the care it takes to support the ideals of fraternity and equality of rights of all men, avoiding privileges of race, religion, groups, sexes or individuals.[9]

This section was reproduced in its entirety a year later, in the fifth amendment to the same Article 3, published on 5 March 1993.[10]

A few years later, a constitutional reform of August 14, 2001 reinstated this expression in Mexican constitutionalism:

> Any discrimination based on ethnic or national origin, gender, age, disability, social status, health conditions, religion, opinions, preferences, marital status or any other grounds that violate *human dignity* and are intended to nullify or impair the rights and freedoms of the individual shall be prohibited.[11]

As can be seen from the content of the text itself, the reform of the Constitution limited itself to considering it as a principle that cannot be contravened in the discriminatory sense. It thus connected the concepts of human dignity and discrimination,[12] but said nothing about its basis,[13] notion, scope and extent.

On June 10, 2011, a new text was included in Article 1, giving full expression to human dignity. To the text of the aforementioned reform of 2001 ("All discrimination based on ethnic or national origin is prohibited. . ."), three important preceding paragraphs were incorporated, which introduced the *pro persona* principle into

thank Dr. José Luis Soberanes for making me aware of the existence of this constitutional reform of 1946, which has sometimes been ignored by scholars of human dignity in Mexican constitutionalism; unless otherwise stated, the italics in the transcribed texts are mine.

[9] Article 3, paragraph I, section c), CM 1917; the reproduced text reflects the reform published on 22 January 1992 (see http://www.diputados.gob.mx/bibliot/publica/inveyana/polint/cua2/evolucion.htm)

[10] Article 3, clause I, fr. c), CM 1917; the reform published on March 5, 1993 included the text of 1992 (see http://www.diputados.gob.mx/bibliot/publica/inveyana/polint/cua2/evolucion.htm)

[11] Article 1, Paragraph Three, CM 1917; this reform was published in the *Official Journal of the Federation* on August 14, 2001 (I use the version of the Mexican constitutional text found at http://www.diputados.gob.mx/LeyesBiblio/htm/1.htm)

[12] In this regard, see Torre (2006), pp. 40–53, which discusses human dignity as a basis for non-discrimination.

[13] Saldaña (2006), pp. 57–80.

Mexican constitutional law,[14] within Chapter I, under the heading 'Human Rights and their Guarantees').[15]

Shortly afterwards, when Article 3 on education was amended, another express reference to the 'dignity of the person' was introduced by stipulating that education:

> It will contribute to a better human coexistence, in order to strengthen the appreciation and respect for cultural diversity, *the dignity of the person*, the integrity of the family, the conviction of the general interest of society, the ideals of fraternity and equality of rights for all, avoiding privileges of races, religion, groups, sexes or individuals.[16]

On June 5, 2013, when Art. 25 of the constitutional text was amended, it was established that it is up to the State to create a series of conditions that allow "the full exercise of freedom and *dignity of individuals*, groups and social classes."[17]

Later, thanks to another reform, Article 2A, section II, referring to the "dignity and integrity of women" was later amended on 22 May 2015. Specifically, the provision provides that the Mexican Fundamental Law "[...] recognises and guarantees the right of indigenous peoples and communities to self-determination and,

---

[14] On the introduction of the *pro persona* principle in Mexican constitutional law, see Saltalamacchia and Covarrubias (2012); Caballero (2012); Saucedo (2013); Galindo (2016); Hidalgo (2016), pp. 2–3.

[15] Article 1, Paragraph Three, CM 1917; Decree published in the *DOF* of México on 10 June 2011: "Any discrimination based on ethnic or national origin, gender, age, disabilities, social status, health conditions, religion, opinions, sexual preferences, marital status or any other that violates human dignity and is intended to nullify or impair the rights and freedoms of persons shall be prohibited"; the only difference in this paragraph with respect to the 2001 paragraph was the introduction of the expression 'sexual' (after the term 'preferences').

Article 1 should read as follows:

> In the United Mexican States all persons shall enjoy the human rights recognised in this Constitution and in the international treaties to which the Mexican State is a party, as well as the guarantees for their protection, the exercise of which may not be restricted or suspended, except in the cases and under the conditions established in this Constitution.
>
> The norms relating to human rights shall be interpreted in accordance with this Constitution and with the relevant international treaties, favouring at all times the broadest protection for individuals.
>
> All authorities, within the scope of their competencies, have the obligation to promote, respect, protect and guarantee human rights in accordance with the principles of universality, interdependence, indivisibility and progressiveness. Consequently, the State must prevent, investigate, punish and redress human rights violations, under the terms established by law.
>
> Slavery is prohibited in the United Mexican States. Slaves from abroad who enter the national territory shall, by this sole fact, attain their freedom and the protection of the laws.
>
> [followed by the final paragraph at the beginning of this note].

[16] Article 3.B.II.c CM 1917 (Subsection amended DOF 09-02-2012, 26-02-2013).

[17] Article 25 CM 1917: "The State is responsible for guiding national development to ensure that it is comprehensive and sustainable, that it strengthens the Sovereignty of the Nation and its democratic regime and that, through competitiveness, the promotion of economic growth and employment and a fairer distribution of income and wealth, it allows the full exercise of freedom and dignity of individuals, groups and social classes, whose security is protected by this Constitution. Competitiveness shall be understood as the set of conditions necessary to generate greater economic growth, promoting investment and the generation of employment".

consequently, to autonomy in order to: [. . .] II. Apply their own normative systems [. . .] subject to the general principles of this Constitution, respecting [. . .] the *dignity* and integrity of women [. . .]."[18]

2.2.2 *Switzerland*

In 1999, the Federal Constitution of the Swiss Confederation was promulgated.[19] Its Art. 7, under the title 'Human Dignity', provides that "*Human dignity* must be respected and protected."

This constitutional text includes, for the second time, the expression 'human dignity' by stipulating that "The Confederation shall draw up regulations on the use of the human genetic and embryonic heritage; in this way it shall ensure the protection of *human dignity*, the personality and the family" (Article 119. 2 CFCS 1999).

2.2.3 *Poland*

Two years earlier, the Constitution of the Republic of Poland of 2 April 1997 expressly provided—in Article 30—that "The inherent and inalienable dignity of the person shall be a source of freedom and rights of individuals and citizens. It shall be inviolable".

2.2.4 *Portugal*

Two years earlier, Portugal had promulgated its Constitution (2 April 1976), which included an express mention of dignity in article 1:

> Portugal is a sovereign Republic, based on the *dignity of the human person* and the will of the people, and committed to the construction of a free, just and united society.

Article 13.1, in enshrining the principle of equality, states that "All citizens have the same social *dignity* and are equal before the law", although this provision does not properly refer to natural dignity (hence the expression 'social dignity'); otherwise, such dignity could not derive from the status of a citizen of a country.

---

[18] Article 2.A II: "To apply their own normative systems in the regulation and resolution of their internal conflicts, subject to the general principles of this Constitution, respecting individual guarantees, human rights and, in a relevant manner, the dignity and integrity of women. The law will establish the cases and procedures for validation by the corresponding judges or courts".

[19] Federal Constitution of the Swiss Confederation of 18 April 1999.

In Title II ('On rights, freedoms and guarantees'), Chapter I ('On personal rights, freedoms and guarantees'), Article 26 of the Portuguese text contains two explicit references to natural human dignity:

> The law shall establish effective guarantees against the abuse, or use contrary to *human dignity*, of information relating to individuals and families (Article 26.2 PC 1976).

> The law shall guarantee the *personal dignity* and genetic identity of the human being, especially in the creation, development, use of technology and scientific experimentation (Article 26.3 CP 1976).

Article 67, in regulating "the family as a fundamental element of society", provides that it is incumbent on the State to "regulate assisted procreation in terms that safeguard the *dignity of the human person*" (Article 67.5 CC 1976).

Finally, Article 206 ("Court hearings") provides that hearings are public "except when the Court itself decides otherwise, by reasoned order, in order to safeguard the *dignity of persons* and public morals or to ensure the normal functioning of the Court".

2.2.5 *Greece*

A year earlier, the Greek Constitution (of 11 June 1975), in its Title 'Human Dignity', had provided that "Respect for and protection of *human dignity* constitutes the primary obligation of the State" (Article 2 GC 1975).[20]

The Greek Constitution contains two more provisions with express references to human dignity:

> Torture, all corporal cruelty and any attack on health or psychological pressure, as well as any other attack on *human dignity*, are prohibited and shall be punished in accordance with the provisions of the law (Article 7.2 GC 1975).

> Private economic initiative is not allowed to develop to the detriment of freedom and *human dignity*, nor to the detriment of the national economy (Article 106. 2 GC 1975).

2.2.6 *Germany*

The first national—or state—constitution that gave human dignity a prominent place as the cornerstone of the entire constitutional edifice was the Bonn Basic Law.[21] The

[20]This Art. 2.1 of the Greek Constitution was amended on 27 June 2008 to read as follows: "Respect for and protection of the value of the human person constitute the primary obligation of the State".

[21]The Parliamentary Council, in public session on May 23, 1949 in Bonn, ascertained that the Basic Law for the Federal Republic of Germany, agreed upon on May 8, 1949 by the Parliamentary Council, was approved during the week of May 16 to 22, 1949 by the representations of the people

enshrinement of the principle of the protection of human dignity in Article 1 of the German constitutional text was a clear and forceful response to the violations of human rights carried out within the framework of the National Socialist political regime:

Article 1
[Protection of *human dignity*, binding public authorities to fundamental rights].

(1) *Human dignity* is intangible. Respecting and protecting it is the duty of every public authority.
(2) The German people therefore recognises the inviolable and inalienable human rights as the foundation of every human community, of peace and justice in the world.
(3) The following fundamental rights bind the legislature, executive and judiciary as directly applicable law.

The Bonn text contains no further references to human dignity. However, its insertion in Article 1 as a device of constitutional openness expresses a fundamental feature of the new democratic order and the rule of law established by the constitutional text. Hence, Article 79.3, regulating the 'Reform of the Fundamental Law', prevents the possibility of reforming this constitutional principle, protecting the dignity of the person as the original principle and value of every human being.[22]

Human dignity entails, as the aforementioned provision states, the recognition of "inviolable and inalienable human rights as the foundation of every human community" (Article 1). Hence, Articles 2 to 19 enshrine the recognition of such rights, beginning with 'Freedom of action and of the person', that is, the right to life and liberty:

Article 2
[Freedom of action and of the person]

(1) Everyone has the right to the free development of his personality provided that he does not violate the rights of others or infringe upon the constitutional order or the moral law.
(2) Everyone has the right to life and physical integrity. The liberty of the person is inviolable. These rights may only be restricted by virtue of a law.

It is precisely human dignity that demands that the person be able to act autonomously, exercising his own freedom ("development of his personality"), although not in an unlimited manner ("provided that he does not violate the rights of others or violate the constitutional order or the moral law").

Here it is not a question of developing the notion of human dignity in the German constitutional text.[23] It is sufficient for our purpose to underline that the Bonn Basic Law was the first state constitution to include the expression and notion of human

---

of more than two thirds of the participating German *Länder. On the* basis of this verification, the Parliamentary Council, represented by its President, adopted and promulgated the Basic Law (*Grundgesetz*). It was the third constitutional text in German history, after those of 1871 and 1919.

[22] "No amendment of this Basic Law is permitted which affects the organisation of the Federation into *Länder*, or the principle of the participation of the *Länder* in legislation, or the principles set out in Articles 1 and 20" (Art. 79.3 LFB 1949).

[23] In this regard, see Starck (2005).

dignity, and that it constituted an important precedent for other constitutional texts in Europe and Latin America, which would follow the example of the German text, although in a different way. It should be noted that the Bonn Basic Law was not, however, the first legal text to include human dignity. In other words, the legal notion of human dignity was not born in Bonn, but in San Francisco two years earlier, not in the framework of (national) constitutional law, but in the sphere of international public law.

Nevertheless, it is worth remembering—as we have seen—that it was México, and not Germany, that was the first country to make an express reference to [human] 'dignity' in its constitutional text.[24]

2.3 The Origin of the Legal Notion of Human Dignity in the Aftermath of World War II

The expression 'human dignity' was not taken up—as will be seen—in the inception of modern constitutionalism. It can be affirmed, then, that the history of this expression in this context is quite brief, but at the same time intense and successful, both in constitutional law—national constitutions—and in public international law—international declarations and instruments. Intense, because of its (omni)-presence, as we have seen, after the Second World War and, in particular, from 26 June 1945 onwards. Successful, because it has become the foundation of all public law. The Bobbio's expression of the 'age of rights' could well be applied to human dignity, naming the stage that began in the second half of the twentieth century as the 'age of human dignity'.

In fact, the history of 'human rights' and the history of 'human dignity' present interesting parallels: (i) both expressions are recent, even though their meaning and sense enjoy a long historical evolution; (ii) both expressions triumph, but at a time when it is difficult—not to say impossible—to agree on the basis,[25] meaning and scope of their content[26]; (iii) both expressions are claimed and defended in theory -or

[24]See footnote n. 229 in Part I as well as the corresponding main text.

[25]In this regard, it is worth recalling the event that took place at one of the preparatory meetings for the drafting of the text of the Universal Declaration of Human Rights, narrated by Maritain (1949), p. 15: "... someone was astonished to see that people of such different and opposing ideologies had agreed on the approved table of rights. But, in reality, what happened was that they all agreed, as long as they were not asked why and how they had reached this agreement, since the dispute began with the why".

[26]On the various conceptions of human dignity in the Western tradition, from its origins to the Protestant Reformation, see the study by Baker (1947); logically, the notion of dignity is closely related to the question of what man is; in this regard, see Buber (1956); on the dialogical condition of man, see Buber (1979): "Through the Thou a person becomes I"; "Another human being is a neighbor not only on the basis of a generic feeling of humanity, but primarily on the basis of his being 'another I'" (Wojtyla, K., "Participation or alienation?", *El hombre y su destino*, Madrid:

in the abstract-, but in practice—or in concrete circumstances—their respect or protection is often unequal and insufficient; and (iv) both expressions seem to have a clear meaning—as presuppositions that do not require any demonstration -, but this is betrayed or questioned by certain currents of the philosophy of Law or political philosophy. What happened to the notion of 'fundamental rights' in the eighteenth and nineteenth centuries has also affected 'human dignity' and 'human rights' in the twentieth and twenty-first centuries.

What was the reason for the 'positivisation' or 'constitutionalisation' of 'human dignity'? Why was this expression used in the legal texts of international and constitutional law after the Second World War? The answer is well known: to show rejection of the horrific consequences of that war, which claimed the lives of 50 million civilians and 20 million combatants. Human history had never known an episode that had caused so much human loss, so much human suffering and so much destruction and material damage.

Totalitarian political regimes, aided by certain philosophical tides of thought, political and legal thought, caused great damage to the whole of humanity. The first enemy to be defeated was logically the National Socialist political regime, which was primarily responsible for the war and its dramatic consequences. This was the only way to defend the dignity that had been degraded, denigrated and trampled underfoot during the war. This is how a well-known German economist expressed himself in 1944:

> There is but one means to save our civilisation and to preserve the dignity of man. It is to annihilate Nazism radically and pitifully. Only after the total destruction of Nazism can the world resume its efforts to improve social organisation and to build a better society. The alternatives are humanity or bestiality, peaceful human cooperation or totalitarian despotism. All plans for a third solution are illusory. [27]

However, it was also necessary to reduce those philosophical, political and legal doctrines which, in one way or another, had defended or justified an arbitrary and despotic use of political power. How was it possible to defend human dignity and human rights within the framework of currents of thought dominated by utilitarianism, instrumentalism, consequentialism, legal positivism, the philosophical-political theses of Karl Schmidt or Marxism-Leninism? Was it possible to avoid a repetition of the tragedy of the War by simply eliminating National Socialism as a political regime, but without eradicating the doctrines which served this political cause, providing the necessary substratum and justification for an unlimited exercise of political power?

With the creation of the *United Nations Organization*—and its *Charter of San Francisco*—in 1945, and the drafting of the *Universal Declaration of Human Rights* in 1948, it became clear that the guarantee and protection of fundamental rights—the texts began to be called 'human rights'—could not depend on national States,

Palabra, 1998); Wojtyla (1998): "Another human being is a neighbor not only on the basis of a generic feeling of humanity, but primarily on the basis of his being 'another I'".

[27] Mises (1944), p. 267, the translation is mine.

because such rights are common to all men. And they are common to all because every human being possesses the same 'natural dignity'. The expressions 'inherent' or 'intrinsic' refer precisely to this 'natural dignity', common to every human being (as distinct from 'moral dignity', which depends on the conduct of each person). This explains why international declarations and texts often use the expressions 'inherent' or 'intrinsic' when referring to human dignity, as did the first modern constitutional texts—in the eighteenth and nineteenth centuries—when referring to 'natural rights' or 'fundamental rights'.

The consequences of the denial and violation of human dignity in the Second World War were terrible. The resurgence of the concept of human dignity after 1945 was a reminder of what humanity had forgotten and pointed the way forward for the construction of a just and peaceful world or global society. Indeed, after the Second World War, human rights became the *lingua franca of* international relations. Both international declarations—or legal instruments—and national constitutions established human rights as the basis of legal systems.[28] In doing so, the legal texts explicitly cited, for the first time, human dignity as the origin and foundation of human rights.

The first text of a legal nature that took up the notion of human dignity was the *Charter of the United Nations*, signed on 26 June 1945 in San Francisco (hence also called the '*San Francisco Charter*'), at the end of the United Nations Conference on International Organization, coming into force on 24 October of the same year. This is how its Preamble reads:

> WE THE PEOPLES OF THE UNITED NATIONS DETERMINED
> - to save succeeding generations from the scourge of war, which twice in our lifetime has brought untold suffering on mankind, and
> - *to reaffirm faith in fundamental human rights, in the dignity and worth of the human person*, in the equal rights of men and women and of nations large and small, and
> - to establish conditions under which justice and respect for the obligations arising from treaties and other sources of international law can be maintained, and
> - to promote social progress and better standards of life in larger freedom...".

The text recognises, in addition to fundamental human rights, "the dignity and worth of the human person". The Charter no longer contains any reference to human dignity.

This was done three years later, and in a particularly emphatic and eloquent way, in the most emblematic text of the recently created UN, that is, its *Universal Declaration of Human Rights* (*UDHR*).[29] From the outset, the Preamble includes

[28] In this regard, see, for example, the study by Soberanes (2009); see also Saldaña (2006), pp. 61–64.

[29] The *Universal Declaration of Human Rights* is a declaratory document that was adopted by the *General Assembly of the United Nations* in its Resolution 217 A (III), on December 10, 1948 in Paris; in its 30 articles it gathers the human rights considered basic, from the San Francisco Charter (June 26, 1945). As is well known, the original title of the text in English was "Universal Declaration of Human Rights"; Later, the General Assembly, in its resolution 548 (VI) of 5 February 1952, decided to modify all the working documents in Spanish, to use the expression "human

the expression on two occasions (the second being a partial—not complete—literal reproduction of the text of the *San Francisco Charter*):

> Whereas *recognition of the inherent dignity* and of the equal and inalienable rights of all members of the human family (...) is the foundation of freedom, justice and peace in the world (...).
>
> Whereas the peoples of the United Nations have in the Charter reaffirmed their faith in fundamental human rights, in *the dignity and worth of the human person* and in the equal rights of men and women, and determined to promote social progress and better standards of life in larger freedom (...).

After the Preamble, three other articles contain an express reference to 'human dignity'. The most relevant is undoubtedly the first:

> *All human beings are born free and equal in dignity and rights.* They are endowed with reason and conscience and should act towards one another in a spirit of brotherhood (Article 1 UDHR).

The article includes a notion of natural human dignity ("All human beings are born free and equal in dignity"), since dignity derives from the mere fact of being born as a human being, a condition characterised by being endowed with "reason and conscience."[30] The precept has a Kantian influence, but it goes further, as will be seen below. Moreover, since *noblesse oblige*,[31] all human beings, precisely because of their dignity as beings endowed with reason and conscience, "must behave fraternally towards one another".

The other two express references to dignity refer to the right of every person to "the realisation of the economic, social and cultural rights indispensable for his dignity and the free development of his personality" (Article 22),[32] as well as "to just

---

rights" instead of "rights of man", taking into account that the content and purpose of the Declaration "have a broad meaning that does not fit within the Spanish title of 'rights of man', bearing in mind also that the body of the instrument alludes to the expression 'human rights' and that distinguished Spanish-American representatives "have expressed their preference for the terminology used in the Charter"; Loewenstein (1945): "In recognizing human rights and fundamental freedoms as a legitimate objective of international law and world order, the San Francisco Charter took a momentous step forward. But the path is beset with enormous difficulties which no sober appraiser will easily underestimate" (p. 283); on the San Francisco Charter, see Humphrey (1984), Sohn (1995), Burgers (1997), Morsink (1999) and Sarah (2007–2008), among others.

[30] See, for example, the study by Bloch (1987); see also the study by López Guerra (2003).

[31] A reality that was forgotten in the twentieth century, as Marías (1964), p. 99, makes clear: "What defines the mass man is not to make demands on himself. His morality is the inverse of the motto *noblesse oblige*. For this reason, he affirms himself as he is, he believes that he has the right to everything, that everything is due to him, that he does not have to strive for anything: to be just, to be intelligent, to be right. He counts on the things he enjoys as if they existed automatically and without further ado, as if they were unproblematic and due to invention, talent, work and sacrifice. He does not listen, he does not admit that others can be right—strictly speaking, he does not even admit that there can properly be others irreducible to him -, and that is why he tries to violently impose his points of view or his desires; more precisely, he pretends that they are spontaneously accepted, without even making an effort to impose them"; see also Arriola (2003), p. 31.

[32] Article 22 UDHR: "Everyone, as a member of society, has the right to social security and is entitled to realisation, through national effort and international cooperation and in accordance with

and favourable remuneration ensuring for himself and his family an existence worthy of human dignity" (Article 23)[33]

The UDHR was a major step forward in the recognition of human dignity and fundamental rights.[34] It is also the first international instrument with a comprehensive catalogue of fundamental rights and freedoms of universal scope adopted by the international community at the global level.[35]

It should not be forgotten that, a few months before the formal approval of the Universal Declaration of Human Rights, the recently created Organization of American States had approved the American Declaration of the Rights and Duties of Man (ADRDM), which was, in fact, the first international catalogue with universal pretensions, albeit promoted by a regional organisation. In fact, the ADRDM was adopted at the Ninth International Conference of American States in Bogotá, Colombia, on May 2, 1948.[36]

The text of this American Declaration contains two express references to 'human dignity'. The first appears in the Preamble and is very similar—almost verbatim—to the formulation that was later adopted in the aforementioned UDHR:

> All men are born free and equal in dignity and rights *and being endowed by nature with reason and conscience, they should conduct themselves as brothers to one to another.*
>
> *The fulfilment of duty by each individual is a prerequisite to the rights of all. Rights and duties are interrelated in every social and political activity of man. If rights exalt individual liberty,* duties express the dignity of that liberty.
>
> Duties of a juridical nature presuppose others, of a moral nature which support them in principle and constitute their basis.

The differences between the two texts are clear. Thus, for example, the UDHR chose not to include the express reference to 'nature', as the American Declaration had done ("endowed as they are by nature with reason and conscience"). Moreover, the idea of interrelatedness between rights and duties is not so explicit in the UDHR,[37] let alone the affirmation that the moral order constitutes the substratum or foundation

the organisation and resources of each State, of the economic, social and cultural rights *indispensable for his dignity* and the free development of his personality.

[33] Article 23 UDHR:

(1) Everyone has the right to work, to free choice of employment, to just and favourable conditions of work and to protection against unemployment.
(2) Everyone, without any discrimination, has the right to equal pay for equal work.
(3) Everyone who works has the right to just and favourable remuneration ensuring for himself and his family an existence worthy of *human dignity*, and supplemented, if necessary, by other means of social protection.
(4) Everyone has the right to form and to join trade unions for the protection of his interests.

[34] In this regard, see, for example, the study by Carrillo (1999), or the work of Bobbio (1996).

[35] On the origins, drafting process and content of the UDHR, see the studies Morsink (1999, 2004, 2009).

[36] In this regard, see the study by Gros (1995).

[37] In this regard, see the study by d'Agostino (2000); this correlativity was clearly stated in the title of the *American Declaration of the Rights and Duties of Man* (2 May 1948).

of the duties of the legal order. It is evident that the philosophical doctrines of Hume—for whom being ethical or moral norms cannot be inferred—and Kant—for whom Law and morality must be kept separate because the former belongs to the sphere of the contingent and the latter belongs to that of the necessary, legal norms are followed 'coercively' and moral norms by mere 'respect'—, exerted their influence on the UDHR.[38]

The second—and last—reference to human dignity in the ADRDM appears in Article 23, when it enshrines the 'Right to property' in the following terms:

> Everyone has a right to own such private property as meets the essential needs of decent living and helps to maintain the dignity of the individual and of the home.

The impact of these first two Declarations of 1948—ADRDM and *UDHR*—was remarkable. Since then, many international documents, national constitutions and philosophical doctrines began to consider human dignity as the "source of human rights" [39] and the foundation of public law.[40] It is eloquent to note how international human rights instruments have emphasised the close relationship between human rights and human dignity and, more particularly, the extent to which they have explicitly recognised that "human rights derive from the inherent dignity of the human person." [41]

It is appropriate to dwell now precisely on the explicit reference to the 'inherent' character of human dignity. While most international human rights instruments refer to 'human dignity', some of them have chosen to add the expression 'inherent'. The additional expression of this adjective ('inherent') is particularly significant. As is well known, 'inherent' can be defined as "a basic or essential characteristic that gives something its character," [42] "a natural or basic part of something," [43] "that which is permanent, essential, or a characteristic attribute of something." [44] In other words, "a quality that is inherent in something is a natural part and cannot be separated from that something." [45] In short, qualifying human dignity as 'inherent' means that persons deserve to be respected for who they are (natural dignity), not for their behaviour or capacities (moral dignity). Natural dignity is common to all individuals

---

[38] In this regard, see, for example, the study by Carpintero (2000), pp. 76–80.

[39] Mieth (2014), p. 11; on this issue, see also Griffin (2008); Nussbaum (2006).

[40] In this regard, read the Preface to Volume 23 of Studies in International Law, Capps (2009): "A State, in turn, must be understood as the recipient of a legitimacy that comes ultimately from the pursuit of the human dignity of the community it governs, as well as the dignity of those human beings and States are affected by its actions in international relations".

[41] International Covenants on Civil and Political, and on Economic, Social and Cultural Rights (1966), Preambles; on this, see Barak (2015), chapter 3; see also Alzina (2011), pp. 1 ff; Andorno (2014), pp. 49–50.

[42] See http://www.macmillandictionary.com/dictionary/british/inherent; last accessed 30 July 2020.

[43] See http://dictionary.cambridge.org/dictionary/british/inherent; last accessed 30 July 2020).

[44] See http://www.oxforddictionaries.com/es/definicion/ingles/inherent; last accessed 30 July 2020).

[45] See http://www.ldoceonline.com/dictionary/inherent; last accessed 30 July 2020).

and this is the kind of human dignity that is considered to be the source of human rights. [46]

The first reference to the 'inherent' character of human dignity in public international law is found after the Second World War, in the Preamble of the *Universal Declaration of Human Rights* (1948):

> Whereas recognition of the inherent dignity and of the equal and inalienable rights of all members of the human family is the foundation of freedom, justice and peace in the world [...].

A few years later, in 1966, the Preamble to the *International Covenant on Civil and Political Rights* (*ICCPR*) and the *International Covenant on Economic, Social and Cultural Rights* (*ICESCR*) recognises the inherent nature of human dignity:

> Recognition of the inherent dignity and of the equal and inalienable rights of all members of the human family is the foundation of freedom, justice and peace in the world.

Moreover, Article 10 of the *ICCPR* refers to the "inherent dignity of the human person," [47] an expression identical to that used in 1984 by the *Convention against Torture and Other Cruel, Inhuman or Degrading Treatment or Punishment*, which states that "human rights derive from the *inherent dignity of the* human person." [48]

Likewise, the *International Convention on the Protection of the Rights of All Migrant Workers and Members of Their Families* (1990) proclaimed that "migrant workers and members of their families who are deprived of their liberty shall be treated with humanity and with respect for the inherent dignity of the human person and their cultural identity" (Article 17.1).

The *World Conference on Human Rights* held in Vienna (14–25 June 1993) drafted the *Vienna Declaration and Programme of Action* (12 July 2003), with the following Preamble:

> All human rights derive from the inherent dignity and worth inherent in the human person.

The preamble to the *Convention on the Rights of Persons with Disabilities* (2007) states that any discrimination against any person on the basis of disability would violate "*the inherent dignity and worth of the human person*." Furthermore, Article 3 establishes "*respect for inherent dignity*" as one of the basic principles of the *Convention*.

UNESCO has adopted several declarations concerning human rights, including in the field of bioethics, in which human dignity is considered as the basic principle. In this regard, Article 1 of the *Universal Declaration on the Human Genome and Human Rights* states that "[t]he human genome underlies the fundamental unity of

---

[46] See note n. 2.

[47] Art. 10 of the ICCP: "*All persons deprived of their liberty shall be treated with humanity and with respect for the inherent dignity of the human person.*"

[48] Two years later, in 1986, the General Assembly adopted another text as a guideline for new human rights conventions. The text affirms that human rights "derive from the inherent dignity and worth of the human person."

all members of the human family as well as the recognition of *their inherent dignity* and diversity."

There are also regional texts that mention the inherent nature of human dignity. In Europe, in the context of the reforms to the *European Convention for the Protection of Human Rights and Fundamental Freedoms* (1950), which abolished the death penalty (1983 and 2002), [49] the Preamble to the reforms states that the abolition of the death penalty is essential "for the full recognition of the *inherent dignity* of all human beings." [50] In 2009, the Council of the European Union issued *Guidelines on Human Rights and International Humanitarian Law*, stating that the "[p]romotion and protection of the rights of the child is a priority of EU human rights policy. The European Union (EU) considers it critically important to address the issue of children and armed conflict, not only because children are suffering today and will shape the future, *but because they have inherent and inalienable rights*, as set out in the Convention on the Rights of the Child, its Optional Protocols and other international and regional human rights instruments." [51]

In the Americas, Article 2 of the *American Convention on Human Rights* (adopted in 1969 by the *Organization of American States*—the *OAS*—and in force since 1978), declares that "[e]very person deprived of liberty shall be treated with the respect due to the *inherent dignity of the human person*." The Preamble of the *International Convention on the Prevention, Punishment and Eradication of Violence against Women* (1994) states that every woman has the "right to be respected in the *inherent dignity of her person* and to have her family protected."

In Africa, the *African Charter on Human and Peoples' Rights* (1986; drafted by the *Organisation of African Unity—OAU*), refers to the inherent nature of human dignity in two articles. Article 5 stipulates that "every individual shall have the right to respect for the *inherent dignity of a human being* and to the recognition of his legal personality". Article 3 of one of the protocols that added rights to the charter, more specifically one on women's rights in Africa, states that "[e]very woman has the right to the *inherent dignity of the human person* and to the recognition and protection of her human and legal rights." Only the *Arab League* and the *Organisation of Islamic Cooperation* have chosen not to use the adjective 'inherent' when referring to human dignity.

---

[49] Protocol No. 6 concerning the abolition of the death penalty: 28-04-1983; entry into force: 01-03-1985; Protocol No. 6 concerning the abolition of the death penalty in all circumstances: 03-05-2002; entry into force: 01-07-2003); on the genesis of the European Convention, see Simpson (2001).

[50] *Protocol No. 13 to the Convention for the Protection of Human Rights and Fundamental Freedoms concerning the abolition of the death penalty in all circumstances* (Vilnius, 3 May 2002), Preamble.

[51] Some rights are inherent to individuals because they derive simply and plainly from their human condition, that is, because they possess a natural human dignity.

2.4 The Historical Precedents of the Notion of 'Human Dignity' (from the Nineteenth to the Fifteenth Century)

2.4.1 The Absence of the Expression 'Human Dignity' in Early Modern Constitutional Texts

What was the precedent for the legal notion of 'human dignity' in the various Declarations—especially the Bills of Rights—and other national constitutional texts after the Second World War?

The first declarations of modern constitutionalism contained no reference to human dignity. Indeed, the expression 'dignity' or 'human dignity' is neither found in the *Declaration of Virginia* (1776), nor in the American *Declaration of Independence* (1776), nor in the *Declaration of the Rights of Man and of the Citizen* (1789). Nor is it to be found in the various modern constitutions which, after the first ones were approved—in particular, the French and the American—at the end of the eighteenth century, were promulgated throughout the nineteenth century, both in the continental tradition (Europe and Latin America) and in the Anglo-Saxon tradition (United Kingdom, United States, Canada, Australia, New Zealand, etc.).

For the texts of modern constitutionalism, rights—and not human dignity—were the fundamental element for establishing limits to political power. Hence the content of Article 16 of the *Declaration of the Rights of Man and of the Citizen* (1789):

> Any society in which no provision is made for guaranteeing rights or for the separation of powers, has no Constitution.

Today, this provision would be inconceivable without the insertion of the notion of human dignity ('A society in which human dignity is not recognised, the guarantee of rights is not assured...'). But the expression—not the idea of—'human dignity' was unnecessary for those who drafted the first modern declarations and constitutional texts. It was simply taken for granted. If rights derived from the dignity of the human being, their recognition and protection entailed respect for human dignity. If the recognition of rights was the most powerful and genuine way of limiting the power of the State, there was no need to appeal to the dignity of every human being.

Indeed, the liberal constitutions that emerged in the West after the American Declaration of Independence and the French Revolution set clear limits to political power after the abuses of the absolutist political regimes of the *Ancien Régime*.[52] The transition from monarchical absolutism to a constitutional liberal system meant, precisely, the recognition of the existence of fundamental—or human—rights that corresponded to every individual (natural dignity) and whose protection, as they constituted the raison d'être of political power, legitimised the existence of the State. This was expressed in Article I of the *Virginia Declaration of Rights* (1776):

[52] In this line, see Masferrer and Obarrio (2012), pp. 15 ff.; Masferrer and Obarrio (2014), pp. 965 ff.; as well as the critique of Sieyès (1988).

> That all men are by nature equally free and independent and have certain inherent rights, of which, when they enter into a state of society, they cannot, by any compact, deprive or divest their posterity; namely, the enjoyment of life and liberty, with the means of acquiring and possessing property, and pursuing and obtaining happiness and safety.

As can be seen, the text leaves no room for doubt that such rights correspond to every human being and are, therefore, 'inherent' in proceeding from (human) nature itself. Such rights had, consequently, a pre-political origin and character; hence, they could not "henceforth be deprived or dispossessed by any covenant." Moreover, the protection of such rights constituted precisely the raison d'être of political power itself.

This was reflected in the text of the American *Declaration of Independence* (1776). After insisting on the inalienable character of rights, he added "that to secure these rights, Governments are instituted among Men, deriving their just powers from the consent of the governed."[53] Therefore, it is the function of governments, whose power derives from the consent of the governed (sovereignty of the people or nation), to ensure or guarantee such rights.

In the French context, the *Declaration of the Rights of Man and of the Citizen* (1789) stated in its very Preamble its purpose to "set forth, in a solemn Declaration, the natural, unalienable and sacred rights of man, to the end that this Declaration, constantly present to all members of the body politic, may remind them unceasingly of their rights and their duties." Finally, after pointing out that "men are born and remain free and equal in rights" (Article 1), it used a formula similar to the American *Declarations* of 1776:

> The aim of every political association is the preservation of the natural and imprescriptible rights of man. These rights are liberty, property, security and resistance to oppression (Article 2).

The content of this provision is clear and leaves no room for interpretation. Not in vain has it been pointed out that "respect for natural rights is objectively imposed on the social pact, thus marking its limits and giving it meaning", given that "the affirmation, defence and protection of such rights (...) as the authentic *prius* and foundation of society, will constitute the criterion of legitimacy of all human coexistence, the limit and, at the same time, the meaning of the social pact."[54] Precisely because such rights were declared natural and imprescriptible, the French Constitution of 1791, by guaranteeing several of them in its Title I, provided that "the legislature may not make laws that diminish and hinder the exercise of the natural and civil rights set forth in the present title and guaranteed by the Constitution."

In short, the drafters of the first modern constitutional texts understood that, while the recognition of national sovereignty was a more than sufficient title for the organisation of the State with its various powers, on the understanding that these

---

[53] Paragraph II of the Preamble to the *Declaration of Independence of the United States* (July 4, 1776).

[54] Díaz (1977), p. 238.

had been 'created' or constituted by the people or the sovereign nation, the same could not be said with respect to fundamental rights. These did not emanate from sovereignty but from nature, so that they could only be recognised or declared, making it clear that such rights were natural, that is, belonging to nature or inherent to the human being and, in any case, not susceptible to deprivation or dispossession by any covenant.

The expressions 'natural rights' or 'inherent rights', included in the first modern constitutional texts, make clear the origin and anchorage of rights in human nature and, consequently, their pre-political character or, better said, unavailable to political power.[55] For the drafters of these first constitutional texts—as well as for the jurists, philosophers or politicians of the time—, to introduce an express reference to 'human dignity' would have been vain, superfluous or redundant. Hence, although the expression was not included, the notion was present—in an implicit way—as a non-visible basis of the foundation, as it was, precisely, buried, giving consistency to the whole constitutional building. This foundation—the dignity of every human being -, as well as the recognition and protection of his 'natural' or 'inherent' rights, were at the basis of modern constitutionalism,[56] conferring, at the same time, the necessary legitimacy to political power.

In contrast to German National Socialism, which understood that not every human being enjoys the same dignity or is deserving of the same rights, the first modern constitutional texts started from the premise that any legal system must guarantee respect for the fundamental rights of individuals, not because they are intelligent, qualified or well endowed, but because of their mere human condition or, if one prefers, their natural dignity. From this perspective, they understood that if laws did not recognise and respect the natural dignity of all individuals on an equal footing, serious harm would be done to people, especially the most vulnerable. Laws and states would lose all legitimacy and societies would collapse.

2.4.2 The Resurgence and Influence of the Kantian Doctrine of Human Dignity

We have seen how the notion of human dignity was expressly taken up in international declarations and instruments, how it found its way into national

[55] As aforementioned, no one, no human reality, can be 'pre-political. The human being has many natural faculties, but they are not therefore pre-political. Although the expression 'pre-political' is intended to designate a reality "prior to the State" and unavailable to the power of the State, this expression does not seem to be the most adequate. It is more correct to affirm that these rights are 'inherent', 'natural' (with certain reservations for the same reason), intrinsic or, even better, that they derive from the dignity of man. In reality, the most atomic human datum is dignity sifted by objective human needs.

[56] In this regard, see Masferrer (2011b), pp. 191 ff.; on the notion of constitutionalism and its inescapable historical dimension, see the studies by Clavero (1986); Clavero (1989).

constitutions—the Bonn Basic Law (1949) being the first—and how it came to be used in the aftermath of the Second World War. It is now worth asking where this notion of human dignity came from. In other words, what are the historical and philosophical roots of this notion?

It is often claimed that the philosophical foundations of the notion of human dignity taken up by legal texts since the mid-twentieth century are to be found in Immanuel Kant. Is this thesis true? Was Kant the thinker who most influenced the notion of 'constitutionalised' human dignity after 1945? More specifically, was Kant the first to defend the 'natural dignity' of every human being or to relate dignity and rights to human nature?

My thesis in this regard could be summarised as follows: (i) the notion of 'human dignity' in legal texts is largely indebted to Kantian doctrine; (ii) Kant was not, however, the pioneering thinker to link human dignity and rights to human nature, but he took up the legacy of the previous tradition. In fact, in the seventeenth and eighteenth centuries, authors before Kant used the expression 'dignity of human nature'; and (iii) the interpretation that some authors give to the Kantian doctrine of human dignity, presenting the autonomy of the will as unlimited and morality as a mere exercise of freedom, does not do justice to the thought of this German philosopher.

Kant held, in effect, that autonomy was the basis of human dignity. For the German philosopher, the Kantian notion of moral autonomy consisted in obeying the law for its own sake, so that the subject, in obeying it, obeys objective reason, which is also his reason, and thus remains free, not subject to the will of another person or group. However, it is important not to forget his insistence on the need for "a good will". Not all choices are equally good, nor do they reflect "a good will". What did Kant mean by "good will"?

> That, which we now know, *is a good will whose maxim, if it were to become universal, would not be repugnant to itself.* This principle is its supreme law: 'Act in accordance with this maxim whose universality, as a right, you can at the same time will.' This is the only condition on which the will can never contradict itself; and this imperative is categorical. And since such a will, if considered as the realisation of its maxims, is analogous to the uniform and systematic order of events in the physical system which we call nature, the categorical imperative may be expressed thus: 'Act in conformity with those maxims which may be regarded as universal laws of nature.' These are the formulas which indicate what an absolute good will is. [57]

Kant recognised that, along with "the physical system we call nature," there are "universal laws of nature" (non-physical). In his view, a good will should always behave according to such universal laws of nature: "Act in accordance with those maxims which can be regarded as universal laws of nature." The well-known Kantian principle that no man should ever be treated as a means (but as an end) is rooted in the dignity of humanity or human nature:

[57] Kant (1796), Ch. II ('On the a priori spring of the will'), p. 52; italics are mine.

> …every intelligent being, being by nature an end in itself, should subordinate to this end the maxims of all its causal and arbitrary ends. [58]

The Kantian requirement of subordinating to this end—founded on human nature—the maxim of the other "causal and arbitrary ends" came to set limits to the libertarian or utilitarian conception of free will or autonomous will.[59] Not all alternatives are good. The goodness of moral acts does not come simply from free will.[60] There are some norms that are grounded in human nature, and autonomy should move within these "universal laws of nature." Thus, Kant linked autonomy, human dignity, and human nature. In doing so, he took up the legacy of seventeenth-century political philosophy and law, which argued for the need for a social order based on a natural order, a new secularised society, based on a rational and philosophical foundation (and not theological or based on the authority of the biblical text).

After World War II, Kantian doctrine experienced a resurgence and led to what George P. Fletcher called the "glorification of autonomy." [61] Autonomy was used to explain that people should never be treated as a means but as an end in themselves. Many tragedies of the Second World War were caused by treating thousands of human beings as mere means and not as ends. In the face of this sad episode in the History of Humanity, Kantian legal thought was used to defend itself against the threat of utilitarianism which, together with instrumentalism and consequentialism, constituted the philosophical basis of a totally different conception of human dignity: a human dignity related to autonomy, but completely distant and detached from human nature. Utilitarianism and natural law (and natural rights) are incompatible. In this line, it is worth remembering that while Kant showed a remarkable respect for nature, the laws of nature and natural law, Jeremy Bentham completely rejected these notions:

> What are these natural laws, which no one has made, and which everyone supposes in his fancy? [62]

While Kant related 'human nature' to a moral order, based on the (non-physical) laws of nature, Bentham's utilitarianism conceived 'human nature' from a radically

---

[58] Kant (1796), Ch. II ('On the a priori spring of the will'), pp. 51–52; italics are mine.

[59] In this regard, see Saldaña (2006), pp. 61–64; on the problematic aspects of the Kantian foundation of human dignity, see Gallego (2005), in particular, pp. 253–256; Torre (2006), pp. 46–48; for an example of a Kantian basis for human dignity, see Gallego (2005). 46–48; for an example of how the quasi-limited autonomous will can become the characteristic feature of human dignity, affirming—taking the Kantian thesis to an extreme that Kant himself would hardly share—that dignity should be recognised only to those beings who are capable of determining themselves, of self-legislation or of proposing to themselves norms of ethical conduct, see Singer (1993).

[60] In this regard, see the study by Starck (2002), p. 181: "Human dignity does not mean unlimited self-determination, but self-determination which is exercised on the basis that everyone-not simply the person claiming the right to self-determination-is of value in his or her own right".

[61] Expression taken from Fletcher (1984), p. 171.

[62] Bentham (1843), General view of a complete code of laws, Ch. I.

different perspective. Unlike Kant, Bentham harshly criticised natural law scholars—such as Grotius and Pufendorf—for pretending to be the legislators of the human race (a curious criticism indeed, since Bentham himself spent his whole life in precisely this attempt).[63]

The revival of the Kantian conception of human dignity after the Second World War sought to reject the utilitarian approach to human rights, according to which the moral rightness of an act is measured only by its consequences, or, in other words, that an act is right if it will generate a benefit in the form of pleasure or to the well-being of those affected. In more economic terms, one might say that an act is right if its benefits outweigh its costs. After the Second World War it was concluded that human rights and human dignity could not be founded on mere utilitarian principles,[64] although some twentieth century authors are still determined to keep these philosophical tides of thought alive.[65] The tragedy of two World Wars in barely half a century proved Bentham's mistake in calling natural rights 'nonsense upon stilts'.[66]

Referring to natural rights as 'nonsense', or to 'fundamental rights' as mere creations of the State that it imposes with no other legitimacy than the binding force of the law (understood as a simple mandate of the State), seems to be the best 'legitimation' to violate rights when the State considers them as inconvenient for whatever reasons, as recent experience shows.[67]

On the contrary, when fundamental rights are recognised and protected by States and international instruments because their source is pre-political, as are human beings and their dignity, the threat of the totalitarian State diminishes considerably. A solid foundation of human rights does not resolve the danger of their possible violation, but it helps to protect them when they are sought to be violated in the name

[63] Bentham (1843), 'Pannomial Fragments', Ch. III: 'Expositions', p. 221: 'Behold the professors of natural law, of which they have dreamed—the legislating Grotii—the legislators of the human race: that which the Alexanders and the Tamerlanes endeavoured to accomplish by traversing a part of the globe, the Grotii and the Puffendorffs would accomplish, each one sitting in his arm chair: that which the conqueror would effect with violence by his sword, the jurisconsult would effect without effort by his pen. Behold the goddess Nature!—the jurisconsult is her priest; his idlest trash is an oracle, and this oracle is a law".

[64] The main works of the utilitarian philosophical tide of thought of the nineteenth century can be found in Bentham (1789); John Austin (1832); Holmes (1881).

[65] The most representative figure in this respect is probably Posner (2010); see also Álvarez (2009).

[66] Bentham (1843), p. 502: "Natural rights is simple nonsense: natural and imprescriptible rights, rhetorical nonsense—nonsense upon stilts. But this rhetorical nonsense ends in the old strain of mischievous nonsense: for immediately a list of these pretended natural rights is given, and those are so expressed as to present to view legal rights. And of these rights, whatever they are, there is not, it seems, any one of which any government can, upon any occasion whatever, abrogate the smallest particle".

[67] In the fight against terrorism, for example, it is clear that States have gone beyond what can be assumed to be reasonable in the framework of a constitutional democracy; on this, see Masferrer (2012); Masferrer and Walker (2013); Masferrer (2011a).

of a false "public interest" (such as national security) or in the name of political or economic interests.

Kant, partly aware of this need, elaborated his theory of human dignity. [68] Indeed, by relating human dignity to the laws of nature and human nature, [69] he took up the legacy of the sixteenth and seventeenth centuries. In fact, the jurists of this period had in mind the idea of human dignity, [70] but they did not come to use the expression 'dignity' so assiduously. It was Kant who took the term from his predecessors, and began to use it frequently. However, it should be emphasised that numerous authors before Kant had already been using the expression 'dignity of human nature' since the seventeenth and eighteenth centuries.

2.4.3 The (Pre-Kantian) Expression and the Notion of 'Human Dignity' in the Eighteenth and Seventeenth Centuries

As has been said, the main works in which Immanuel Kant developed his concept of human dignity were written from 1781 onwards.[71] Let us now see which authors, in what context and in what sense, used the expression 'human dignity' and, more specifically, that of 'dignity of human nature', linking human 'dignity' and 'nature'. Following the retrospective chronological method, we will start from some authors contemporary to Kant, and we will go down in time until we reach the seventeenth century.[72]

---

[68] The main works in which Immanuel Kant developed his concept of human dignity were written from 1781 onwards [Kant (1781, 1785, 1788, 1797)]; however, some observations on human dignity can be found twenty years earlier, in Kant (1764); on Kant's human dignity, see Cattaneo (1981); Cattaneo (2002); Shell (2003).

[69] This does not mean that Kant based human dignity on human nature, as if he were endorsing a scholastic approach to human dignity. As has been said, and rightly so, "Kant and the notion of 'natural right' is not based on an idea of human nature, but on reason and rationality. That Kant still refers to it as 'natural right' cannot hide the fact that it is more a right of reason than a right of nature. This qualification is necessary. It does not mean, however, that those reflections on human nature and capacity have no significance for Kant" (Reinhardt 2014, p. 145); on this, see also Thornhill (2013); though it is true that "with the emphasis on subjective rights, Kant completes a central shift from classical to modern subjective law, 'a shift from the metaphysics of natural law to natural rights'"(Haakonsen (2006), p. 280), he did not deny the 'laws of nature' and, in fact—as has been said—connected human dignity with the laws of nature and human nature.

[70] In this regard, see the classic work of Finnis (1980); for a historical perspective, see Lauren (2003); Helmholz (2005); Tierney (2008); Helmholz (2010).

[71] See footnote n. 31.

[72] For a more complete overview of this section, but without employing the retrospective method followed here, see my studies: Masferrer and García-Sánchez (2016); Masferrer (2016).

The sources show how throughout the eighteenth century, and prior to Kant, numerous authors (philosophers, politicians, jurists, doctors, etc.) used both the notion and the expression of human dignity.

In Scotland, David Hume (1711–1776) had devoted a short essay to human dignity ("*of the dignity or meanness of human nature*"). [73] The Edinburgh philosopher argued that those who offer a positive view of human dignity are closer to the truth than those who defend the meanness of human nature. [74] In his view, although man may sometimes "be led blindly by instinct," [75] man and animals have different natures. He argued that those who "have insisted so much on man's selfishness" have failed to understand the importance of virtue in human life, [76] holding that "friendship and virtue cannot be disinterested," [77] or that virtuous people pursue vanity, praise, and "the applause of others." [78] Hume went so far as to admit that to behave in a free and rational manner is most appropriate or "*in accordance with the dignity of* human *nature*." [79]

Shortly before, the Irish philosopher and politician Edmund Burke (1729–1797) had referred, in a speech delivered on 22 March 1775, to "all the essential rights, and the *intrinsic dignity of* human *nature*." [80]

[73] Hume (1777); as Eugene F. Miller noted in his Foreword, "the preparation and revision of his essays occupied Hume throughout his adult life. In his early twenties, after completing the three books of the Treatise, Hume began to publish essays on moral and political topics. His Essays, Moral and Political was published in late 1741 by Alexander Kincaid, principal editor of Edinburgh". This edition included the following essays: (1) "Of the Delicacy of Taste and Passion"; (2) "Of the Liberty of the Press"; (3) "Of Impudence and Modesty"; (4) "That politics may be reduced to a Science"; (5) "Of the First Principles of Government"; (6) "Of Love and Marriage"; (7) "Of the Study of History"; (8) "Of the Independency of Parliament"; (9) "Whether the British Government Inclines more to Absolute Monarchy, or to a Republic"; (10) "Of Parties in General"; (11) "Of the Parties of Great Britain"; (12) "Of Superstition and Enthusiasm"; (13) "Of Avarice"; (14) "Of the Dignity of Human Nature"; and (15) "Of Liberty and Despotism." The title of Essay 14 became "Of the Dignity or Meanness of Human Nature" in the 1770 edition of his Essays and Treatises on Several Subjects (*ibid.*, note 5).

[74] Hume (1777), p. 82: "I am of opinion, however, that the sentiments of those who are inclined to think favourably of humanity, are more advantageous to virtue, than the contrary principles, which give us a mean opinion of our nature. When a man is predisposed with a high conception of his rank and character in creation, he will endeavour to act naturally, and will despise to do a base or vicious action, which might sink him below that figure which he makes in his own imagination. Accordingly, we find, that all our polite and fashionable moralists insist on this matter, and endeavour to represent vice as unworthy of man, as well as odious in itself."

[75] Hume (1777), p. 83.

[76] Hume (1777), p. 86.

[77] Hume (1777), pp. 86–87: "In the first place, they found that every act of virtue or friendship was attended with a secret pleasure; whence they concluded that friendship and virtue could not be disinterested. But the fallacy of this is obvious. The virtuous sentiment or passion produces the pleasure, and does not arise from it. I feel a pleasure in doing good to my friend, because I love him; but I do not love him for for the sake of that pleasure".

[78] Hume (1777), p. 89.

[79] Hume (1777), p. 509.

[80] Burke (1775), p. 223.

The English philosopher John Cartwright (1740–1824), in his *The Legislative Rights of the Commonality Vindicated* (1777), based the extension of the right of suffrage to all men of full age on the 'dignity of human nature'. Rejecting that the election of representatives should be made to depend on the wealth or property of individuals, he points out that...

> ...the poor have surely as much interest as the rich [in exercising the right of suffrage] (...). Their poverty is undoubtedly the worst of all the reasons that can be given for depriving them of their *natural rights*; on the contrary, we must try to reconcile them to the many harshnesses of their situation by showing them that it does not degrade them below the level of human nature. Since they have no reason to be proud, let them at least retain the *dignity of human nature*, knowing that they are free and that they share in the privileges which are inseparable from freedom. [81]

Criticising the position of John Locke, who defended the importance of property in order to exercise the right of suffrage, Cartwright asserts that it is not property that is...

> ...what truly constitutes freedom. No; it is undoubtedly a gift made to the whole human species by God, who added free will to rationality, in order to make men responsible for their actions. *All are by nature free and equal; freedom implies choice; equality excludes degrees of freedom.* Therefore, all members of the commonwealth have an equal right to vote to elect those who are to be the guardians of their liberties; and no one can have the right to more than one vote (...). My concept of truth compels me to believe that *personality is the only foundation of the right to be represented*; and that property has, in reality, nothing to do with this problem... [82]

The second American president, John Adams (1735–1826), had resorted to the expression 'dignity of human nature' in his works. In his *Reflections on Government*, he argued that "the happiness of mankind, as well as the *true dignity of human nature*, consists in virtue." [83] Adams seemed to be convinced—as he wrote in a letter to the Senate—that "Virtue, gifts, talents, and attainments, which constitute the *dignity of human nature*, and laid the foundation for the prosperity or longevity of empires." [84] He too linked the 'dignity of human nature' with the assertion that rights

---

[81] Cartwright (1777), pp. 28–30; (text collected by Carlyle (1941), p. 254).

[82] Cartwright (1777), secs. 39, 41, 42, pp. 31–32; (text collected by Carlyle (1941), p. 254–255); on the human condition as a free being and the consequent need to exercise—*velis nolis*—that freedom, see Ortega y Gasset (1987), t. 4, p. 171; collected by Arriola (2003), p. 57: "To live is to feel fatally forced to exercise freedom, to decide what we are going to be in this world. Not a single instant is our decision-making activity allowed to rest. Even when in desperation we abandon ourselves to whatever wants to come, we have decided not to decide. It is therefore false to say that in life 'circumstances decide'. On the contrary, circumstances are the dilemma, always new, before which we have to decide. But it is our character that decides."

[83] Adams (1851), p. 205: "All moderate truth-seeking inquirers, ancient and modern, theologians, moralists, and philosophers, have agreed that the happiness of mankind, as well as the true dignity of human nature, consists in virtue; if there is a form of government whose principle and foundation is virtue, will not any wise man recognise that it is more likely to promote general happiness than any other?"

[84] Adams (1854a), vol. 9, p. 149.

"derive only from nature and the author of nature; that they are inherent, inalienable, and irrevocable by any laws, covenants, contracts, conventions, or stipulations, which man could devise." [85] He also resorted to the 'dignity of human nature' to extol the wisdom and humanity of English law a few years before American independence. Indeed, in his *Revolutionary Writings* (1763), he noted that the *common law* of England, unlike other legal traditions (such as Spanish and French), was characterised by a high regard for "liberty, the inalienable and indefeasible character of the rights of men, the honour and dignity *of* human *nature*". [86] He further asserted that the English system of government "was more conformable to the *dignity of human nature*, than any (...) in Europe." [87]

Henry Home, Lord Kames (1696–1782), one of the leaders of the Scottish Enlightenment and a judge in the supreme courts of Scotland, also wrote about human dignity before Kant. In his *Elements of Criticism* (1762), Chapter IX ('Dignity and Grace'), he pointed out that the expression 'dignity of human nature' had different meanings and there were different levels of 'dignity.' [88] It stated that the expressions 'dignity' and 'meanness' "must belong to [sentient]/sensitive beings, probably to man alone." [89] Furthermore, after stressing that "we never attribute dignity to any action, but to what is virtuous" [90] and that "every action of dignity creates respect and esteem for the author," [91] he argued that "*dignity and meanness are founded on a natural principle*", meaning that "man is [endowed with]/endued of a sense of *the [dignity]/worth and excellence of his nature*: he deems it more perfect than that of the other beings around him; and he perceives that the perfection of his nature consists in virtue, particularly in the virtues of the highest rank." [92] In this way, this illustrious Scotsman related human dignity to virtue and human nature. In his opinion, the perfection of man consists in virtue. [93]

Thomas Gordon (1692–1750) was a radical liberal who defended, in the early eighteenth century, constitutionalism and the freedom of the individual against political corruption, imperialism and militarism. He referred to the "*Dignity of Human Nature*, and the Superiority which omnipotent God bestowed on Man over other Beings", despite man's weakness and imperfection, "to [make him conscious]/

[85] Adams (1854b), vol. 10, pp. 316–317.

[86] Adams (1763), p. 15.

[87] Adams (1763), p. 26.

[88] Home (1762), p. 245.

[89] Home (1762), p. 245.

[90] Home (1762), p. 246.

[91] Home (1762), p. 246.

[92] Home (1762), p. 246.

[93] And he added: "To express that sense, the term *dignity* is appropriated. Further, to behave with dignity, and to refrain from all mean actions, is felt to be, not a virtue only, but a duty: it is a duty every man owes to himself. By acting in that manner, he attracts love and esteem: by acting meanly, or below himself, he is disapproved and contemned." Home (1762), p. 246.

put him in mind of his mortality, to humble his pride, and to excite his diligence." [94] According to this thinker, man should oppose everything that was "an affront to common sense, and beneath the *Dignity of Human Nature*" and "this can be done because we [human beings] enjoy freedom or knowledge." [95]

A few years earlier, the Dutch physician Bernard Mandeville (1670–1733), in his most famous work, entitled *The Fable of the Bees or Private Vices, Public Benefits* (1714), [96] had referred to the "*Excellence of our nature above other animals*", although he acknowledged that human nature presents "Strengths and Weaknesses." [97] In dealing with human beings, he stated "how unbecoming it was the *dignity of such sublime creatures to* be solicitous about gratifying those appetites which they had in common with the brutes." [98] Further on, he pointed out that man, unlike the beasts, "setting a true value upon themselves, took no delight but in embellishing the part in which their excellency consisted; such as despising whatever they had in common with irrational creatures, opposed by the help of reason their most violent inclinations; and making a continual war with them to promote the peace of others, aimed at on no less than the public welfare and the conquest of their own passion." [99]

Nor were these eighteenth-century authors, who predated Kant, the first to use both the notion and the expression 'human dignity'. As is well known, the jurists of the previous century exerted a notable influence on the legal philosophy and legal doctrine of the eighteenth century. The notions of 'natural rights' (or rights of man) and 'human nature' occupied a central place in seventeenth-century legal thought. Along with Grotius and Pufendorf, thinkers such as Thomasius [100] and Wolff, [101]

---

[94] Gordon (1743), pp. 210–211.

[95] Gordon (1743), pp. 280–281.

[96] Mandeville (1732); this work was edited more than half a dozen times and became one of the most controversial works of the eighteenth century for its assertions about the moral foundations of modern commercial society.

[97] Mandeville (1732), pp. 43–44.

[98] Mandeville (1732), p. 44.

[99] Mandeville (1732), pp. 43–44: "To introduce, moreover, an emulation among men, which divides the whole species into two classes, very different one from the other: One consisted of the most abject, low-minded people, who are always hunting immediate enjoyment, were wholly incapable of self-denial, and without regard to the good of others, had no higher aim than their private advantage; as enslaved by voluptuousness, yielded without resistance to every gross desire, and made no use of their rational faculties, but to heighten their sensual pleasure. These vile growling wretches, they said, were the dross of their kind, and having [44] only the shape of men, differed from brutes in nothing but their outward figure. But the other class was made up of lofty high spirit creatures, that free from sordid selfishness, esteemed the improvements of the mind to be their fairest possessions; and setting a true value upon themselves, took no delight but in embellishing the part in which their excellency consisted; such as despising whatever they had in common with irrational creatures, opposed by the helpof reason their most violent inclinations; and making a continual war with them to promote the peace of others, aimed at on no less than the public welfare and the conquest of their own passion."

[100] Thomasius (1705); see also Thomasius (1688).

[101] Christian Wolff (1740–1749).

among others, linked the notions of 'natural rights' and 'human nature', and these with the idea of 'human dignity'. In this sense, the expression 'dignity of human nature' appears frequently in the doctrinal sources of the seventeenth century. Hence, as we have seen, not a few thinkers of the eighteenth century used the expression 'dignity of human nature', without providing a definition or an explanation of the term, as if it were taken for granted. As we have just seen, the authors used the expression in a positive way, with rare exceptions. [102] Some extolled both divine and human nature. [103] However, most authors related the 'dignity of human nature' to the moral dignity of human beings, that is, to virtue, not only to uphold the dignity of virtuous persons, but to emphasise that the practice of virtue was the behaviour most in keeping with the 'dignity of human nature', seen as a source of requirement (or moral duty), obliging one to act accordingly and to lead a virtuous life. In other words, 'the natural dignity of human nature' constituted a call to moral excellence, [104] and was the source of the 'common inalienable rights and privileges of mankind.' [105] However, it did not escape the authors' notice that, despite this 'dignity of human nature', man could denigrate his reason, [106] and degrade himself by the pursuit of sensual pleasures or by disregarding the dictates of his own conscience. [107]

Seventeenth-century jurists already used the expression 'dignity', although less frequently than in the eighteenth century. Samuel Pufendorf was the one who used the expression 'human dignity' most frequently, placing this notion—according to Welzel's opinion—at the centre of the natural law doctrine. [108] However, he was not the first, as will be seen.

Samuel von Pufendorf (1632–1694) used the expression 'dignity', 'dignity of man' or—like Grotius a few years earlier—'dignity of human nature' more frequently.[109] Discussing—in his *Elementorum jurisprudentiae universalis libri duo*

[102] John Trenchard (England, 1662–1723) would be one of these exceptions. Besides stating that many authors use the expression without understanding it, he gave a rather negative view of the 'dignity' of human nature; Trenchard and Gordon (1721).

[103] See, e.g., Cooper (1737), p. 195.

[104] Turnbull (1740), vol. 1, pp. 13–14.

[105] Turnbull (1740), vol. 2, p. 700.

[106] Turnbull (1740), vol. 2, p. 611.

[107] Turnbull (1740), vol. 2, p. 705; see also Turnbull (1742), p. 108.

[108] Welzel (1971), p. 146, note 113; Welzel's view is highly questionable and, however much his work has been republished, his efforts to disqualify the Catholic Church and Catholic thinkers are evident and undisguised. He was translated, as is logical, by Felipe González Vicén, who also shares his point of view to a large extent. Welzel wanted to give a lot of importance to Pufendorf. The reason? Pufendorf repudiates all the above and calls the Church, already in the prologue of his *De jure naturae et gentium*, 'Kingdom of darkness' ('*Regnum Tenebrarum*'). As is well known, Pufendorf was very controversial, so much so that he was dismissed from his University. It was not clear whether he had Faith or not, but in any case, he severed all relation between the reason of God and that of men, from which it follows that the natural law (*entia moralia*) which we men know through our reason, is a '*jus inutile*'; on this, see Carpintero (2013), p. 225.

[109] In this regard, see the study by Saastamoinen (2010).

(1660) [110]—the principle according to which a man is destined by nature to live in society, Pufendorf argued that there are no living beings who have greater need of society than human beings. Stating that "[n]othing is gloomier for a man than perpetual solitude," the German jurist described the various ways by which men and animals obtain the necessary food for themselves, while acknowledging that "the ability to obtain food for the stomach is only a very small part [or of little value] in the merit of the *dignity of the so-called* man." [111]

In Pufendorf's view, reason dictates that a man should take care of himself, so that human society is not thrown into disorder. [112] It is this dictate of reason that leads to the knowledge of the law of nature, [113] and from it arises the obligation to behave in conformity with it. [114] After basing the obligation to follow the laws of nature—or the dictate of reason—on the authority (or will) of the Creator ('voluntarism'), [115] he maintained that the fundamental laws of nature, as well as the others that emanate from them, are reduced to two: self-preservation and not to disturb human society. [116]

In this context, Pufendorf made explicit reference to the 'dignity of human nature' when discussing the first law of nature, in relation to self-preservation. In his view, one of the consequences was that 'everyone must omit everything that might both weaken the use of reason and harm or injure the body.' [117] He argued that the natural law "enjoins on the members of society the protection of themselves, to take care not to be a burden to themselves or to society." [118] Ultimately, "from that law emanate the precepts of the law of nature as to how to deal with the emotions and bring them under the command [rule] of reason, since they prevent us from forming a right judgment about things, and often lead us to what is harmful, both to ourselves and to others." [119] One of the areas which, according to Pufendorf, should be regulated by positive laws is modesty (or a feeling of shame) with regard to the acts of marriage. It was, in his view, a requirement of 'the dignity of man':

---

[110] We use an English edition: Pufendorf (1931).

[111] Pufendorf (1931), Observation III, p. 235: 'A man is destined by nature to lead a social life with men'. The italics are mine.

[112] Pufendorf (1931), Observation IV, pp. 240 ff.: 'reason dictates that a man should take care of himself, so that human society is not led into disorder.'

[113] Pufendorf (1931), Observation IV, pp. 240–241.

[114] Pufendorf (1931), Observation IV, pp. 241–242.

[115] Pufendorf (1931), Observation IV, pp. 242–243.

[116] Pufendorf (1931), Observation IV, pp. 243: (1) *That anyone should protect his own life and limbs as much as possible and save himself and what is his.* (2) *That he should not disturb human society,* or, in other words, *that he should do nothing that would make society among men less peaceful.* These laws ought so to conspire, and, as it were, be intertwined with one another, as to coalesce, as it were, into one law, namely, *That each should be zealous so to preserve himself, that society among men be not disturbed.*"

[117] Pufendorf (1931), Observation IV, pp. 247–249.

[118] Pufendorf (1931), Observation IV, pp. 247.

[119] Pufendorf (1931), Observation IV, pp. 247.

> For the rest, although it was a requirement of *man's dignity* not to be procreated like cattle by unregulated sexual intercourse, and it contributes very greatly to a decorous order in states for the cohabitation of males and females to be fortified, as it were, with the scrupulous observance of a pact; still it assuredly seems strange, that, among the more civilised nations, at least, a most sensitive modesty attaches both to the members destined for procreation, and to the act of generation itself, although that modesty seems to arise neither from some natural deformity of the members or an absurd shape; and the act itself is conformable to nature, and altogether necessary for the preservation of the human species, and suitable to produce a being of *such dignity*. [120]

Our Saxon jurist was fully convinced that the laws of nature had to be followed in order to achieve the necessary social order, a social order in conformity with a natural order that could be grasped by right reason. Hence, he attached so much importance to the laws of nature. He argued that positive laws were necessary to ensure respect for the laws of nature. And even positive law, coming from the free decision of the sovereign (or legislator), had to conform "to a definite *status* [or condition] of men." [121] In short, they had to respect and conform to human nature or—to use Pufendorf's expression—to the 'dignity of human nature'.

Some years later, he developed—in his *De iure naturae et gentium* (1672) [122]—his notion of human dignity. [123] His voluntarist approach to morality and ethics led him to emphasise the role of freedom in both human nature and human dignity. He distinguished between physical beings (*entia physica*) and moral beings (*entia moralia*). Regarding the latter, he followed Aristotle in affirming that all realities in the universe have their own essential characteristics and principles, coming from the Creator. Each of them has properties that emanate from its substance and its capacities (or virtues). [124] He held that man, unlike other living beings, was the only one whose conduct/operation depends on his free will, rather than being subject to the yoke of nature. He stressed the importance of reason—as an excellent light that enables one to know things, to judge, to make decisions, etc.—and of the will. Both reason and will distinguish man from the beasts. Hence, men—unlike beasts (or irrational animals)—were not subjected to uniform and automated behaviors. Men were—unlike beasts—moral beings (*entia moralia*).

It should be noted that Pufendorf at first indicates that the commandments of the Decalogue, which human beings discover naturally in reason, make up "*entia moralia*". Later, however, he points out that nature does not, through its laws, lend man the power to act. Pufendorf does not, therefore, consider natural data to compose natural laws in a moral or legal sense. He therefore denied the normativity of nature. [125] He broke completely with the jurisprudence of the jurists, which started

---

[120] Pufendorf (1931), Observation V, p. 279.

[121] Pufendorf (1931), Observation V, p. 279.

[122] I use here a French version: Pufendorf (1762 & 1759).

[123] For an exhaustive overview in this regard, see the study by Pelé (2006), pp. 839 ff.; whom I follow in the analysis of the Pufendorfian work cited in the previous note.

[124] Pufendorf (1762 & 1759), Préliminaires, § II, p. 2.

[125] Carpintero (2013), pp. 235–237.

from the consideration of justice as a *medium rei*, a matter of things and not only a moral quality proper to the person. Pufendorf was interested, above all, in the freedom of the person, "an incommunicable and solitary being,"[126] to an "isolated and free individual."[127]

After comparing man's physical superiority over animals, Pufendorf emphasised a characteristic feature of human beings, namely, the perfect inner order reflecting the unity of reason and will. Reason was the light without which the will could not carry out its task. [128] Free will also played an important role because thanks to it men had the ability to develop their primitive (biological) nature. In this way, people could be the protagonists of their full realisation as human beings. [129] Human nature permanently pushes man towards his perfection, [130] a tendency that does not occur in an automatic way—like the *entia physica* -, but by the impulse—guided by reason—of free will. In this sense, Pufendorf exalted freedom because it empowers men, granting them the power to exercise effective control over their own conduct and even over themselves.

Pufendorf argued that what distinguishes human freedom from that of animals is morality. It was precisely in this context that he used the expression "*the dignity and excellence of* man." [131] It could be said that human freedom constitutes, in his view, the foundation of man's moral dignity. This does not mean that he denied the human dignity of those who acted immorally or chose to live immorally. According to the German jurist and philosopher, all men possess an innate dignity because of the moral freedom that was granted to all—as human beings—regardless of the particular conduct that the subject then deployed in his concrete moral life.

From the principle that all human beings are equal by nature—even if their particular choices were unlawful or immoral [132]—flowed the obligation—incumbent on all—to respect and treat others as equals, to which Pufendorf devoted an entire chapter. [133] In this regard, he stated that the expression 'man' contains within itself the idea of dignity. This was also the strongest argument he made when confronted with insults and abuse, reminding his authors that, "I am not a dog, however; I am a man like you." [134] There is no doubt that he was defending the idea of natural (or intrinsic) human dignity.

---

[126] Carpintero (2013), p. 238; on Pufendorf's contradictions, see pp. 228 ff.

[127] In this respect, see Carpintero (1987), pp. 477–522; Carpintero (2013), pp. 237–243.

[128] Pufendorf (1762 & 1759), L. I, Chap. III, § I & III, pp. 38–39.

[129] Pufendorf (1762 & 1759), L. I., Chap. I, § IV & VI, pp. 5–6.

[130] Pufendorf (1762 & 1759), Préliminaires, § III, p. 4.

[131] Pufendorf (1762 & 1759), L. II, Chap. I, § V, pp. 145–146.

[132] Pufendorf (1762 & 1759), L. III, Chap. II, § I, p. 308, where recourse was had to the idea that God wrote the law in the heart of man.

[133] Pufendorf (1762 & 1759), L. III, Chap. II.

[134] Pufendorf (1762 & 1759), L. III, Chap. II, § I, p. 309; according to the opinion of J. Barbeyrac, Pufendorf here drew his inspiration from the poetry of Statius, *Thebaid,* Lib. XII, v. 556 ff.

This idea of dignity demanded equality, which did not go along with slavery. Hence, he rejected that some men could have the natural status of slaves. Slavery is a violation of the natural equality of all men. [135] To permit slavery was to deny both the natural equality and the natural liberty of all men. Therefore, no man should be subject to the will of others without their free consent. [136] If all men are equal and possess a common natural liberty, men who had been invested with other qualities or faculties lacked the right to subjugate others. [137] As our author states, civil inequalities could never be used to legitimise or justify the violation or destruction of the natural equality of all men. [138]

Before Pufendorf, Hugo Grotius (1583–1645), had already used the expression 'dignity of man' or 'dignity of human nature'. Indeed, in analysing the common custom of burying the dead and unravelling the reasons for it, he concluded by pointing out that "the most obvious explanation is to be found in the *dignity of* man." [139] According to this illustrious Dutch jurist, the right to be buried stemmed from the "*dignity of* human *nature*," [140] and such a duty could be requested by anyone, even by mortal enemies. [141] In short, both the right to burial and the duty to perform this service were not founded on religious grounds, but were due to the just recognition of the 'dignity of human nature'.

As we have seen in the preceding pages, in the eighteenth and seventeenth centuries' legal philosophy maintained the idea of moral excellence and natural dignity of human beings, even though later individual conduct might not reflect that natural human dignity in a clear-cut way. The expression 'dignity of human nature', of Ciceronian origin and so often found in seventeenth and eighteenth century sources,[142] shows the remarkable attention that authors paid to human nature and its dignity. Their doctrine could be synthesised in the following principles: (1) natural dignity derives from human nature; (2) this natural dignity implies the obligation to act accordingly, thus forging a moral dignity whose degree depends on the practice

---

[135] Pufendorf (1762 & 1759), L. III, Chap. II, § VIII, p. 316.

[136] Pufendorf (1762 & 1759), L. III, Chap. II, § VIII, p. 317.

[137] Pufendorf (1762 & 1759), L. III, Chap. II, § VIII, p. 317.

[138] Pufendorf (1762 & 1759), L.III, Chap. II, § VIII, p. 319.

[139] Grotius (1625), Book II, Ch. XIX: 'On the Right of Burial', II, p. 216: "But the most obvious explanation is to be found in the dignity of man, for whom surpassing other creatures, this would be a shame, if it be an act of compassion then, said Quintilian, to preserve the bodies of men from the ravages of birds and beasts. To be torn by wild beasts, as Cicero observes in his first book On Invention, must be deprived of those honors, in death, because of our common nature..."

[140] Grotius (1625), II, XIX, II, 4.

[141] Grotius (1625), II, XIX, II, 5; this idea can be found in Seneca (1989); on this subject, see also Griffin (1991); Pelé (2006), pp. 366 ff.

[142] In fact, Cicero, in *De Officiis*, explicitly included this expression when he stated the convenience of one's own conduct being in accordance with "the superiority and dignity of our [human] nature" (Book I, n. 30); in Book I, n. 17, he stated as follows: "For if we bring a certain amount of propriety and order into the transactions of daily life, we shall be conserving moral rectitude and moral dignity" (I used the English version available at http://www.stoics.com/cicero_book.html)

of virtues; and (3) natural dignity, which comes from human nature, must always be recognised, even when someone's conduct might seem petty or vicious. Let us look briefly at each of these.

(1) According to most philosophers of law of the eighteenth and seventeenth centuries, natural dignity emanates from human nature. According to these thinkers, natural dignity comes from the simple fact of being human. Nothing else is needed. Moreover, natural rights are based on natural dignity, whether or not the individual is capable of exercising or enjoying them. Incapacity would not affect the natural dignity that corresponds to everyone by the mere fact of being human, that is, of possessing human nature. The philosophers of these centuries related human nature and the condition of being human to natural dignity and natural rights. While in the sixteenth century thinkers (jurists, philosophers and theologians) established the connection between human nature and natural rights (Francisco de Vitoria, Domingo de Soto, Francisco Suárez, etc.), from the seventeenth century onwards authors began to use the expression 'dignity' to underline the idea of respect and consideration that every individual deserves for the mere fact of being human, or, if one prefers, for possessing human nature. In beginning to use the expression 'dignity of human nature', the aim was precisely to show in a clear way the consideration and respect that humanity in general and any singular individual in particular deserves. In this sense—as we have seen—, some seventeenth-century authors declared that natural rights emanated from the 'dignity of human nature', while others continued to affirm—in line with the doctrine of the School of Salamanca—that natural rights were rooted in human nature. These were two ways of expressing the same idea, namely, that natural rights belong to human beings (or those who share human nature), whose natural dignity came from the mere fact of being human.
(2) The authors of the eighteenth and seventeenth centuries considered natural dignity not only as the origin of natural rights, whose protection constituted the *raison d'être* of any political power. Natural dignity was also the source of duties and obligations. In this sense, human nature conferred a natural dignity from which emanated rights for the individual, but also the obligation to lead a life in accordance with his dignity. "Noblesse oblige", the saying goes. Natural dignity implies the duty to lead a virtuous life. Indeed, with the practice of virtue there is a gradual increase in the moral dignity of each individual. From this perspective, freedom or autonomous will is understood as the human faculty that enables a person to conduct himself in a manner consistent with his natural dignity, thus progressively increasing his moral dignity (or esteem among his peers). Freedom and autonomy were seen as the principal human faculty without which man could not honour his natural dignity by freely pursuing that which is proper or "in accord with the *dignity of* human *nature*." [143] The more a man

[143] See footnote n. 42.

practices virtue, the more he honours his human dignity, and the happier he will be, because happiness cannot be pursued or attained apart from that which is in accordance with the 'dignity of human nature'.

(3) Natural dignity, which comes from human nature, should not be confused with moral dignity or the public esteem that a virtuous life produces in the eyes of others. Natural dignity obliges one to act accordingly. Bad conduct, or leading a mean life, could tarnish, overshadow, or even almost destroy an individual's moral dignity, but never diminish his natural dignity in the least, since he cannot cease to be human (even if his conduct does not honour or reflect the 'dignity of human nature'). [144]

2.4.4 The Notion of Human Dignity in the Sixteenth Century

The fact that it was from the seventeenth century onwards that authors began to assiduously use the expression 'human dignity', 'dignity of man' or 'dignity of human nature', does not mean that the history of this notion—or of the expression itself, probably—began in that century.[145]

As is well known, the jurists, philosophers and theologians of the sixteenth century, in relating human nature and natural rights, defended that the dignity of man emanated precisely from human nature. The concept of human nature came from antiquity, but it was particularly developed in the sixteenth century, in the context of the Spanish colonisation of America (Francisco de Vitoria, Domingo de Soto, Francisco Suárez, etc.). [146] It would make no sense to make the history of the notion of human dignity depend on that of its expression, especially when this notion can be defended without using the term 'dignity'. In this sense, the famous sermon delivered by Fray Antonio Montesinos on December 21, 1511, on the fourth Sunday of Advent, criticising the practices of the colonial system of *encomienda*, as well as "the cruelty and tyranny" with which some treated the indigenous people, is paradigmatic:

---

[144] Some authors distinguish between 'intrinsic dignity' (that which everyone possesses by the simple fact of being human, and not that reserved for the virtuous) and 'extrinsic dignity' (which depends on the mentality and behaviour of persons); in this regard, see Stetson (1998), pp. 15–18; Andorno (2012), p. 73 distinguishes between 'intrinsic dignity' and 'ethical dignity', basing the concept of human dignity on the former.

[145] According to the opinion of Alonso (1986), t. II, p. 956, the expressions 'dignidad' and 'dignitat', understood as 'calidad de digno' or 'merecedor de dignidad', come from the end of the fifteenth century (1495); I thank Dr. María del Refugio González Domínguez, who suggested me to investigate this point and with whom I could consult this *Dictionary* in her work office.

[146] In this regard, see Stuurman (2017), ch. 5, including the protest against the Spanish treatment of the Native Americans voiced by the Dominican friar Antonio de Montesinos (1511), the justification and critique of the Spanish Empire by Francisco Vitoria in the mid-sixteenth century and the criticism of Spanish rule by Bartolomé de Las Casas (1514–1566); see also the study by Sánchez de Movellán (2014).

> This voice (he said) tells you that you are all in mortal sin and in it you live and die because of the cruelty and tyranny that you use with these innocent people. Tell me, by what right and by what justice do you hold these Indians in such cruel and horrible servitude? By what authority have you waged such detestable wars against these people who were in their meek and peaceful lands, where you have consumed so many of them with death and havoc never heard of? How do you keep them so oppressed and fatigued, without feeding them or curing them of their diseases, in which, from the excessive labours you give them, they incur and die, and, to put it better, you kill them to extract and acquire gold every day? And what care you for those who teach them, and who teach them to know their God and Creator, to be baptised, to hear mass, to keep the feasts and Sundays? Are they not men? Have they not rational souls? Are you not obliged to love them as yourselves? Do you not understand this? Do you not feel this? How are you in such a depth of sleep, so lethargic, asleep? Be assured that in the state you are in, you can no more save yourselves than the Moors or Turks who lack and do not want the faith of Jesus Christ.[147]

Indeed, the text of the sermon does not include the expression 'dignity', but it is undeniable that this notion was at the heart of Montesinos' message, just as it was well present in the thinkers of the second Spanish scholasticism, regardless of the fact that the expression 'dignity' [human] might not be expressly included in their works. This is not to say that no sixteenth-century author used this expression. It can be found in some texts, but not with the assiduity that has been found in the sources of the seventeenth and eighteenth centuries. In spite of this, that is, although the sources of the sixteenth century did not include the expression 'dignity of human nature', the concept and its meaning were very present throughout that century.

The defence of the Indians carried out by Francisco de Vitoria—as well as Fray Bartolomé de las Casas, as will be seen—constituted a defence of natural human dignity,[148] and of its consequences. Let us now look at the doctrine of these two authors.

2.4.4.1 Francisco de Vitoria

Francisco de Vitoria asked himself whether the Indians were the owners of their property, both in the public and private sphere.[149]

To defend that the human dignity of the indigenous people came from nature, and not from grace, was a notable advance in the development of the expression 'dignity of human nature' that authors would use in the seventeenth and eighteenth centuries. In fact, although Thomas Aquinas clearly stated the well-known distinction between

---

[147] I handle here the text available at http://www.dominicos.org/kit_upload/file/especial-montesino/Montesino-gustavo-gutierrez.pdf; for a more modern version of the sermon, see the one collected in the main text of footnote n. 70 in Part I.

[148] In this regard, see the study by Savignano (2011); see also the work of Hanke (1970); Brufau (1997).

[149] Vitoria (1967), p. 17.

nature and grace,[150] it was "to Vitoria's credit that he saw in his own time its political"[151] and legal implications. In this line, it has been affirmed—and rightly so—that "although the bases flowed from the preceding doctrine of Thomas Aquinas, [Vitoria] knew how to bring them down to the field of practical theology and law, giving legal form to the principles of the Gospel message: equality, universal fraternity of men and their dignity as free persons."[152]

The Thomistic distinction between nature and grace led Vitoria to defend that the nature of the Indians could also be "fully realised by the grace of God: the dignity and value of the nature of the Indian are supported by the disposition of that nature in every human being, a disposition that can be fully realised by the grace of God. In other words, the fact that Indians can be converted to Christianity shows that God has given them a nature that is open to divine grace. Indians, then, must have the same created nature as Europeans, since they are endowed with sufficient reason to understand the meaning of the gospel. The foundation of the human dignity and rights of Indians is found in the fact that they have a nature that is obviously endowed with sufficient reason to understand the gospel, and therefore they are images of God."[153]

The fact that the professor of the University of Salamanca distinguished nature from grace does not mean that he founded human dignity apart from God, especially when man enjoyed dignity because he was *imago Dei.* In his opinion, "[b]ecause of his condition as a rational and free being, he is not a mere vestige of his Creator, but is his image. Being *imago Dei* entails, by its elevation to the supernatural order, the divine filiation attained by the redemptive work of Christ."[154]

Vitoria's development of the political and legal implications of the distinction between grace and nature had important consequences. In this line, it has been affirmed—and rightly so—that "[t]his conception leads him to establish a far-reaching principle: that the rights he enunciates do not depend on or belong to a religion, nor to a culture, nor to a particular people, but have their foundation in

---

[150] Thomas Aquinas, *In III Sententiarum*, d. 29, q. 1, a. 7: grace does not modify nature, but fully realises it; Vitoria took from Thomas Aquinas some ideas in applying to the Indians the following three principles: "(1) Every man, in so far as *imago Dei*, has a personal dignity and therefore is the subject of fundamental rights independently of whether or not he shares the Christian faith, to which he is free to adhere, as he is also free for the choice of political government; (2) The forms of power and dominion were introduced with human right, which is not annulled by divine right; (3) The Church has no power over infidel peoples who are not subject to her *de iure et de facto*, or who do not occupy lands of Christian kings. Therefore, she cannot force them to choose or change their political regime. This does not exclude an indirect intervention of the Church itself, appealing to its spiritual purposes" (Savignano (2011) p. 107).

[151] Justenhoven (2011), p. 89; on this, see also Matz (1968), p. 277.

[152] Mora (2013), p. 37; see also Pereña (1992), pp. 106–109, where it is stated that Vitoria, according to Thomistic doctrine, states that reason inclines to the knowledge of truth and virtuous life in society -accepting that these are "natural inclinations".

[153] Mora (2013), p. 90; see also Justenhoven (1991), pp. 60 ff.; see also the study by Goti (1999).

[154] Vitoria (1967), p. 18; according to Mora (2013), p. 38, Vitoria "lays the foundation of the dignity of man, and this because he is the image of God through his rational powers".

human nature itself—rational—and, therefore, can be established as universal criteria for all men and peoples. It is a human being who distinguishes between the natural and supernatural planes, on the principle that grace does not destroy nature, but only perfects it."[155]

And human nature is characterised, according to Vitoria, by three notes or traits: rationality, language and sociability. Indeed, for Vitoria "rationality is the radical constitutive characteristic; but reason in the case of man, at least, is needed by another equally constitutive characteristic, although derived from reason or demanded by it: language. And that through the word, implies and demands a third reality, equally constitutive characteristic: sociability. Then, rationality, since, being the specific, the really constitutive characteristic of being man, of every man, brings indissolubly united, in a compact braid of unity, the word and sociability. Hence, for Vitoria, if the Indians are men, it cannot be said that they lack rationality, nor, consequently, reason; reason that will be manifested by language and by the social organisation in which they live; it is rationality that will demonstrate that they are participants of the same human nature as the Spaniards, endowed, consequently, with the same rights and prerogatives that derive from such nature."[156]

If the indigenous person, like all human beings, was characterised by rationality, language and sociability, he must enjoy freedom. Indeed, "[i]t is he who decides freely in his life, it is a created freedom and, therefore, limited and dependent; but authentic freedom."[157]

Moreover, Vitoria maintained that since possession and dominion were based on natural law, they could not be destroyed by theological—or faith—questions. If the Indians were right, as was the case, they could claim the same natural rights as any Christian. These natural rights gave them the power to be possessors of their property before the arrival of the Spaniards, both in the private and public sphere."[158]

God, in creating the human being in his image and likeness, placed man at the centre of creation as a responsible subject of law because of his rational nature, as well as a holder of rights as a rational being, apart from faith and culture.[159] Hence Vitoria departed "from the moral and faith thesis, to reason from natural law, because man continues to be the image of God even if he ignores him and even mocks him."[160] For Vitoria, the fact that the Indians had not had the opportunity to know the Christian faith could not lead to the deprivation of rights that correspond to every human being according to the natural order.[161]

---

155 Mora (2013), pp. 37–38.

156 Ocaña (1996), pp. 78–79 (collected by Mora (2013), p. 38, footnote n. 3).

157 Vitoria (1967), p. 19 (collected by Mora (2013) p. 38, footnote n. 4).

158 Vitoria (1967), pp. 14–31; see also Mora (2013), p. 38, footnotes nn. 6 and 7.

159 Vitoria (1967), pp. 14–31.

160 Mora (2013), p. 39.

161 Vitoria (1967), p. 31.

It has rightly been stated that, "[w]ith this formulation[,] [Vitoria] conceptualises the dignity of the human being—rationality, language and friendly sociability, free will—as the source of rights, characterised as innate and personal and, at the same time, establishes the principles of freedom and equality. Consequently, he can be considered to have left the unfinished task of describing and defining the human rights that are inherent to human nature, but we must still add that he has qualified these rights with the notes of: inalienability, inviolability, equality and universality."[162]

Vitoria maintained that "the duty to evangelise entailed respect for the freedom to adhere to the faith; since the act of faith, to be such, must be essentially free."[163] On the other hand, this natural dignity was not compatible with slavery. In this sense, in defending the dignity of persons, he distinguished between natural slavery and civil or legal slavery, affirming—contrary to the opinion of Aristotle—that no one could be a slave by nature, not admitting legal slavery either, nor for those Indians who, for lack of education, might seem stupid or idiots.[164]

2.4.4.2 Friar Bartolomé de las Casas

Bartolomé de las Casas also defended the natural dignity of the Indians,[165] rejecting "with forcefulness the recourse to irrationality and coercion so that the other is inserted into a community of communication, in which it is necessary to advance with the rational method and with dialogue, from the basic presupposition of recognition of equal dignity and equal rights."[166] In effect, Las Casas made a

[162] Mora (2013), p. 44.

[163] Savignano (2011), pp. 105–106; and adds: "The defence of the rights of the Indians seems evident when he puts the question of the principle, in the three fundamental chapters [of Vitoria (1967)]: those referring to the recognition of the 'human dignity' of the Indians, to the right of those peoples to defend their sovereignty (*dominium*), and to the right of the world to collaborate constructively in solidarity among peoples".

[164] Savignano (2011), pp. 108–109; on this subject, see Vitoria (1967), pp. 30–31.

[165] In this regard, see Beuchot (1996), pp. 87–95; Beuchot (2013).

[166] Savignano (2011), p. 113, where it is cited, in a footnote, the work Las Casas, (1975), p. 343; one might celebrate Vitoria's rejection of slavery for the Indians, lamenting at the same time the absence of public debate on the African / Trans-Atlantic slavery in the sixteenth-century Spain. How can this be explained? Antonio Montesino, Bartolomé de Las Casas and Francisco de Vitoria, among others, touched upon the Indians because they encountered a real, close problem (human, social and political) that needed to be addressed and solved, they feel responsible for it and saw themselves in the position to find a solution to such a serious moral issue. The fact that they did not tackle the African / Trans-Atlantic slavery should not be seen as if they undervalued African / Trans-Atlantic slaves (in comparison with the American ones). It rather reveals that their intellectual and doctrinal efforts were not due to their academic curiosity and love for abstract categories, but to their commitment to real and practical moral issues that arose in the context of a colonization carried out by their own monarchy.

defence of human freedom and dignity that prevented forcing the conversion of the indigenous people:

> But the rational creature has a natural aptitude to be led, directed or attracted in a soft, gentle, delicate and soft way, in virtue of his free will, so that he voluntarily listens, voluntarily obeys and voluntarily gives his adhesion and his obeisance to what is heard. Therefore, the way to move, direct, attract or direct the rational creature to good, to truth, to virtue, to justice, to pure faith and to true religion, must be a way that is in accord with the way, nature and condition of the rational creature himself, that is, a gentle way, gentle, soft, and mild, so that from its own motive, with a free will and with a natural disposition and faculty, it listens to all that is proposed and reported to it concerning faith, true religion, truth, virtue, and the other things that pertain to faith and religion.[167]

The idea that evangelisation should be carried out with respect for freedom, with reasons and persuasive ways, proper to rational beings with free will, appears constantly in Lasallian thought:

> ...it is one, alone and the same, the way which divine Providence established to notify its truth and to attract and invite men to the true religion at all times; namely, a way persuasive by reason as to the understanding, and gently attractive as to the will.[168]

In his *Apologetic summary history* (1539), Bartolomé de Las Casas argued that natural and human rights derive from a nature "predicated on all individuals marked by equal dignity. Every man is defined as a rational animal having intelligence, will and free will."[169] That equal dignity led him—like Francisco de Vitoria—to reject slavery.[170]

After insisting that what defines man is his rationality,[171] "that all have understanding and will and free will as they are formed in the image and likeness of God,"[172] "that all the lineage of men is one, and all men as to their creation and to natural things are alike and no one is born taught,"[173] that "all the nations of the world have understanding and will, and what results from both these powers in man is free will,"[174] Las Casas went further. He did not limit himself to defending the natural dignity of all human beings, but went so far as to use the expression 'dignity' in that sense:

[167]Las Casas (1975), § II, p. 15.

[168]Las Casas (1975), § XIII, p. 339; in this regard, see in particular §§ XV-XVI, p. 373–393; see also pp. 17–23, 35, 39, 45, 51, 63, 79–81, 87–89, 111–115, 203, 211, 307, 327, 335, 343, 343, 349, 357–359, 363, 367; in this regard, see Castañeda (1990), XVII-XLII.

[169]Savignano (2011), p. 114, collecting in note 58 the work of Las Casas (1967), t. III, c. 48.

[170]Savignano (2011), p. 114, footnote 60, where is cited another work of Las Casas (1965), pp. 1249–1250, making it clear that all men, equal by nature, are free, rejecting slavery; see also Las Casas (1965), t. II, pp. 1069–1071.

[171]In this regard, see the study by Beuchot (1994), pp. 45–47.

[172]Las Casas (1967), book III, chap. 48, pp. 257–258.

[173]Las Casas (1967), p. 258.

[174]Las Casas, (1967), p. 258.

> ...rational creatures, since they are formed in the image and likeness of God, their dignity and excellence over other creatures...[175]

Although it would require dealing with more authors and a more exhaustive analysis of the sources,[176] which here and now would completely exceed the limits of the present study,[177] it seems clear that the authors of the sixteenth century made a defence of natural human dignity, as derived from human nature itself, using the expression 'dignity' to a lesser extent than the authors of the seventeenth and eighteenth centuries, which does not mean that the former gave less importance to this notion, its meaning and foundation.

2.4.5 The Notion of Human Dignity in the Fifteenth Century

The same could be said with regard to the development of this notion prior to the sixteenth century. Giovanni Pico della Mirandola's *Discourse on the Dignity of Man*, published only six years before the Discovery of America, is well known.[178] A careful reading of the text is enough to confirm that, in spite of the author's beautiful apology for the 'dignity of man'—as reflected in the title of the work itself—he did not consider it opportune or necessary to use the expression 'dignity' throughout the work. In distinguishing, in clear and elegant prose, between the human condition and that of the animal, he thanks God for having given human beings freedom and autonomy ("the supreme and admirable good fortune of man to whom it has been granted to obtain what he wishes, to be what he wishes!"),[179] but he did not use the

[175] Las Casas, (1967), p. 259.

[176] The reader may miss the study of other great authors, internationally known, such as Domingo de Soto (*qui scit Sotum, scit totum*), Martín de Azpilcueta (El Navarro), Luis de Molina (apostle of individual freedom) or Diego de Covarrubias (the *Bartolus hispanus*), but this has not been our purpose from the beginning.

[177] In this regard, see, for example, the studies by Beuchot, Beuchot (1999); Beuchot (2000), co-authored with Javier Saldaña; Beuchot (1995); Beuchot (2004).

[178] Mirandola (2006).

[179] "The excellent Artificer, therefore, established that he whom he could endow with nothing of his own, should have in common with all that had been given to him separately from the others. He therefore took man thus constructed, a work of indefinite nature, and having placed him at the center of the world, He spoke to him in this way:

> O Adam, I have given you neither a definite place, nor an aspect of your own, nor a peculiar prerogative in order that you may possess the place, the aspect, and the prerogative which you consciously choose and which in accordance with your intention you obtain and retain. The definite nature of other beings is constrained by the precise laws prescribed by me. You, on the other hand, not constrained by any narrowness, will determine it according to the will to whose power I have consigned you. I have placed thee in the center of the world so that thou mayest observe more comfortably all that exists in it. I have made thee neither celestial nor terrestrial, neither mortal nor immortal, in order that thou, as arbiter and sovereign artificer of thyself, may inform thyself and shape thyself into the work of thy choice. You

expression 'dignity'. In referring to the duty to conduct oneself in accordance with one's [human] dignity, he did not mention that term either.[180]

The fact that medieval authors used less frequently the expression 'dignity' to express natural human dignity does not mean that they were unaware of this notion, much less that they lacked it,[181] because, as the authors of the centuries studied here affirmed, every human being is the bearer of 'inherent' rights that should be the object of respect and protection in the juridical sphere.[182]

Thus, for example, Thomas Aquinas used the expression 'dignity' in various senses ("Dignity means something that is good in itself"),[183] but also to refer to the dignity of every person or human being.[184] For Aquinas, there is a connection between being a person and having dignity: "[t]he person is always a being with dignity."[185] Precisely because it must be "maintained that personality is the name of

---

> may degenerate into the inferior beings that are the beasts; you may regenerate yourself, according to your will, into the superior realities that are divine.

O supreme freedom of God the Father, O supreme and admirable fortune of man to whom it has been granted to obtain what he wishes, to be what he wishes! Beasts, at the very moment of their birth, bring with them from the womb, as Lucilius says, all that they will afterwards possess. The superior spirits, from the beginning, or soon after, were what they will be eternally. To man, from his birth, the Father bestowed germs of every species and germs of every life, and, according as each man has cultivated them, they will mature in him and give him their fruits" (Mirandola 2006, pp. 5–6); for Stuurman (2017), "[a]n incipient notion of common humanity became thinkable when humans began to demarcate themselves from animals, imagining a hierarchy of sentient beings with humans at the apex of the pyramid. By enumerating the attributes that distinguished humans from animals, such as speech, morality and reason, they summed up the faculties all human beings were supposed to share" (Introduction).

[180] "But what is the purpose of all this? Why, that we may understand, since we are born in the condition of being what we will, that it is our duty to take care of all this: that it may not be said of us that, being in so high a degree, we have not realised that we have become like brutes and stupid beasts of labour" (Mirandola 2006, pp. 7–8).

[181] Beuchot (1999), where he deals with human dignity and human rights in Thomas Aquinas (pp. 49–60), Francisco de Vitoria (pp. 61–69), Fray Bartolomé de Las Casas, (pp. 70–79), Fray Alonso de la Vera Cruz (pp. 80–89), Jacques Maritain (pp. 90–98), in the Social Doctrine of the [Catholic] Church (pp. 99–110); in this regard, see also Gonzalo (2016), p. 2446.

[182] The 'inherent' character of human rights constitutes another reason that makes it advisable to historicise the evolution of such rights, as stated by Escudero (2015), pp. 1046–1047: "And if *human rights* are those inherent to the person, and the man of the glebe or the galley oarsman was the bearer in his tribulation of such an egregious moral deposit, it does not seem reasonable to throw into the attic the seventeen centuries prior to the eighteen centuries (with their Declarations) or the eighteen previous ones (with their Constitutions). *Human rights* have been historically recognised or denied in many ways and not only *sub specie* of Declarations and Constitutions. That is why I, who am not a medievalist, call for more attention to the medieval and the ancient world, as did a rather little-known section of German historiography in the 1930s".

[183] Rosen (2012), shows how Thomas Aquinas, for example, uses this expression; according to Aquinas, "Dignity means something that is good in itself".

[184] In this regard, see the study by Carpintero (2016).

[185] Summa Theologica, II-II, q. 63, art. 1: "In nomine enim personae intelligitur personae dignitas" (taken up by Carpintero (2016), p. 104, footnote n. 11).

dignity", he affirmed that "...the dignity of the human nature of Christ is no less than in us."[186] Moreover, the human being becomes more dignified to the extent that he freely follows the end for which he was created.[187]

Other authors of the current—or context of—*ius commune*, contemporaries and prior to Thomas Aquinas, referred to human dignity more or less expressly. Thus, for example, some jurists, such as Bulgarus, "left abundant sentences, especially known because they used to be at the beginning of the commentaries to the Digest and the *Instituta*, in which they maintained that, in accordance with natural law, the slave is always a free man, so that when he is manumitted he is not granted his freedom, but is given it back."[188] Along the same lines, Accursius included in his Magna Glossa—or Glossa Ordinaria, Glossa Magistralis, or Glossa Accursii, 1234/35), the following affirmation: "*Homo est dignissima creaturarum*", aware that every human being possesses this personal quality. This affirmation comes from Irnerius, who, commenting on the term persona in the *Institutes* of Gaius, wrote "*Nam homo est dignissima creaturarum*", relying on Boethius and on various verses of Ovid and Virgil.[189] His disciples followed him in this respect.

2.5 Final Considerations

At this point, we can make the following statements by Carpintero our own:

> Our history has been very paradoxical on this point because when the equal dignity of all men was not recognised, jurists and theologians proposed explanations on the basis of the equal freedom of all, and later, when there was a clamour for this universal respect, anthropological explanations abandoned the theological bases and were not able to find a sufficient basis for this dignity that belongs to all. The researcher has the (moral) certainty that the moderns took the fruits of medieval works without mentioning their origins, or often despising them; but the inertia that came especially from the Jus Commune as well as from the works of the philosopher-theologians we know as the Nominals, led Luis de Molina, Francisco Suárez, Hugo Grotius and Samuel Pufendorf to popularise what others had created. Of course, the secular notion of dignity would not have been possible without the theological foundations that preceded them from centuries before. Only once the term 'dignitas' had been emancipated from one another and had remained a cliché to which

[186] "...the dignity of the human nature of Christ is not less than in us, and that it must be maintained that personality is the name of dignity: *Personalitas autem ad dignitatem pertinet*" ("...natura humana non est minoris dignitatis in Christo quam in nobis. Personalitas autem ad dignitatem pertinet, ut in primo habitum est", Summa Theologica, III, q. 2, art. 2; collected by Carpintero (2016), p. 114, footnote n. 55).

[187] "His most general statement expresses that *Dignitas eorum quae sunt ad finem, praecipue consideratur ex fine*: man's life has an end, which is the contemplation of God, and human dignity is measured from this end" ("Respondeo dicendum quod dignitas eorum quae sunt ad finem, praecipue consideratur ex fine", Summa Theologica, II-II, q. 174, art. 2; collected by Carpintero (2016), p. 111, footnote n. 40).

[188] Carpintero (2016), p. 100.

[189] Moschetti (1969), p. 41 (collected by Carpintero (1981), p. 69, footnote n. 108).

anyone could, in fact, turn, could everyone speak of freedom, dignity and respect. Today we have made no progress in these approaches. . .[190]

An approach to the origins and historical evolution of human dignity in general,[191] and to its notion between the 15th and 18th centuries in particular,[192] reveals how most philosophers and jurists of that period, including Immanuel Kant (1724–1804), defended the existence of a natural or intrinsic dignity—deriving from the same nature or human condition -, different from moral dignity—forged by one's own conduct—.

The expression 'inherent dignity' or 'intrinsic dignity' in many Declarations and international instruments after the Second World War, when referring to human dignity, is in fact linked to the notion of natural human dignity of the authors of the seventeenth and eighteenth centuries, who, as we have seen, frequently used the expression 'dignity of human nature'.

The expressions 'inherent', 'inviolable', 'natural' or 'imprescriptible', taken up by the first modern constitutions when referring to fundamental rights, implicitly included the concept of human dignity, even though none of these early modern constitutional texts included the expression 'human dignity'.

If the notion of human dignity has been present in an implicit way in much of the Western cultural tradition, particularly from the sixteenth century onwards, and in an explicit way from the seventeenth and eighteenth centuries onwards, the following two questions can be asked:

(1) Why did 'natural rights' not serve to respect and protect the dignity of persons until the eighteenth century? The answer has to do with the existence of an absolutist political system in which political power lacked, in practice—and, according to some authors, even in theory—limits.
(2) Later, after the advent of the liberal regime, and with the recognition of 'fundamental rights', why did such rights, conceived in theory by modern Constitutionalism as limits to political power, not prevent the horrors of World War II? In my opinion, this was due to the fragility of 'fundamental rights' that were notably relegated after identifying Law with law, the latter being understood as a mere 'expression of the general will.'[193]

It could be said that, in the nineteenth century, the utilitarianism and legal positivism tides of thought prevailed over the natural law one, leading to a voluntarist conception of Law. It is important not to lose sight of the fact that the rationalist conception of Law, which meant understanding Law as an expression of reason, had to face another radically opposite one, that is, the one that considered Law as an expression of will. Both conceptions converged in the origins of modern

[190] Carpintero (2016), p. 103.

[191] On this subject, see Pelé (2006); Sánchez de Movellán (2014).

[192] On this subject, see my studies, already cited in footnote n. 72.

[193] See the bibliography in footnote n. 22 in Part I.

constitutionalism.[194] History shows how, with the passage of time, the voluntarist conception of Law prevailed over the rationalist one. In fact, legal positivism, the philosophical-political theses of Karl Schmidt and German national socialism (which provoked the Second World War) constitute concrete manifestations of this conception of Law, understood as mere "expression of the popular will" (Rousseau) or mere "mandate of the State" (John Austin). If Law is mere procedure,[195] formality or continent, devoid of any material or substantive requirement, and individuals lack a dignity or rights inherent to human beings, the State ceases to be the 'guarantor' of a reality prior to its very existence, and becomes the 'founder', the 'creator' of human dignity and rights, whose content can change radically if certain 'reasons of State', 'national security' or 'cultural conjuncture' so require.

This is precisely what helps to explain, to a large extent, why, after the Second World War, and despite the theoretical recognition and the express consecration of human dignity in international instruments and national constitutions, such dignity is often, in practice, so little protected.

In my opinion, the triumph of the voluntarist conception of Law not only explains the fragility—and consequent failure—of fundamental rights as a limit to political power in the early days of modern constitutionalism, despite the fact that the constitutional texts themselves enshrined the pre-political nature of rights—with the expressions 'natural', 'inherent' or 'intrinsic'—. The expression 'human dignity' in these texts was not expressly included, being taken for granted, because such rights of a pre-political nature could only be anchored in human nature and its dignity.

After the Second World War, the expression 'human dignity' was used to reinforce the respect and protection of 'human rights' (an expression that underlined their universal, supranational or global character, thus distinguishing them from 'fundamental rights', which until then had been more the preserve of national constitutions). The problem lies in the fact that the rights of individuals are not effectively respected and protected by the mere use—more or less fortunate—of expressions, categories or labels, but rather when those obstacles that prevent understanding the true sense and meaning of the notions or concepts are removed. In other words, those utilitarian and positivist tides, defenders of a voluntarist conception of Law, have led to a postmodernist culture which, in my opinion, is incompatible with a more humane notion of human dignity. It is not humane to reject the universality of human dignity, nor to deny the most vulnerable their dignity as human beings.

If human nature is denied, it is difficult—if not impossible—to defend the natural or inherent dignity of every human being. For those who defend this position, "man

[194] In this regard, see Masferrer (2013b), pp. 277 ff; see also Masferrer and Taitslin (2014).

[195] On the 'proceduralisation' of law as a false alternative, see Ollero (2007), pp. 347–348.

is simply what he does (. . .), there is no human nature at all, only human behaviour." [196] Human dignity is, according to this conception, a mere historical and cultural construction. If there is no natural equality between individuals, egalitarian dignity must be constructed by political power, that is, by the State through laws. There are no laws or rights of pre-political origin. The consequences of this line of thought are that political power only has the limits it wants to impose on itself, and the rights of individuals are neither recognised nor guaranteed, but totally designed and created by the State. [197]

The problem is that enacting laws outside the reality of the human condition—with its basic needs, frailties and vulnerabilities—makes people more fragile and vulnerable. As Heyd points out, "if we have no concept of human nature, can we speak of human rights or human rights that rest on human nature?" [198] As Griffin asserted, once the metaphysical and epistemological context that natural rights entails "is abandoned, as it was in the course of the Enlightenment, what is left? Is what that is left enough?" [199]

Denying the transcendence of the human being and his dignity—as a reality prior to the political and juridical-positive order—, not only makes it difficult to find a solid foundation for human rights and a rigorous definition of human dignity, but also poses serious problems when it comes to establishing limits to the power of the State. Postmodernism began by declaring the death of God in order to free people from moral and other religious and irrational constraints,[200] and ended by

[196] Mitchell (1972), pp. 23–24: "There are, of course, not universally accepted conclusions about human nature. Many scholars, especially since John Locke, are under the impression that the term 'human nature' is a real irony and, in fact, there is no such reality. Like other fictitious inventions, 'human nature' is nothing but a claim, which does not correspond to reality in the material world (. . .). A more modern theory suggests that man is simply what he does. Some are domesticated, some are wild. Some share, others accumulate; some monogamous, others polygamous (. . .). As you see, he goes on to reason, there is no human nature at all, only human behavior. The possibilities are infinite, in terms of the behavior that a given person or a given society can engage in. This view, which I call 'man-as-neutral concept of human nature', is probably the most widely accepted position on human nature in the scientific community of the twentieth century".

[197] On this issue, see Masferrer (2013a), pp. 37 ff., arguing that fundamental rights have a pre-political character, in the sense that their recognition and protection is what justifies the existence of the political order itself.

[198] Heyd (2003), p. 168.

[199] Griffin (2008), p. 14: "Natural law began as part of a teleological metaphysics capable of supporting strong interpretations of how morality is rooted in nature, and which ended at the close of the eighteenth century in something akin to vacuity. Not that the strong, non-vacuous conception of natural law is without its own considerable problems. Still, many scholastic conceptions of natural law gave us at least *something* to decide what natural rights exist. Once the metaphysical and epistemological background they provided is abandoned, as it was in the course of the Enlightenment, what is left, and is there enough left?"; on the enlightened roots of human rights, see Hunt (2007).

[200] Nietzsche (1974), Section 125: "God is dead. God remains dead. And we have killed him. How can we comfort ourselves, the murderers of all murderers? That which was holiest and mightiest of all that the world has yet possessed has bled to death under our knives: who shall cleanse this blood

announcing the death of man. [201] As has been rightly pointed out, "Foucault announces the death of man during the 1960s, and sees no other way than to destroy the 'anthropological' quadrilateral at its very foundation. (...), Foucault speaks of the death of man as a necessary result of the death of God. Man and God belong to each other, the death of the latter is synonymous with the disappearance of the former." [202]

I do not think it is necessary to take things so far as to predict the death of man or the destruction of humanity, but it is undeniable that there is a link between the denial of the inherent or natural dignity of human beings and their rights and the difficult task of setting limits—both in theory and in practice—to political power. Express recognition of natural human dignity is necessary if we are to build a just and peaceful global society whose law respects and protects all people, especially the most vulnerable. This requires a change in the current model, which, "with its emphasis on success and self-sufficiency, does not seem to be conducive to investment in efforts to help the slow, the weak or the less gifted to find opportunities in their lives as well." [203]

If constitutional democracies recognise and protect fundamental rights in the terms set forth in international instruments, aware that their origin (or foundation) is pre-political, as is every human being and his dignity, the threat of the totalitarian State diminishes considerably. We understand that the recognition of the pre-political nature of human dignity and fundamental rights does not resolve the danger of their possible violation, but it contributes significantly to their due protection and safeguarding, especially when they are sought to be violated in the name of a false "public interest" (such as national security) or other interests of a political or economic nature. [204]

Every human life possesses natural dignity and deserves unconditional respect. This is very much the legacy of the sixteenth-, seventeenth- and eighteenth-century notion of human dignity, on whose fidelity depends the dignity of humanity itself and respect for the dignity of each and every human being in it.[205]

---

of ours? What water is there that we may be cleansed? What festivals of atonement, what sacred games shall we invent? Is not the greatness of this act too great for us? Shall we ourselves be no gods simply to appear worthy of it?"

[201] Foucault (1994), pp. 341–342.

[202] Tepe (2014), p. 64.

[203] Pope Francis (2013), n. 209.

[204] In this sense, see, for example, Knox (1821), where the author describes how the political despotism of a state can claim to be justified by being at war; referring to 'natural rights' as 'nonsense', or to 'fundamental rights' as mere creations of the state which it imposes with no other legitimacy than the binding force of the law (understood as a simple mandate of the state), seems to be the best 'legitimation' for violating rights when the state considers them inconvenient for whatever reasons, as recent experience shows; in the fight against terrorism, for example, it is evident that States have gone beyond what can be assumed to be reasonable in the framework of a constitutional democracy; on this point, see the bibliography cited in footnote n. 67.

[205] Some examples of how human dignity has been applied in German and French jurisprudence in recent years can be found in Gonzalo (2016), pp. 2449–2453.

Some Cited Normative Sources and Declarations

Spain

Fueros locales del Reino de León (910–1230). Antología, Madrid: Boletín Oficial del Estado, 2018 (available at https://www.boe.es/biblioteca_juridica/publicacion.php?id=PUB-LH-2018-61).

Leyes políticas españolas fundamentales (1808-1978) (compiled and prologue by E. Tierno Galván). Madrid, Tecnos, 1984.

Las Constituciones de España (compilation and foreword by Jorge Esteban). Madrid, CEPC, 2000.

International

Textos básicos de la Historia constitucional comparada (ed. and prologue by J. Varela Suanzes). Madrid, CEPC, 1998.

Virginia Declaration of Rights (June 12, 1776).

Declaration of Independence of the United States (July 4, 1776)

Constitution of the United States of America (1787).

Declaration of the Rights of Man and of the Citizen (1789)

French Constitution of 1791.

Amendment to the American Constitution (December 15, 1791).

Charter of the United Nations (San Francisco, 26 June 1945).

American Declaration of the Rights and Duties of Man (May 2, 1948).

Universal Declaration of Human Rights (Paris, 10 December 1948).

Protocol No. 13 to the Convention for the Protection of Human Rights and Fundamental Freedoms concerning the abolition of the death penalty in all circumstances (Vilnius, 3 May 2002).

References

Doctrinal and Bibliographical Sources

Adams J (1763) Revolutionary Writings. http://oll.libertyfund.org/titles/592#Adams_0284_82

Adams J (1851) Novanglus, thoughts on government, Defence of the constitution. In: The works of John Adams, vol 4. http://oll.libertyfund.org/titles/2102#Adams_1431-04_591

Adams J (1854a) Letters and State Papers 1799-1811. In: The Works of John Adams, vol 9. http://oll.libertyfund.org/titles/2107#Adams_1431-09_430

Adams J (1854b) Letters and State Papers 1811-1825. In: The Works of John Adams, vol 10. Available at http://oll.libertyfund.org/titles/2127#Adams_1431-10_1058

Álvarez I (2009) Utilitarismo y derechos humanos: la propuesta de John S. Mill. Plaza y Valdés, Madrid

Alzina J-P (2011) Human dignity according to international instruments on human rights. Revista Electrónica de Estudios Internacionales 22:1–24. http://www.reei.org/index.php/revista/num22/notas/human-dignity-according-to-international-instruments-on-human-rights

Andorno R (2012) Bioética y dignidad de la persona. Tecnos, Madrid

Andorno R (2014) Human dignity and human rights. In: Have HAMJ, Gordijn B (eds) Handbook of global bioethics. Springer, Dordrecht, pp 45–57

Arriola J-F (2003) La libertad, la autoridad y el poder en el pensamiento filosófico de José Ortega y Gasset. Universidad Nacional Autónoma de México, México

Austin J (1832) The province of jurisprudence determined. John Murray, London

Baker H (1947) The dignity of man. Harvard University Press, Cambridge

Barak A (2015) Human dignity: the constitutional value and the constitutional right. Cambridge University Press, Cambridge

Bentham J (1789) The principles of morals and legislation

Bentham J (1843) The works of Jeremy Bentham

Beuchot M (1994) Bartolomé de las casas, indigenous humanism and human rights. Anuario Mexicano de Historia del Derecho 6:37–48

Beuchot M (1995) Derechos humanos, iuspositivismo y iusnaturalismo. Universidad Nacional Autónoma de México, México

Beuchot M (1996) El fundamento de los derechos humanos en Bartolomé de las Casas. Revista Portuguesa de Filosofía 52(1/4):87–95

Beuchot M (1999) Derechos humanos, historia y filosofía. Distribuciones Fontamara, México

Beuchot M, Saldaña J (2000) Derechos humanos y naturaleza humana. Universidad Nacional Autónoma de México, México

Beuchot M (2004) Filosofía y derechos humanos. Siglo XXI, México City

Beuchot M (2013) Filosofía y política en Bartolomé de las Casas. San Esteban, México City

Bloch E (1987) Natural law and human dignity (trans: DJ Schmidt). The MIT Press, Cambridge

Bobbio N (1996) The age of rights. Polity Press, London. (reprinted by John Wiley & Sons, 2017)

Brufau J (1997) Juan Ginés de Sepúlvera y su controversia con Bartolomé de las Casas. In: Fartos M (coord) La filosofía española en Castilla y León: de los orígenes al Siglo de Oro, t. 1. Universidad de Valladolid, Valladolid, pp 207–217

Buber M (1956) Yo y tú. Galatea Nueva Visión, Buenos Aires

Buber M (1979) What is man? Fondo de Cultura Económica, México City

Caballero J-L (2012) La cláusula de interpretación conforme y el principio pro persona (art. 1, 2° párrafo, de la Constitución). In: Carbonell M, Salazar P (eds) La reforma constitucional de los derechos humanos. Un nuevo paradigma. UNAM-Ed. Porrúa, México City, pp 103–133

Capps P (2009) Human dignity and the foundations of international law. Hart Publishing, Oxford

Carlyle A-J (1941) Political liberty: a history of the conception of middle ages and modern times. Oxford University Press, Oxford. (I used the Spanish translation entitled *La libertad política*, México City: Fondo de Cultura Económica, 1942)

Carpintero F (1987) La independencia y autonomía del individuo: los orígenes de la persona jurídica. Anuario de Filosofía del Derecho 4:477–522

Carpintero F (2000) Igualdad y simetría: la selección de los derechos. In: Saldaña J (coor) Problemas actuales sobre Derechos humanos. Una propuesta filosófica. UNAM, México, pp 61–90

Carpintero F (2013) La ley natural. Una realidad aun por explicar. UNAM, México City

Carpintero F (2016) La dignidad humana en Tomás de Aquino. Persona y Derecho 74:97–116

Carrillo J-A (1999) Dignidad frente a barbarie. La Declaración Universal de Derechos Humanos, cincuenta años después. Trotta, Madrid

Cartwright J (1777) The legislative rights of the commonalty vindicated; o, Take your choice

Castañeda P (1990) Las doctrinas sobre la coacción y el 'idearium' de Las Casas. In: Catañeda P, García A (eds) "De unico vocationis modo", en Obras completas de Fray Bartolomé de las Casas. Alianza Editorial, Madrid, pp XVII–XLII

Cattaneo M-A (1981) Dignità umana e pena nella filosofia di Kant. Giuffrè, Milan
Cattaneo M-A (2002) Dignità unama e pace perpetua: Kant e la critica della política. CEDAM, Milan
Clavero B (1986) Evolución histórica del Constitucionalismo español, 2nd edn. Tecnos, Madrid
Clavero B (1989) Manual de historia constitucional de España. Alianza Editorial, Madrid
D'Agostino F (2000) Los derechos y deberes del hombre. In: Saldaña J (coord.), Problemas actuales sobre Derechos humanos. Una propuesta filosófica. UNAM, México, pp 91–106
de Vitoria F (1967) Relectio de Indis. Consejo Superior de Investigaciones Científicas, Madrid
Díaz E (1977) Libertad-igualdad en la Declaración de Derechos del Hombre y del Ciudadano de 1789. In: Filosofía y Derecho. Studies in honour of professor José Corts Grau, vol I. University of Valencia, Valencia
Díaz J (2008) El principio de la dignidad humana y su repercusión en la Constitución de los Estados Unidos Mexicanos. Conferencia magistral del Primer Congreso Internacional sobre Justicia Constitucional y Quinto Encuentro Iberoamericano de Derecho procesal constitucional, May 16. UNAM, México, pp 189–205. https://www.yumpu.com/es/document/view/14719494/diaz-romero-juan-quotel-principio-de-la-dignidad-humana-y-su-
Escudero J-A (2015) Sobre los derechos humanos. In: Hermida C, Santos J-A (coords), Una filosofía del Derecho en acción. Homenaje al profesor Andrés Ollero. Congreso de los Diputados-Universidad Rey Juan Carlos, Madrid, pp 1045–1050
Fernández F (1995) La dignidad de la Persona en el ordenamiento constitucional español. Revista Vasca de Administración Pública 43:49–80
Finnis J (1980) Natural law and natural rights. Oxford University Press, Oxford
Fletcher G-P (1984) Human dignity as a constitutional value. U W Ontario L Rev 171:171–182
Foucault M (1994) The order of things. An archaeology of the human sciences. Vintage Books, New York
Galindo J-A (2016) Los derechos naturales del hombre. Su disponibilidad y la Tesis por contradicción 293/2011. In: XV Congreso Nacional de Abogados de la Barra Mexicana. A cien años de la Constitución de 1917. Ed. Themos, México City, pp 899–952
Gallego G-M (2005) Sobre el concepto y fundamento de la dignidad humana. In: Velásquez F (coord), Derecho penal liberal y dignidad humana. Libro homenaje al doctor Hernando Londoño Jiménez. Editorial Temis, Bogotá, pp 245–271
García A (2008) La Dignidad Humana: Núcleo Duro de los Derechos Humanos. Ius Revista Jurídica 28
Gómez Y (2005) Dignity and the legal order. Rev Eur Constitutional Law (ReDCE) 4:219–254
Gonzalo I (2016) La Dignidad como Valor y como Derecho en la Perspectiva Constitucional. In: XV Congreso Nacional de Abogados de la Barra Mexicana. A cien años de la Constitución de 1917. Ed. Themis, México City, pp 2441–2455
Gordon T (1743) The independent Whig, 7th edn, vol 2. http://oll.libertyfund.org/titles/2382#Gordon_1563-02_299
Goti J (1999) Del Tratado de Tordesillas a la doctrina de los derechos fundamentales en Francisco de Vitoria. Universidad de Valladolid, Valladolid
Griffin J (2008) On human rights. Oxford University Press, Oxford
Griffin M (1991) Seneca. A philosopher in politics. Oxford University Press, Oxford
Gros H (1995) La Declaración Americana. Raíces conceptuales y políticas en la historia, la filosofía y el derecho americano. In: Gros H (ed) Derechos humanos y vida internacional. UNAM / CNDH, México
Grotius H (1625) The rights of war and peace, 1901 edition. Paris
Haakonsen K (2006) German natural law. In: Goldie M, Wokler R (eds) Cambridge history of eighteenth-century political thought. Cambridge University Press, Cambridge, pp 251–290
Hanke L (1970) Aristotle and the American Indian. A study of race prejudice in the modern world. University of Indiana Press, Bloomington/London
Helmholz R-H (2005) Natural law and human rights in English law: from Bracton to Blackstone. Ave Maria L Review 1:1–22

Helmholz R-H (2010) Human rights in the canon law. In: Witte J, Alexander F-S (eds) Christianity and human rights: an introduction. Cambridge University Press, Cambridge, pp 99–112
Home H (1762) Dignity and grace. In: Home H (ed) Elements of criticism. http://oll.libertyfund.org/titles/1430#Home_1252-01_641
Heyd D (2003) Human nature: an oxymoron. J Med Philos 28(2):69–151
Hidalgo J-D (2016) Problemáticas procesales. Estudio, análisis y soluciones al Código nacional de procedimientos penales. 206 cuestiones con respuestas. Editorial Flores, México City
Holmes O-W (1881) The common law. Macmillan & Co., London
Justenhoven H-G (1991) Francisco de Vitoria zu Krieg und Frieden. Bachem, Köln
Justenhoven H-G (2011) Las raíces teológicas del Derecho internacional según Francisco de Vitoria. In: Cruz J (ed) Razón práctica y Derecho. Cuestiones filosófico-jurídicas en el Siglo de Oro español. EUNSA, Pamplona, pp 87–98
Kant I (1764) Observations on the Feeling of the Beautiful and Sublime -Beobachtungen über das Gefühl des Schönen und Erhabenen
Kant I (1781) Critique of Pure Reason -Kritik der reinen Vernunft, 2nd ed.
Kant I (1785) Groundwork of the metaphysics of morals -Grundlegung zur Metaphysik der Sitten
Kant I (1788) Critique of practical reason -Kritik der praktischen Vernunft
Kant I (1797) Metaphysics of morals -Metaphysik der Sitten. Meiner, Hamburg
Kant I (1796) The metaphysics of ethics
Knox V (1821) The spirit of despotism, 2nd edn. William Hone, London
Lauren P-G (2003) Philosophical visions: human nature, natural law, and natural rights. In: Lauren P-G (ED) The evolution of international human rights: Visions Seen. University of Pennsylvania Press, Philadelphia
López Guerra R (2003) Afirmar a la persona por sí misma. La dignidad como fundamento de los derechos de la persona. Comisión Nacional de los Derechos Humanos, México City
López Sánchez R (2009) El tardío desarrollo de la dignidad humana y libre desarrollo a la personalidad en el Estado constitucional mexicano. Derecho en Libertad. Revista del Centro de Investigaciones Jurídicas de la Facultad Libre de Derecho de Monterrey 3:127–151
Maritain J (1949) Los derechos del hombre. Estudios y comentarios en torno a la Nueva Declaración de los Derechos del hombre. Fondo de Cultura Económica-UNESCO, México City
Masferrer A (ed) (2011a) Estado de Derecho y derechos fundamentales en la lucha contra el terrorismo. Una aproximación multidisciplinar (histórica, jurídico-comparada, filosófica y económica). Thomson-Aranzadi, Cizur
Masferrer A (2011b) Legislación anti-terrorista, Estado de Derecho y Derechos fundamentales: una aproximación a los límites del Estado en el constitucionalismo moderno. In: Masferrer A (ed) Estado de Derecho y derechos fundamentales en la lucha contra el terrorismo. Una aproximación multidisciplinar (histórica, jurídico-comparada, filosófica y económica). Thomson-Aranzadi, Cizur, pp 191
Masferrer A (ed) (2012) Post 9/11 and the state of permanent legal emergency: security and human rights in countering terrorism. Springer, Dordrecht
Masferrer A (2013a) The fragility of fundamental rights in the origins of modern constitutionalism: its negative impact in protecting human rights in the 'war on terror' era. In: Masferrer A, Walker C (eds) Counter-terrorism, human rights and the rule of law. Edward Elgar Publishing, London, p 37 ff
Masferrer A (2013b) The 'Fundamental Rights' – 'national sovereignty' antinomy in the origins of modern constitutionalism. GLOSSAE European Journal of Legal History 10:277–302
Masferrer A (2016) Taking human dignity more humanely: a historical contribution to the ethical foundations of the constitutional democracy. In: Masferrer A, García-Sánchez E (eds) Human dignity of the vulnerable in the age of rights: interdisciplinary perspectives. Springer, Dordrecht, pp 221–256
Masferrer A, García-Sánchez E (2016) Vulnerability and human dignity in the age of rights. In: Masferrer A, García-Sánchez E (eds) Human dignity of the vulnerable in the age of rights: interdisciplinary perspectives. Springer, Dordrecht, pp 1–25

Masferrer A, Obarrio J-A (2012) The state power and the limits of the principle of sovereignty: an historical approach. In: Masferrer A (ed) Post 9/11 and the state of permanent legal emergency. Springer, Dordrecht, pp 15–51
Masferrer A, Obarrio J-A (2014) El principio de soberanía: una aproximación histórica a sus límites. In: Historia y Derecho. Studies dedicated to Professor Santos coronas, vol 2. KRK Ediciones- University of Oviedo, pp 987–1010
Masferrer A, Taitslin A (2014) The ill-fated union: constitutional entrenchment of rights and the will theory from Rousseau to Waldron. In: Hickey J-E, Silkenat J-R (eds) The legal doctrines of the rule of law and the legal state (Rechtsstaat). Springer, Dordrecht, pp 105–128
Masferrer A, Walker C (eds) (2013) Counter-terrorism, human rights and the rule of law: crossing legal boundaries in defence of the state. Edward Elgar Publishing, London
Matz U (1968) Vitoria. In: Maier H, Denzer H (eds) Klassiker des politischen Denkens. Beck, München
Mieth C (2014) The double foundation of human rights in human nature. In: Albers M, Hoffman T, Reinhardt J (eds) Human rights and human nature. Springer, Dordrecht-Heidelberg-London-New York
Mirandola GP d (2006) Discurso sobre la dignidad del hombre (1486). Editorial π, Medellín (Colombia). http://editorialpi.net/ensayos/discursosobreladignidaddelhombre.pdf
Mitchell J-J (1972) Why study human nature. In: Mitchell J-J (ed) Human nature: theories, conjectures, and descriptions. The Scarecrow Press, Metuchen, pp 23–24
Mora C-B (2013) Los derechos humanos en Francisco de Vitoria. En-claves del pensamiento, Vol. 7, n° 14: 35–62
Morsink J (1999) The universal declaration of human rights. Origins, drafting and intent. University of Pennsylvania Press, Philadelphia
Morsink J (2004) The universal declaration of human rights as a norm for societies in transition. In: Horowitz S, Schnabel A (eds) Human rights and societies in transition. Causes, consequences, responses. United Nations University Press, Tokyo, pp 29–51
Morsink J (2009) Inherent human rights. Philosophical Roots of the Universal Declaration. University of Pennsylvania Press, Philadelphia
Moschetti G (1969) Eticità nella glossa di Accursio sotto l'aspetto della libertà dell'uomo. Studia et documenta historiae et iuris 35:23–50
Moyn S (2014) The secret history of constitutional history. Yale Human Rights and Development Journal 17.1: article 2
Nietzsche F (1974) The gay science: with a prelude in rhymes and an appendix of songs. Vintage Books, New York
Nussbaum M-C (2006) Frontiers of justice: disability, nationality, species membership. Harvard University Press, Cambridge
Ocaña M (1996) El hombre y sus derechos en Francisco de Vitoria. Pedagógicas, Madrid
Ollero A (2007) Derechos humanos. Entre la moral y el Derecho. UNAM, México City
Ortega y Gasset J (1987) Obras completas. Alianza y Revista de Occidente, Madrid
Pelé A (2006) Filosofía e historia en el fundamento de la dignidad humana. Instituto de Derechos Humanos 'Bartolomé de las Casas'. Getafe. http://e-archivo.uc3m.es/bitstream/handle/10016/3052/Tesis_Pele.pdf?sequence=7
Pereña L (1992) La idea de justicia en la conquista de América. Mapfre, Madrid
Pope Francis (2013) Evangelii gaudium, November 24th
Posner R (2010) Economic analysis of law, 8th edn. Little, Brown and Company, Boston
von Pufendorf S (1931) Two books of the elements of universal jurisprudence. Clarendon Press, Oxford (also available at http://oll.libertyfund.org/titles/pufendorf-two-books-of-the-elements-of-universal-jurisprudence)
Reinhardt J (2014) Human rights, human nature, and the feasibility issue. In: Albers M, Hoffman T, Reinhardt J (eds) Human rights and human nature. Springer, Dordrecht, pp 137–158
Rosen M (2012) Dignity: its history and meaning. Harvard University Press, Cambridge

Saastamoinen K (2010) Pufendorf on natural equality, human dignity and self-esteem. J Hist Ideas 71:39 ff

Saldaña J (2006) La dignidad de la persona. Fundamento del derecho a no ser discriminado injustamente. In: Torre C de la (coord), Derecho a la no discriminación. UNAM-CONAPRED-CDHDF, México, pp 57–80. http://ru.juridicas.unam.mx/xmlui/handle/123456789/26854

Saltalamacchia Ziccardi N, Covarrubias Velasco A (2012) La dimensión internacional de la reforma de los derechos humanos: antecedentes históricos. La reforma constitucional de los derechos humanos. Un nuevo paradigma. UNAM-Ed. Porrúa, México City, pp 1–38

Sánchez de Movellán I (2014) La dignidad humana como base de los derechos humanos fundamentales: de los escritos de teólogos-juristas del s. XVI a la Carta de Derechos Fundamentales de la Unión Europea. In: Goizueta J, Cienfuegos M (dirs), La Eficacia de los Derechos fundamentales de la UE. Advanced Issues. Aranzadi-Thomson Reuters, Pamplona, pp 593–611

Saucedo J-I (2013) Implicaciones filosóficas de las resoluciones de la Corte Interamericana de Derechos Humanos. AAPAUNAM, Academia, Ciencia y Cultura, p 4

Savignano A (2011) Diálogo intercultural y derechos humanos. El debate entre Sepúlveda, Vitoria y Las Casas. In: Juan Cruz Cruz (ed) Razón práctica y Derecho. Cuestiones filosófico-jurídicas en el Siglo de Oro español. EUNSA, Pamplona, pp 99–115

Seneca L-A (1989) Carta LXXXVIII. In: Seneca L-A (ed) Cartas Morales a Lucilio. Planeta, Barcelona, p 270-ff

Shell S-M (2003) Kant on human dignity. In: Kraynak R-P, Tinder G (eds) In defense of human dignity. University of Notre Dame Press, Indiana

Sieyès E (1988) What is the third estate? Available at https://revolution.chnm.org/d/280

Singer P (1993) Practical ethics. Cambridge University Press, Cambridge

Soberanes J-L (2009) Sobre el origen de las declaraciones de derechos humanos. UNAM, Instituto de Investigaciones Jurídicas / Comisión Nacional de los Derechos Humanos, México

Starck C (2005) Introducción a la dignidad humana en el Derecho alemán. Anuario Iberoamericano de Justicia Constitucional 9:489–497

Starck C (2002) The religious and philosophical background of human dignity and its place in modern constitutions. In: Kretzmer D, Klein E (eds) The concept of human dignity in human rights discourse. Brill, Leiden, pp 179–193

Stetson B (1998) Human dignity: rhetoric versus reality. In: Stetson B, human dignity and contemporary liberalism. Praeger, Westport, pp 3–42

Tepe H (2014) Rethinking human nature as a basis for human rights. In: Albers M, Hoffman T, Reinhardt J (eds) Human rights and human nature. Springer, Dordrecht, pp 57–77

Thornhill C (2013) Natural law, state formation and the foundations of social theory. J Class Sociol 13(2):197–221

Tierney B (2008) Natural law and natural rights. In: Witte J, Alexander FS (eds) Christianity and law: an introduction. Cambridge University Press, Cambridge, pp 89–103

von Mises L (1944) Omnipotent Government: the rise of the total state and total war. http://oll.libertyfund.org/titles/2399#Mises_OmnipotentGovt1579_873-874

von Pufendorf S (1762 & 1759) De jure naturae et Gentium. Francofurti – Lipsiae

de la Torre C (2006) El Derecho a la no discriminación en México. Ed. Porrúa-Comisión Nacional de los Derechos Humanos, México City

Welzel H (1971) Introducción a la Filosofía del Derecho. Aguilar, Madrid

Wojtyla K (1998) ¿Participación o alienación? In: El hombre y su destino, Palabra, Madrid

Chapter 3
Looking Forwards to the Future of Dignity and Human Rights: New Generation Rights

3.1 'New Generation Rights'? What 'Generation' (Third, Fourth, Fifth, Sixth, etc.)?

With this chapter as an epilogue, after having presented the formation of human dignity and human rights in a retrospective manner, starting from the present and moving towards the increasingly remote past, I intend to return again to the present, and in its most recent moment, analysing the rights of the new generation. In this way, the reader will be able to become aware of the danger that human rights run today, of the historical roots of some of their great problems, as well as of the historical references or models that the legislator should take into account in order to stop their current process of trivialisation.

To affirm that Law—including current Law—is a historical reality, or is essentially historical, does not mean defending that Law is a merely historical product, as did the German Historical School of Law (nineteenth century). According to this school, in Law everything can change, everything is ephemeral or circumstantial, and there is nothing that remains outside of dynamism, nothing is permanent.

Those who sustain this thesis need to prove why the Law of different traditions, civilisations and epochs has so many common aspects. The fact that man is in constant progress, just as Law is in permanent development, does not mean that man has ceased to be human and that Law, consequently, can cease to be the reflection—more or less faithful—of the human being, the inescapable framework and reference of Law and rights.

If Law in general has its history, human rights in particular also have theirs. Accepting the existence of natural rights—as Bartolomé de las Casas, Vitoria, Suárez, Grotius, Locke, Pufendorf and so many others did—does not mean denying or undervaluing the historical context in which the recognition and protection of such rights became a reality. To affirm that the recognition of human rights is the result of a historical process does not mean to maintain that their origin and

A. Masferrer, *The Making of Dignity and Human Rights in the Western Tradition*, Studies in the History of Law and Justice 29,
https://doi.org/10.1007/978-3-031-46667-0_3

foundation are historical. To defend the contrary would be to erect history as a source of legitimacy for law and rights, as if history were the source of morality on which to base social peace and justice. Experience shows the opposite. Not every historical episode constitutes a model of morality that can serve as a reference for universalisable human conduct that promotes just and peaceful societies.

In fact, the history of human rights shows this reality. The recognition of certain rights has been, on many occasions, the response to morally unsustainable social situations. Untenable was the treatment of the indigenous people in America by some colonists (sixteenth century); untenable were the abuses of religious freedom and the consequent wars of religion (sixteenth and seventeenth centuries); untenable was the omnipotent power of absolute monarchies (eighteenth to nineteenth centuries); untenable were the conditions of the majority of workers the undignified treatment of women, children, unemployed, sick or disabled people (nineteenth to twentieth centuries); unsustainable is the global dualism that exists today, where some live in the most complete opulence at the expense of many others who lack the essentials to live with a minimum of dignity (drinking water, food, housing, education, communication, etc.), while the rest contemplate—or even justify—the two world wars (twentieth century). It is unsustainable that a part of the world leads a consumerist and hedonistic life, justifying the trampling of the rights of the defenceless, of the most vulnerable beings,[1] of those who cannot fend for themselves, or of those who when they come will no longer be able to enjoy the world and the environment that we enjoy today.

If human rights can be defined as "a core of morality based on the idea of human dignity,"[2] it is clear that the referent or foundation of human rights is not history—especially when history itself does not show the convenience of giving a charter of nature to everything that happens in time—, but human dignity—or the 'dignity of human nature', as the authors of the seventeenth and eighteenth centuries used to say[3]—, despite the fact that these always arise as an achievement in a precise historical context. History is essential to explain the emergence and evolution of human rights, but they transcend history; hence history cannot give an explanation of their origin and foundation, nor, on many occasions, of their content and scope.

The expression 'new generation rights' is as cautious as it is ambiguous. It is cautious because it avoids saying what generation it is talking about, and is content to use the cautious formula 'new generation'. For some it would be the rights of the third generation, for others of the fourth, for others of the fifth, for others of the sixth, and so on. And not all those who agree on the same generation are talking about the same rights. Let's take an example. For some, the fourth generation refers to solidarity rights; and this is so because, according to them, the rights of the first generation are composed only by civil rights—not including political rights—; those of the second generation by political rights; those of the third generation by

[1] Masferrer and García-Sánchez (2016).

[2] Peces-Barba (2004), p. 148.

[3] Masferrer (2016).

economic, social and cultural rights); and those of the fourth generation by solidarity rights.[4] However, according to others, the fourth generation would affect only a part of cultural rights, that is, rights related to ICTs and cyberspace:

> The development of the fourth generation of human rights is intrinsically linked to the empowerment of citizens to enjoy the possibilities of personal fulfilment that ICTs bring. Today, being digitally excluded means being socially excluded. As information is wealth, the lack of access to ICTs, or the lack of knowledge of their use, becomes a fundamental factor of social discrimination, a new gap that divides rich and poor. This creates the categories of *info-rich* and *info-poor*.[5]

For others, the fourth generation refers rather to "rights linked to technological progress, which mainly concern issues related to bioethics—euthanasia, abortion, etc.—and genetic treatments."[6]

For Pérez Luño it is preferable not to use the expressions "new rights", "solidarity rights", "rights of the technological era", "rights of the global society", as well as "fourth, fifth, etc. generation rights", because all these rights are part of the "third generation rights."[7]

As can be seen, there is no consensus on the content of each of the generations. The expression 'generation' is currently confusing. Perhaps for this reason, some authors prefer to avoid it, and resort to the expression 'new rights',[8] although this is not free of problems either. Even so, an important part of the doctrine continues to use it, sometimes without specifying which generation is being referred to.[9] The title of this chapter is a good example of this.

The expressions 'new [rights]' or 'new generation' [of rights] pose problems similar to those that have arisen with the terms 'modern', 'modernity', 'modern age' (to distinguish it from the medieval), or 'contemporary age' (to distinguish it from the modern). They may be more or less useful when coined at a specific historical moment, but with the passage of time—which is unforgiving—they end up becoming anachronistic, generating considerable confusion and ambiguity.

---

[4]In this regard, see, for example, the position of Gómez (2008); in this regard, the sections of Chapter 2 are eloquent: 3. 3.1. The Liberal State of Law: the first and second generations of rights. 3.2. The social State: the third generation. 3.3. The social State: the fourth generation of rights; Peces-Barba (1991), pp. 156 ff; Martínez de Pisón (1997), p. 157, footnote n. 117: "Those who consider that there are four generations divide the first generation of rights into the first and the second. Those who consider that there are four generations divide the first generation into two, so that the temporal succession would be as follows: first, civil rights that would reflect liberal freedom; the second, composed of political rights based on democratic freedom; the third, articulated around social rights and reflecting the concept of egalitarian freedom or socialist freedom and, finally, the fourth generation composed of the last rights inspired by the synthesis between egalitarian freedom and the value of solidarity"; see also Vidal (1993), pp. 89–110.

[5]Bustamante (2007), p. 17; in this regard, see also Morello (1998), pp. 943–951; Bustamante (2001a, b); Riofrío (2014): see also Peces-Barba (2004).

[6]Martínez de Pisón (1997), p. 157.

[7]Pérez Luño (1997); by the same author, Pérez Luño (1995); see also Pérez Luño (2006).

[8]Squella (2002), Corchete (2007), Bustamante (2007).

[9]See, for example, Rodríguez (2010).

In the case of the expression 'generation', used to explain the evolution of human rights, the ambiguity is rooted in its very origin. The term 'generation' is a metaphorical expression whose simplicity and apparent rigour have enabled it to gain currency not only in the field of education—there is not a single textbook that does not use it—but also in historiography. This way of explaining and classifying human rights chronologically is presented as something indisputable and unquestionable, often ignoring not only their origin but also the assumptions and problems they raise.[10]

The recourse to this expression arose in the 1960s, when the search was on for a way to regulate—and name—the 'right to development' or, if one prefers, the rights referred to with the original notion of the third generation. This is how Rabossi explains it:

> The discussions lasted more than a decade and included other themes: peace, the environment, the common heritage of humanity, the self-determination of peoples. As in the case of development, there was an insistence on considering them not only as rights, but as human rights. The need thus arose to justify this expansion of the extensive list already set out in international declarations and conventions. It was then argued that this was not an arbitrary creation, but one more stage in the historical process initiated at the end of the 18th century, with the consecration of civil and political rights, and continued in the 20th century, with the establishment of economic, social and cultural rights.[11]

Karel Vasak, Director of UNESCO's Legal Department, was the one who formally put forward the thesis in 1977. He defended it in an article published in the *Unesco Courier*:

> The rights set forth in the Universal Declaration fall into two categories: civil and political rights, on the one hand, and economic, social and cultural rights, on the other. The question arises as to whether the recent evolution of human societies does not call for the development of a third category of human rights, which the Director-General of UNESCO has described as 'third-generation human rights'. Whereas first-generation rights (civil and political) are based on the right to oppose the State and second-generation rights (economic, social and cultural) on the right to make demands on the State, the third-generation human rights now being proposed to the international community are the rights of solidarity.[12]

A few years later, Vasak himself would be in charge of developing and polishing the contours of this theory.[13] A theory that, as has been said, would end up imposing itself, becoming topical and a *cliché*. The topical cliché reads as follows:

> Human rights have come in three generations: the first encompassed civil and political human rights (late 18th and 19th century); the second, economic, social and cultural human rights (20th century); the third encompasses human rights of solidarity (recent years).[14]

---

[10] In this regard, see, for example, the study by Rabossi (1997–1998), pp. 42: "La sencillez y obviedad que aparece tener la tesis de las generaciones de derechos humanos hace que se pasen por alto por su presuposiciones e implicaciones teóricas y prácticas".

[11] Rabossi (1997–1998), pp. 42–43.

[12] Vasak (1977), p. 29.

[13] Vasak (1984).

[14] Rabossi (1997–1998), p. 42.

3.2 The New Rights: Characteristics and Typology

The use of 'generations' to explain the history of human rights from the eighteenth century to thc present day has become established in the doctrine, as shown by part of the historiography.[15]

It would be reiterative to deal here with the so-called first-and-second- generation rights since they have already been the object of study in the second part—in its second and third sections—of this study. We will therefore deal only with the so-called "new rights" or "new generation rights" which, as we have just seen, are the ones that led to the unfortunate chronological classification of rights into generations. As we have seen, although this way of explaining the history of human rights has prevailed, it has also plunged the doctrine into such a notable disparity of opinions that there is no longer any consensus on the rights affected by the different generations of rights, and in particular from the third generation onwards. While some authors speak of only three generations, others speak of four, five or even six different generations of rights. This, as will be seen later, has eroded and deteriorated the very notion of human rights.

Before listing the various 'new' or 'new generation' rights, it is useful to present, in a succinct manner, the characteristic features of these rights. It is true that the historical context in which these rights emerged helps to explain, to a large extent, their general physiognomy. But it is no less true that the disparity of some rights, as well as the great transformations that Western society has undergone in the last half century, makes it difficult to present a homogeneous picture that characterises all these rights.[16] This perhaps explains why some authors prefer not to speak only of a third (or fourth) generation, and add other supposed generations whose rights would have little to do with those of the third generation that emerged in the sixties and seventies of the last century.

I too will first deal with the human rights that emerged in the two decades mentioned above, and then add other rights whose emergence or vindication came later.

A brief presentation of the previous two generations may facilitate the understanding of the added value of third or new generation rights.

As is well known, **the first generation rights**—civil and political rights[17]—, have their roots in the late eighteenth century, in the context of American Independence and the French Revolution. These rights sought to guarantee the freedom of individuals. This required placing limits on the power of the State, safeguarding a

---

[15] In this regard, see, for example, Pérez Luño (1998); Pérez Luño (2013), Pérez Luño (2007).

[16] Martínez de Pisón (1997), p. 178: "All this anticipates a different world with unknown pretensions and thus justifies this *very varied category of rights in which demands with such different presuppositions are included*"; the italics are mine.

[17] Civil rights include the rights to life, property, ideological and religious freedom, and freedom of expression, among others. Among the political rights, the rights to vote, to strike, to associate freely to form a political party or a trade union, etc., are noteworthy.

person's private sphere, as well as guaranteeing the citizen's participation in public affairs.

If freedom was the fundamental value of first-generation rights, equality was the fundamental value of **second-generation rights**, affecting economic, social and cultural rights. Their recognition and protection were the result of a process that went from the end of the nineteenth century to the second half of the twentieth century. Equality being—as aforementioned—its *leitmotif*, the State is required to promote access for all to minimum living conditions, for which it is necessary to guarantee the exercise of some rights (to education, health, work, decent housing, etc.).

As opposed to the 'freedom' value of first generation rights (civil and political) and the 'equality' value of second generation rights (economic, social and cultural), **third generation rights emphasise** 'solidarity' (or, if one prefers, 'fraternity'),[18] They emerged—as has been said—in the sixties of the last century, are still in full development,[19] and aim to foster solidarity among peoples and individuals around the world. They seek to promote peaceful and constructive relations that allow us to face the new challenges facing humanity. The list of rights that make up this generation "is far from being a closed, precise and clear-cut list. It is, rather, a frame of reference, still *in fieri*, of the most pressing current demands affecting the rights and freedoms of the person."[20] They deal with topics oriented towards the protection of collective interests of a planetary nature.

Third generation rights include self-determination, economic and political independence, national and cultural identity, peace, political coexistence, international and regional cooperation, international justice, the use of advances in science and technology, the solution of food, demographic, educational and ecological problems, the environment, the common heritage of mankind, and development that allows a dignified life. Let us see the enumeration that Pérez Luño makes of them:

> The rights relating to the environment, quality of life, peace, freedom of information, cyber-citizenship, or guarantees in the biotechnological sphere are not the only rights that make up the third generation, although they are perhaps the most representative and consolidated. Along with them, other rights of very heterogeneous significance are also postulated, such as: the right to development, the rights of consumers and users, the right to the enjoyment of historical-artistic heritage, gender claims, as well as the different powers and claims included in the postulation of the so-called 'emerging rights.'[21]

Let's look at a simple comparative Table 3.1 of the three generations of rights[22]:

---

[18] In this connection, it should be recalled that Article 1 of the *Universal Declaration of Human Rights* provides for the desirability of "behaving towards one another in a spirit of brotherhood".

[19] Pérez Luño (2013), pp. 175–176.

[20] Pérez Luño (2013), pp. 175–176.

[21] Pérez Luño (2013), p. 175.

[22] See http://recursostic.educacion.es/secundaria/edad/4esoetica/quincena5/quincena5_contenidos_5.htm (Accessed August 14, 2020).

Table 3.1 Simple comparative of the three generations of rights

Generation of rights	Time of acceptance	Duty rate	Value they stand for	Main function	Examples
First	eighteenth and nineteenth centuries	Civil and political	FREEDOM	To limit the action of power. To guarantee the political participation of citizens.	Civil rights: Right to life, liberty, security, property... Political rights: Right to vote, association, strike...
Second	nineteenth and twentieth centuries	Economic, social and cultural rights	EQUALITY	Ensuring decent living conditions for everyone	Right to health, to education, to work, to decent housing?
Third	twentieth and twenty-first centuries	Justice, peace and solidarity	SOLIDARITY	Promoting peaceful and constructive relations	Right to a clean environment, to peace, to development...

It is not easy to define the characteristic features of third generation rights. Perhaps because they are not all common, nor do all their purported rights seem to reflect a common *leitmotif.* It has been said, and rightly so, that this generation is 'complementary' to the two previous ones, and that it arises as a response to a phenomenon called '*liberties' pollution*', "a term with which some sectors of Anglo-Saxon social theory allude to the erosion and degradation that afflicts fundamental rights in the face of certain uses of new technologies."[23]

Although such a 'contamination of freedoms' is somewhat reductionist—especially when it would only affect the field of new technologies—, it seems clear that third generation rights are a response to a new reality that takes place in a different historical—social, economic, cultural and technological—context. Their origin is to be found "in the new needs and interests emerging in society and in international life at the end of the twnetieth century, in the new movements that demand other forms of organisation (...). In general terms, they are rights that refer to new social demands that are bursting onto the political scene and that are characterised by their plurality, by their reference to fraternity, solidarity, environment, social justice, justice between generations."[24]

A characteristic aspect of this generation of rights is their connection to the 'technological revolution'—also called the 'knowledge revolution' or the 'third

[23] Pérez Luño (2013), p. 168; Pérez Luño (1998), p. 1958.

[24] Martínez de Pisón (1997), p. 177.

industrial revolution'—closely related to the ongoing process of globalisation, which has made the world a 'common home' for all.[25]

The note of globality is particularly relevant for two reasons. Firstly, because the most relevant fields of third-generation rights are global in scope: peace; peaceful coexistence between countries, peoples and individuals; self-determination of peoples; development; the cultural heritage of humanity; the environment or quality of life; freedom of information technology; and so on. Secondly, because these rights of global scope or dimension—no longer governing relations between citizens of a State or between States and their citizens, but between States themselves—"connect [s] with the ideal of universality that is at the root of rights."[26]

Another feature is its critical stance towards the prevailing financial capitalism, the consequences of which are contrary to the 'rights of solidarity' which are intended to bring about a new social sensitivity, mutual aid and help. It is about establishing fraternity as the basis of a new political and legal culture, in order to prevent situations of degradation of people, of workers, of the most vulnerable. It is a response to situations of injustice and social degradation. It has been rightly affirmed that its primary objective consists in "preventing the order from becoming an instrument of domination through which to legitimise situations of social inequality and tyranny of one group over others; its realisation, therefore, goes hand in hand with a democratic deepening that questions the economic, social and political structures on which economic development in the western world was based, calling for their transformation."[27]

One of the most complex aspects of the new generation of rights is the question of who is or who are the holder(s) of these rights. Indeed, it is not easy to know who is the holder of, for example, a right to peace or a right to development: an individual person? a people? a State? a group? a collectivity? The answer is not simple. And the fact is that third generation rights, having expanded their ownership so much, include all human beings on the planet because peace, the environment, development, etc., involve all of humanity, all the citizens of the world. These rights "must have, therefore, a dimension that is not limited to groups or sectors as in the second generation, but are universal rights, in which there is no room for establishing watertight compartments, no room for establishing distinctions, because as soon as these distinctions and watertight compartments arise, the struggle for these rights is lost in advance."[28]

Indeed, there is no doubt that issues such as the environment, peace and poverty, to give three examples, affect everyone:

---

[25] In this regard, the title of Pope Francis' latest encyclical letter, *Laudato Si': On Care for the Common Home* [Pope Francis (2015)] is eloquent; see, in particular, ch. 1: 'What is happening to our home'.

[26] Rey (2011), p. 106.

[27] Rey (2011), p. 106; the italics are mine; in this regard, see Rodríguez (2010), p. 307, who points out that these rights "are aimed at overcoming relations of domination in the internal sphere of States and in international relations."

[28] Pérez Luño (1995), p. 116; Martínez de Pisón (1997), p. 179.

> . . . the deterioration of the environment, for example, affects everyone: it cannot be said that some States recognise it and others do not, because the damage that the latter can do to this good harms everyone. The same is true of peace: situations of war not only cause damage and tension to the disputants, but also permeate the entire planet. (. . .) Instability or poverty in one area of the planet, the deterioration of the ozone layer, pollution, erosion and loss of trees affects everyone. In a world without barriers, what happens in one point on the map spreads, sooner or later, its effects to the rest.[29]

This 'affecting all' includes not only all the people who inhabit the earth at a given moment, such as the present, but also those who are to come. It is particularly clear what harm is done to future generations if we fail to care for the environment, if we fail to eradicate poverty in some parts of the planet, if we fail to avoid conflicts and wars whose effects are devastating for future generations, if we fail to cancel—at least in part—debts that weigh on a political community and that are at least partly owed to it, in part-if debts that weigh on a political community and that prevent its citizens from attaining minimally dignified living conditions, if a consumerist and hedonistic model that is not sustainable is not changed, if in the world—our common home—opulence and the most extreme poverty, the excesses of some with the most absolute shortages of others, are present. Even today, being born in one part of the world or another is a determining factor for living in a more or less dignified way, for being able to enjoy opulence or to survive miserably.

On whom do these rights apply, on humanity in general, on all human beings, present and future, and if so, how can they be enforced? And if so, how can they be enforced, and is there a way to impose sanctions for non-compliance? If so, on whom? This indeterminacy of the holders of third generation rights is what has led the doctrine to speak of 'diffuse rights'. And the fact is that the specific holder who can enjoy these rights—and who can demand their exercise and protection—is not clear. How to convert such generic and important interests (peace, environment, development, etc.), whose addressees are the whole of humanity—present and future—into rights enforceable by specific individuals? Some authors use the expression 'collective rights'. In any case, it is undeniable that "this diffuse or collective character makes it difficult to categorise them as human rights," [30] and that the diffuse and global character of these rights "hinders their effectiveness and their realisation."[31]

Are we not expecting more from rights than they can deliver? The more rights are extended, the less their effective exercise can be guaranteed. With the first-generation rights, although they had a limited real—rather than formal—scope, their enforceability and exercise were more attainable. With second generation rights, which are broader in scope and ambition, their effective exercise and

[29] Martínez de Pisón (1997), p. 179.

[30] Martínez de Pisón (1997), pp. 179–180, and he adds: "There is nothing more distant and contradictory than to speak of "human rights" and to affirm that their ownership is diffuse. That there is no one to whom to assign them!".

[31] Rey (2011), p. 106.

enjoyment is in many cases more difficult. The scope of third-generation rights is so broad and all-encompassing that their effective exercise is, at present, unfeasible.

Perhaps we have taken the wrong path, and we are asking about rights for what only other realities, categories or values can provide. I am referring to the obligations and duties that stem from solidarity and responsibility.[32] In short, these rights will become effective to the extent that all human beings acquire a greater sense of solidarity and responsibility.[33] On the other hand, it will be necessary to study to what extent States and international organisations can use the Law to demand from the States themselves, from the big financial entities and multinational companies, from the different lobbies and from the common citizen, a conduct that contributes to the establishment of peace, to development, to the care of the environment and the heritage of humanity, etc.

If, as aforementioned, human rights are "a core of morality based on the idea of human dignity,"[34] it is congruent to ask ourselves what are the minimum moral requirements necessary for human beings, of today and tomorrow, to be able to live peacefully and with dignity in the whole world.[35] These minimum ethical requirements will be precisely those that will have to be achieved with various means, with a good education in values, but also with the coercive force of a law of global scope.

This poses an additional problem for third generation rights: that of their justification. While first and second generations rights are justified by the values of liberty and equality, respectively, with third generation rights, solidarity—or fraternity—lacks the same legitimating force as liberty and equality.[36]

In the first place, because Law seems to move with greater tact and security in the supposed terrain of freedom and equality than in that of solidarity, which seems to belong more to morality, ethics, beneficence or the religious spirit. It is perhaps mistakenly thought that while freedom and equality belong to justice—and, consequently, to law—, solidarity belongs to a sphere of ethics that is rather alien to the field of law. Perhaps this is due to an erroneous understanding of the relationship between law and morality, or it is one of the pernicious effects of the Kantian distinction between morality and law. It has been forgotten that the human condition, vulnerable or fragile in itself, requires solidarity, and that this is part of justice to the extent that it is essential to live a truly human life and build a just society. Secondly, because it is a very widespread or diffuse solidarity, which embraces the whole of humanity,[37] which makes its legitimising force even more difficult.

[32] On this subject, see the study by Jonas (1984).

[33] Levinas (1994).

[34] See note n. 2.

[35] In this regard, see Cortina (1986).

[36] This has been made clear by Peces-Barba (1991), pp. 156 ff.; Pérez Luño (1995), p. 119; Martínez de Pisón (1997), p. 181.

[37] Martínez de Pisón (1997), p. 181: "...a solidarity extended to all of humanity, to all men and women and to all peoples and corners of the planet and which thus binds and intertwines all in a common interest: that of the global environment, perpetual peace, sustainable development, the enjoyment of the goods proper to humanity, etc. And, at the same time, a solidarity that constitutes

In any case, a more just and peaceful world will not be achieved with a mere list of rights of global or planetary scope, but with a social awareness—also planetary—that includes everyone, starting with those who can do the most, who unfortunately are usually also those who do the most damage (in particular, the political class and rulers with partisan and short-term approaches in order to stay in power; owners—and high-ranking officials—of financial institutions and multinationals that pursue economic profit above all else; and media that put themselves at the service of spurious political, ideological and economic interests, far removed from the task of informing, the only one that dignifies these media).

The achievement of these third generation rights depends, rather—to a good extent—on a global social awareness that promotes solidarity and responsibility for all.[38] If a minimum ethics—also global—is required for this, how to reach an agreement or consensus for a common minimum ethics in a relativistic cultural and philosophical framework, in which personal fulfilment seems to depend on one's own subjectivity, on the gratification of one's own interests and desires?

It is true that it is not possible to understand the third generation of rights without considering the political, social and economic context in which it has emerged. But neither should we forget the cultural and philosophical context, which allows us to explain some paradoxes, the contrast of light and shadow, or the existence of some claims of supposed rights, which are mere arbitrary desires of individuals in developed and opulent societies, 'everyday rights' or 'rights-desire' I call them, as we will see later on.

Let us now see which rights form part of this third generation, knowing—as aforementioned—that not all authors agree that they belong to this specific generation. The main third generation human rights are the *right to the* environment, the *right to peace*, the *right to development*, the *right to the common* heritage *of humanity, the right to* use and benefit from information and communication technologies (ICTs), and other purported rights.

---

the basic platform for modifying and improving many of the realities and miseries of life on the planet and makes it possible to justify these new needs and aspirations that are the rights of the third generation".

[38] Pérez Luño (2013), p. 183: "...the effectiveness of third generation rights does not allow us to contemplate their ownership from the point of view of man in isolation from first generation rights, nor even from the sphere of man situated in the groups and social movements that promoted second generation rights. Today, in the global society, both the individual and the collectivity are insufficient to respond to challenges and aggressions that, because they affect all human beings, can only be counteracted through rights whose holders are aware that the full realisation of their freedoms is something that concerns, actually or potentially, all human beings. The ownership of the third generation of human rights requires, in short, full awareness of the universality and solidarity on which they are based.

3.2.1 The Right to the Environment

Since the middle of the twentieth century, the economic development model—with its production, distribution and consumption of goods and services from a voracious, highly technological and globalised industrial production—has revealed the lack of protection of renewable natural resources caused by deforestation, gas emissions, the indiscriminate use of chemicals and the discharge of toxic waste. All these elements have contributed to the pollution of the water, air and soil of the globe, resulting in a significant deterioration of ecosystems beyond the borders of States and to the detriment of the international community.

How can we respond to the systematic exploitation of finite natural resources? If natural resources are limited and can therefore be depleted,[39] the right to the environment arises from the human need to enjoy the landscape and biodiversity,[40] to breathe clean air,[41] to drink healthy water,[42] to exploit fertile land for the consumption of unpolluted fruits and food. Neglecting the environment would result in a deterioration of the quality of human life and social degradation.[43] Ultimately, it

---

[39] Pope Francis (2015), n. 27, "Other indicators of the present situation have to do with the depletion of natural resources. We are well aware of the impossibility of sustaining the present level of consumption in the most developed countries and in the richest sectors of society, where the habit of waste and throw-away has reached unprecedented levels. Certain maximum limits of exploitation of the planet have already been exceeded, without having solved the problem of poverty.

[40] On biodiversity, see Pope Francis (2015), nn. 32–42, in particular n. 32: "The earth's resources are also being depleted by immediatist ways of understanding the economy and commercial and productive activity. The loss of forests and woodlands implies at the same time the loss of species that could in the future be extremely important resources, not only for food, but also for the cure of diseases and for multiple services. The diverse species contain genes that can be key resources to solve in the future some human need or to regulate some environmental problem".

[41] On pollution and climate change, see Pope Francis (2015), nn. 20–26.

[42] On water, see Pope Francis (2015), nn. 28–31, in particular n. 28: "Drinking and clean water is a matter of primary importance, because it is indispensable for human life and for sustaining terrestrial and aquatic ecosystems. Freshwater sources supply sanitation, agriculture and industry. Water supply has long remained relatively constant, but in many places demand now exceeds sustainable supply, with serious short- and long-term consequences. Large cities that depend on a significant level of water storage suffer periods of water stress, which at critical times is not always managed with adequate governance and fairness. Social water poverty is particularly prevalent in Africa, where large sectors of the population do not have access to safe drinking water, or suffer from droughts that hinder food production. In some countries, there are regions with abundant water and at the same time others with severe water scarcity.

[43] On this subject, see Pope Francis (2015), nn. 43–47, in particular n. 44: "Today we note, for example, the excessive and disorderly growth of many cities which have become unhealthy to live in, not only due to pollution caused by toxic emissions, but also to urban chaos, transport problems, and visual and noise pollution. Many cities are large, inefficient structures that waste excessive energy and water. There are neighbourhoods that, although recently built, are congested and untidy, without sufficient green spaces. It is not befitting for the inhabitants of this planet to live increasingly inundated with cement, asphalt, glass and metals, deprived of physical contact with nature".

refers to the right of every human being, as well as future generations, to enjoy a "*healthy and ecologically balanced environment.*"[44]

3.2.2 The Right to Peace

This right has its roots in the political philosophy of the medieval and modern centuries, although the technological advances of the twentieth century and the horrific experiences of their destructive power in the context of the two world wars—particularly the second, with the use of nuclear weapons—have made the right to peace particularly important. The justification for this right is also related to the risks of total destruction that the use of nuclear weapons, as well as all kinds of weapons of mass and indiscriminate killing through biological weapons, napalm, etc., can entail.

Although the search for a moral basis for this right has not been abandoned, it has been the fear generated by the power and destructive capacity acquired by armaments over the last century, that is, the fear of an atomic conflict, which has most sensitised the international community, and which has led to the vindication of peace as a "priority" and "non-negotiable" right.[45]

The United Nations General Assembly adopted Resolution 33 of 15 December 1978, and with it its *Declaration on the Preparation of Societies for Life in Peace*, as well as Resolution 39 of 12 November 1984, with the consequent *Declaration on the Right of Peoples to Peace.*

However, peace is not achieved through its consecration as a right—even if it is a right—but through the education of a new culture, a culture of peace. Hence, the United Nations General Assembly, through Resolution A/Res/52/13 of 15 January 1998, adopted on 20 November 1997, requested both the Secretary-General of the United Nations and the Director-General of UNESCO for a programme of action for a culture of peace, promoting such a culture as an integral approach to preventing violence and armed conflict. A year later, UNESCO adopted the *Declaration on a Culture of Peace* (1999), Article 1 of which defines a culture of peace as "a set of

[44] See, in this regard, the following conferences and instruments drafted from 1968 to the present: *Water Charter* adopted by the Council of Europe in Strasbourg (1968); *Declaration of the United Nations Conference on the Human Environment (*1972); *Declaration on Safe Drinking Water and Sanitation for the Decade* (1990); United Nations Conference on Environment and Development (*Earth Summit*), Rio de Janeiro (1992); International Conference on Water and Environment (Dublin, 1992); *Copenhagen Declaration on Social Development* (1995); *Marrakech Declaration*, First World Water Forum (1997); Kyoto Convention (1997); Rio+20 Summit (2012); on the ecological question, see also the latest encyclical letter of Pope Francis (2015).

[45] Pérez Luño (1995), p. 111.

values, attitudes, traditions, behaviours and lifestyles based on [and lists a set of principles without which peace would not be possible]."[46]

It should be borne in mind that the danger of a possible atomic conflict has not disappeared with the end of the Cold War, especially since the atomic arsenals have not yet been definitively destroyed, and "research continues in the laboratories for the development of new offensive weapons capable of altering natural balances."[47] On the other hand, the depletion of some natural resources could also lead to the emergence of new armed conflicts.[48]

3.2.3 *The Right to Development*

Since the 1980s, there has been a growing awareness of the misery and poverty of many underdeveloped countries, whose citizens live in conditions of inequality with respect to the enjoyment of civil, political, economic, social and cultural rights. The

---

[46] See the principles contained in Art. 1 of the *Declaration on a Culture of Peace* (1999), without which peace would be impossible to achieve:

(a) Respect for life, ending of violence and the promotion and practice of non-violence through education, dialogue and cooperation.

(b) Full respect for the principles of sovereignty, territorial integrity and political independence of States and non-interference in matters which are essentially within the domestic jurisdiction of States, in accordance with the Charter of the United Nations and international law.

(c) Full respect for and promotion of all human rights and fundamental freedoms.

(d) Commitment to the peaceful settlement of conflicts.

(e) Efforts to meet the developmental and environmental needs of present and future generations.

(f) Respect for and promotion of the right to development.

(g) Respect for and promotion of equal rights and opportunities for women and men.

(h) Respect for and promotion of the right of everyone to freedom of expression, opinion and information.

(i) Adherence to the principles of freedom, justice, democracy, tolerance, solidarity, cooperation, pluralism, cultural diversity, dialogue and understanding at all levels of society and among nations.

and fostered by an enabling national and international environment conducive to peace".

[47] John Paul II (1990), n. 154: "...despite the international agreements which prohibit chemical, bacteriological and biological warfare, the fact is that laboratory research continues to develop new offensive weapons capable of altering the balance of nature".

[48] In this regard, see Pope Francis (2015), n. 57: "It is foreseeable that, in the face of the exhaustion of certain resources, a favourable scenario will be created for new wars, disguised behind noble claims. War always causes serious damage to the environment and to the cultural wealth of populations, and the risks become greater when we think of nuclear and biological weapons (...). Greater political attention is required to prevent and resolve the causes that can give rise to new conflicts. But the power connected to finance is the most resistant to this effort, and political designs are not usually far-sighted. What is the point of preserving today a power that will be remembered for its inability to intervene when it was urgent and necessary?

gap between the haves and have-nots is widening, giving rise to a dual world where few have much and many have rather little. John Paul II expressed this very clearly almost five decades ago:

> The disproportionate distribution of wealth and misery, the existence of developed and undeveloped countries and continents, demand a fair distribution and the search for ways for the fair development of all.[49]

The right to development seeks to remedy the different positions and wealth of States, to put an end to the economic exploitation of the colonising countries, which are only interested in the exploitation and trade of raw materials. In short, the aim is to remedy the current "planetary inequity,"[50] which involves eradicating the situation of poverty and exclusion in which billions of people live:

> I would like to warn that there is often no clear awareness of the problems that particularly affect the excluded. They make up the majority of the planet, billions of people. Today they are present in international political and economic debates, but it often seems that their problems are raised as an appendix, as an issue to be added almost as an obligation or in a peripheral way, if they are not considered as mere collateral damage. In fact, when it comes to concrete action, they often come last. This is partly because many professionals, opinion makers, media and centres of power are located far away from them, in isolated urban areas, without direct contact with their problems. They live and reflect from the comfort of a development and quality of life that are not within the reach of the majority of the world's population. This lack of physical contact and encounter, sometimes favoured by the disintegration of our cities, helps to cauterise the conscience and to ignore part of the reality in biased analysis. This sometimes coexists with a "green" discourse. But today we cannot fail to recognise that *a true ecological approach always becomes a social approach*, which must integrate justice into discussions on the environment, in order to hear *both the cry of the earth and the cry of the* poor.[51]

It is true that the international community has specific organisations and policies with development and incentive programs for certain economic sectors, but these programs are not free, but related to structural adjustment policies aimed at the payment of the foreign debt that makes it very difficult—if not impossible—for citizens to reach minimum levels of welfare.

Specific documents relating to the right to development include the *Declaration on Social Progress and Development* (1969), as well as the *Declaration on the Right to Development* (1986), Article 1.1 of which reads as follows:

> The right to development is an inalienable human right by virtue of which every human person and all peoples are entitled to participate in, contribute to, and enjoy economic, social, cultural and political development in which all human rights and fundamental freedoms can be fully realized.

---

[49] John Paul II (1981), I.2; and he adds: "The teachings contained in the Encyclical *Mater et Magistra* of John XXIII, in the Pastoral Constitution *Gaudium et Spes* of the Second Vatican Council and in the Encyclical *Populorum Progressio* of Paul VI move in this direction".

[50] In this regard, see Pope Francis (2015), nn. 48–52.

[51] Pope Francis (2015), n. 49.

3.2.4 The Right of Peoples to Self-Determination

Related—at least in part—to the right to development, the self-determination of peoples acquired a special prominence after the First World War, and since then—especially after the Second World War—it has occupied an important place in international law, going from being a 'principle' to a 'right'. A right whose holder are the "peoples", without restrictions.[52]

The Charter of the United Nations enshrined the obligation of States to respect the equality and self-determination of all peoples (Articles 1.2 and 55). Moreover, the many cases of decolonisation in the 1960s and 1970s enshrined the right to self-determination, which led to the independence of many territories. In this context, the *Declaration on the Recognition of the Independence of Colonial Countries and Peoples* (1960) enshrined the right of peoples to self-determination:

1. The subjection of peoples to alien subjugation, domination and exploitation constitutes a denial of fundamental human rights, is contrary to the Charter of the United Nations and compromises the cause of world peace and cooperation.
2. All peoples have the right of self-determination; by virtue of that right they freely determine their political status and freely pursue their economic, social and cultural development.[53]

A few years later, the two International Covenants of 16 December 1966 (*International Covenant on Civil and Political Rights* and the *International Covenant on Economic, Social and Cultural Rights*) codified the subjective right of all peoples to self-determination. This right was reiterated in a number of international instruments in the early 1970s. [54]

3.2.5 The Right to the Common Heritage of Mankind

The right to the common heritage of humanity has both a physical dimension (concerning areas excluded from national sovereignty, the ocean floor, the polar ice caps and outer space) and a cultural dimension (concerning particularly significant traces of human activity necessary for understanding the history of

[52] International law does not provide a binding definition of the concept of 'peoples'. It seems that the right of self-determination is not necessarily confined to peoples under colonial rule, but extends to '*all peoples*'. It is, of course, an indeterminate legal concept, which should be clarified in each specific case.

[53] Arts. 1 and 2 of the *Declaration on the Recognition of the Independence of Colonial Countries and Peoples*, adopted by the United Nations General Assembly on 14 December 1960.

[54] *General Assembly Declaration on Principles of International Law concerning Friendly Relations and Cooperation among States in accordance with the Charter of the United Nations* (1970); the Charter of Economic Rights and Duties resolution (1974).

humankind).[55] *Its recognition came from* the *Convention concerning the Protection of the World Cultural and Natural Heritage* (1972),[56] and has been regulated in the *UNESCO Convention concerning the Protection of the World Cultural and Natural Heritage* (1972).

3.2.6 The Right to Information and Communication Technologies (ICTs)

Rights related to information and communication in cyberspace have been the subject of considerable development and study in recent decades.[57] As aforementioned, part of the doctrine maintains that these rights belong to a different generation, to the fourth.[58] It is not the purpose here to enter into this doctrinal controversy.[59] In any case, it is worth noting that this right encompasses a notable plurality of aspects and diversity of rights, namely, the rights that protect privacy,

---

[55] In this regard, see the study by Tello (2012).

[56] The text was adopted at the 17th session of the General Conference of the United Nations Educational, Scientific and Cultural Organization in Paris from 17 October to 21 November 1972.

[57] In this regard, see González (1999); Suñé (2008), pp. 66 ff.; on the right to data protection as a 'new' right and a new response to the challenges of NICTS, see also Martínez (2018), pp. 39–42.

[58] On this point, see the bibliography in note no. 431.

[59] This is how Bustamante Donás describes -or tries to justify it- in Bustamante (2007), pp. 16–17, the transition from third to fourth generation rights: "The so-called *solidarity rights* constitute a third generation that took shape in the second half of the twentieth century, and are based on the action of collectives that claim legitimate rights. They appear in the form of sectoral declarations that protect the rights of discriminated groups, age groups, ethnic or religious minorities, Third World countries, which are affected by any of the multiple manifestations of economic and social discrimination. In the last two decades, these rights have become increasingly important and have led to the development of the concept of North-South dialogue, respect for and preservation of cultural diversity, protection of the environment, preservation of the cultural heritage of humanity, and so on. They are the expression of a new context in which new human needs are emerging and where these demands call for new rights that guarantee universal access to more advanced forms of citizenship and civility, freedom and quality of life. Economic globalisation, as well as ideological and symbolic globalisation, the transition from the *information society* to the *knowledge society*, the integration of the world through the universal extension of the mass media, as well as the phenomena of multiculturalism caused by migratory flows, are clear symptoms that something substantial is changing.

The right to peace and international justice, to be able to intervene from supranational institutions in local armed conflicts, imposing peace from a legitimate force, are beginning to be strongly demanded. The persecution without borders of dictators, the limitation of the right to diplomatic immunity for certain crimes, and the right to create an international tribunal that acts ex officio in cases of genocide and crimes against humanity. The right to choose models of sustainable development that guarantee biodiversity and allow for the preservation of the natural environment as well as the cultural heritage of humanity. The right to a multicultural environment that goes beyond the concept of tolerance, allowing the articulation of societies that are home to different cultures.

equality in the conditions of access to new technologies (or 'universal service'), telecommunications as a support for the exercise of the rights to freedom of expression and information, integration between communication systems and social media, media concentration and the guarantee of pluralism, control of information on the Internet, as well as freedom of information technology.

With regard to the right to the protection of personal data, there is no doubt about the transformation brought about by the computerisation of all areas of society, as well as the dangers associated with possible abuses of the data collected. In this regard, the United Nations adopted the *Guiding Principles for the Regulation of Computerized Personal Data Files* (1990), Article 1 of which enshrined the principles of lawfulness and fairness, which are essential to safeguard the privacy of individuals.[60]

Three North Americans are those who have tried to regulate the most structural questions of the regulation of freedom in cyberspace: John Perry Barlow, Robert B. Gelman and—to a lesser extent—Lawrence Lessig. John P. Barlow was the great architect of the *Declaration of Independence of Cyberspace* (Davos, 8 February 1996), making a courageous defence of freedom against the *Communications Decency Act*, approved the day before in his country. Robert B. Gelman published—on the occasion of the 50th anniversary of the *Universal Declaration of Human Rights*—his draft proposal for a *Declaration of Human Rights in Cyberspace* (12 November 1998), following the model of the Universal Declaration. A few years later, in the framework of the *First International Convention on Computer Law*, a group of cybercitizens drafted a *Political Constitution for Cyberspace* (Bogotá, 18 October 2006). Two years later—and on the occasion of the 60th anniversary of the Universal Declaration of Human Rights—the *Cyberspace Bill of Rights* was published.[61]

These new conditions allow the crystallisation of new rights that aspire to become concrete in declarations such as those of civil and political rights and economic, social and cultural rights. The right to peace and to intervention by a legitimate international power in armed conflicts; the right to create an international tribunal to act in cases of genocide and crimes against humanity; the right to sustainable development that allows the preservation of the natural environment and the cultural heritage of humanity; the right to a multicultural world in which ethnic, linguistic and religious minorities are respected; the right to the free movement of persons, not only of capital and goods, which allows decent living conditions for immigrant workers. This set of rights has been taking shape in recent decades, and opens the way for a major additional challenge in the twenty-first century: the new forms that first, second and third generation rights take in the cyberspace environment, that is, the *fourth generation* of human rights"; on the autonomous nature of the so-called 4th generation rights and simultaneous connection with other personal rights: Martínez López-Sáez (2018), pp. 48–57.

[60] "Principle of lawfulness and fairness. Information relating to individuals should not be collected or processed by unfair or unlawful means or used for purposes contrary to the purposes and principles of the Charter of the United Nations" (Article 1, *Guiding Principles for the Regulation of Computerized Personal Data Files*).

[61] The *Cyberspace Bill of Rights* is available at http://portal.uexternado.edu.co/pdf/7_convencionesDerechoInformatico/documentacion/conferencias/Los_Derechos_Humanos_en_el_Ciberespacio.pdf; Emilio Suñé Llinás is its author, although the original draft was discussed with

This is an important, complex and novel field, which will require special attention from specialists, and whose legal regulation must safeguard a set of rights. Although these, for the most part, come from the values of the first and second generation of rights, that is, freedom (privacy, intimacy, freedom of expression, freedom of information and its limits, pluralism, computer freedom, etc.) and equality (access to new technologies, etc.), the appearance of computer, telecommunications and telematics technologies is creating new spaces which, by aggressively bursting into people's lives, require appropriate legal regulation.

Thus, for example, with the right to freedom of information, the aim is to ensure that information of an intimate or private nature of the individual cannot be manipulated or transmitted by third parties without his or her consent and that it is, where appropriate, suitably rectified and updated. The right to freedom of information, on the other hand, allows its application to new legal realities that could only partially be approached with the traditional notion of 'privacy', and could only partially be framed as a 'very personal right'.

3.2.7 *Bioethics and Biotechnology-Related Rights*

Advances in genetic engineering force us to face new situations and challenges, unimaginable until a few years ago, and which require a legal response that safeguards the dignity and rights of individuals.[62] In effect, realities such as assisted procreation, genetic patents, genetic diagnoses and therapies, cloning, etc., require a normative regulation that is in accordance with human nature or condition.[63] And this explains why these rights, considered by some as fourth generation,[64] are in permanent growth.

In the same vein, the *Universal Declaration on the Human Genome and Human Rights* (1997), in article 10, provides that "no research concerning the human genome or any of its applications, in particular in the fields of biology, genetics and medicine, may take precedence over respect for human rights, fundamental freedoms and human dignity of individuals or, where applicable, of groups of individuals".

---

specialists from Europe and America: Juan Juan Pablo Pampillo (ELD of México), Yarina Amoroso (University of Havana), Paula López Zamora (Complutense University of Madrid) and Fanny Coudert (University of Leuven, Belgium), among others.

[62] Andorno (2012); Gaylin (1984).

[63] In this regard, see Albers et al. (2014).

[64] "The same is true of what are already known as *fourth generation rights*, that is, rights linked to technological progress which affect above all questions related to bioethics—euthanasia, abortion, etc.—and genetic treatments" (Martínez de Pisón (1997), pp. 156–157).

In short, talking about rights related to biotechnology means preventing genetic engineering from having the last word on what can or cannot be done, infringing on the human rights of individuals.[65]

3.2.8 *Other So-Called 'Rights': Non-human Rights and 'Rights-Desire'*

The generic, all-encompassing and diffuse nature of third-generation rights—fourth, fifth, sixth, etc., according to the opinion of some—has led to the vindication of supposed rights that in some cases are not human (given that their holders are nature, flora or non-rational animals), and in others do not seem very consistent with the human condition, which I call 'rights-desire'—not to call them, simply and plainly, 'inhuman rights'—. Some of these supposed rights are the result of individual claims that have little force; others, however, are supported by scholars who have tried to defend their theses with scientific theories, as well as by powerful lobbies that try to shape—or invent—a new world legal order in the image and likeness of their ideology.

Among non-human rights, the vindication of animal rights has had a notable predicament, a thesis that has been defended with particular force by a sector of the doctrine and, in particular, by Peter Singer.[66] According to this author, as some animals enjoy a greater dignity than some human beings, it seems logical that they can—and should, according to him—enjoy rights. If for Singer, following Jeremy Bentham's thesis.[67] what makes a human being dignified is the capacity to obtain pleasure—as the fundamental criterion of dignity—, it is understood that some animals can be more dignified than a foetus, a terminally ill person, an elderly person, etc. This thesis reflects, in short, a merely utilitarian and postmodernist conception of the human being,[68] incompatible with respect for human dignity and human rights.[69] As aforementioned, animals—as well as plants and nature in general—do not require rights for humans to give them the care and treatment they deserve as animals—or as living beings—, conduct that, moreover, corresponds to the human condition.

Among non-human rights, it is also worth mentioning those whose holders are machines, artefacts, robots and intelligent software. Is it possible that there will come

---

[65] See, e.g., Ballesteros (2002); Andorno (2009); Andorno (2014).

[66] Singer (1975); in Spain, see Mosterín (1998).

[67] Bentham (1823), note n. 122: "But a full-grown horse or dog is beyond comparison a more rational, as well as a more conversable animal, than an infant of a day, or a week, or even a month, old. But suppose the case were otherwise, what would it avail? the question is not, Can they reason? nor, Can they talk? but, Can they suffer?".

[68] Álvarez (2009).

[69] Salter (1996), Arslan (1999), Ballesteros (1992).

a time when a robot will be able to behave in an autarkic (or 'free') way with respect to its programmer, and even carry out an illegal act? For some, this possibility is within man's reach, in which case, they say, it would be appropriate to regulate their legal status by granting them a series of rights, including those that would ensure their fair legal protection. In the view of some, these would be fifth-generation rights.

The supposed rights related to transhuman beings—and, in its final phase, 'post-human'—, whose holders would be those people with a genetic-cognitive-informational identity altered by a gano-nano-robo-techno modification, would be—according to the opinion of some—those of the sixth generation.[70] These supposed rights would come to protect transhumans, an expression coined in 1957 by Julian Huxley, the biologist who founded transhumanism, and which currently has Nick Bostrom as one of its main exponents.[71] Transhumanism places all its confidence in biotechnology, 'reifying' the human being.[72] By rejecting human nature and its limitations, it does not accept frailty or vulnerability as part of the human condition.[73] In short, it is a dehumanised conception of man, in which there is no room for normal human beings, that is, the common individual, fragile and vulnerable, with defects and shortcomings, but without being deprived of his natural dignity, from which the human rights of all emanate.

Among the 'rights-desire' it is worth mentioning the "rights to eroticism" (freedom of sexual relations, homosexuality, abortion, etc.),[74] related to 'bedroom issues', or 'codpiece rights', as they are called by a well-known Spanish writer.[75] According to this author, these rights constitute a mode of social control used by a political system placed at the service of "international usury, large organisations and corporations."[76] It is about the "new social rights,"[77] "freedoms and rights of fly" that entertain the citizenship "while the liberal order (...) is dedicated to the only

[70]Transhumanism is a forward-looking school of thought that rejects traditional human limitations such as death, disease and other biological shortcomings. Furthermore, it holds that the human species does not represent the end of our evolution, but only the beginning ('humanity'), passing through transhumanity, to finally arrive at posthumanity.

[71]See, for example, Bostrom (2005).

[72]In this regard, see Ballesteros and Fernández (2007), Negro (2009), Postigo (2009), more recently, Cortina and Serra (2015), Damour (2015).

[73]On this subject, see MacIntyre (2001), Masferrer and García-Sanchez (2016).

[74]Martínez de Pisón (1997), p. 224.

[75]In this regard, see Prada (2015a), where he aims to unveil the strategies employed by the 'immense and tutelary power' that governs the world, prophesied by Tocqueville, to turn peoples into "a hotbed of aphids who are flattered with *wifi* connection and codpiece rights".

[76]De Prada (2015b): "The political system is now at the service of international usury, of large organisations and corporations. In exchange, the people are given the sweet treat of totally empty rights and freedoms. In the end, they are reduced to a few rights that stultify the people with hedonism, as power has always done throughout history."

[77]De Prada (2015c): "...according to Chesterton's prophecy: 'It will not be long before a new religion will be proclaimed which, while exalting lust, will forbid fecundity'. This new religion envisioned by Chesterton (although already proclaimed previously by Sade, with his 'exultant trinity of contraception, sodomy and abortion') is what contemporary progressivism calls 'new

freedom that interests it, which is none other than that of amassing money in a few hands."[78] In short, they are rights with which the political power—in the service of the financier—manages to gain social control.[79] These rights, by forging a more passive and ductile citizenry and reinforcing partitocracy, have generally been supported by the political class, regardless of ideological sign or bias, to the detriment of representative democracy.[80]

These are 'individual claims' that states and international bodies have begun to give legal protection to conduct related to the use and enjoyment of sexuality. Some time ago, the mayor of Paris, Bertrand Delanoë, trying to defend or justify a love affair of Hollande, the president of France, claimed the "right to passion and rapture". He was not referring to a sentimental or platonic rapture but a sexual one. To use the expression "right to passion and rapture" is, in itself—and in this respect—quite eloquent.

To elevate certain merely individual claims or interests—related to sexuality or gender issues—to the category of supposed rights is to slide down a slippery slope that can lead to the death of new generation rights in particular and human rights in general. To elevate to the rank of human right the claim to have a child—by whatever means and at whatever cost—, or to stop having one—that is, to have an abortion—, to get rid of a sick relative, to remake one's own image or aesthetics—to be an attractive person to others—, to undergo a sex change operation, etc., would mean the end of human rights, and we would have to start again, distinguishing between authentic human rights and mere desires that the Law cannot—and should not—protect, and even less regulate them as subjective rights.

social rights', which are nothing but codpiece rights; and their enthronement has no other object than to keep the enslaved 'citizenry' placated and docile."

[78] De Prada (2014a): "The freedoms and rights of the codpiece (adultery, divorce, pornography, contraception, abortion) began as more or less shameful assaults on morality, and little by little they have become that *religion* envisioned by Chesterton, which at once stimulates lust and forbids fertility. Of course, all of these fly-by-night freedoms are nothing more than smokescreens, ventured to keep the people entertained, rejoicing in the pigsty, while the liberal order (transmuted into *progressivism*) devotes itself to the only freedom that interests it, which is none other than that of amassing money in the hands of a few."

[79] De Prada (2014b): "Much more important (...) than achieving political power is achieving social control, because in fact political power is nothing more than the effective exercise of a previous social control, in which the various oligarchies, with their right-wing and left-wing deals, can take turns quietly, admitting from time-to-time new partners in the distribution of the cake. By social control we must understand the sibylline mechanisms of mass psychology that achieve the submission of consciences to the cultural paradigms of each epoch (call them 'financial capitalism', 'rights of the fly', 'consumerism', 'gender ideology', etc.), to which they yield without realising it, with the same naturalness with which we breathe (...). Thus, for example, the flock will be allowed to rebel against the abuses of the financial system, as long as they don't stop demanding abortion and other rights of the fly; because the New World Order knows well that the best way to plunder the people and thus better supply the financial markets is to exalt lust and prohibit fertility, so that people do not have children and the plundering they suffer is not perceived as an attack on their offspring."

[80] In this regard, Ortí (2013).

What causes this tendency? Here I will only say that it is the result of a complex historical, cultural and ideological process, which, erecting freedom—or autonomy of will—, with hardly any limits, at the summit of individuals, communities, peoples and States, has left the notion of common good in the trunk of memories, like a museum antique. According to this individualistic conception, if personal fulfilment is based on the satisfaction of desires, what less than claiming the right to satisfy one's own sexual desires. Moreover, the guarantee of the full and pleasurable exercise of this 'right' must take precedence over other types of personal ties such as that between mother and child (in the case of abortion), or that of fidelity between spouses (in the case of marriage). On the other hand, the current mentality has led to consider as a 'subjective right' everything that the Law allows. Hence, there is talk of a 'right to abortion', of a 'right to euthanasia', of a 'right to have a child—healthy, beautiful and smart', 'a right to change sex', etc., when, in reality, these rights do not exist as such.

3.3 From the Inflation of Rights to Their Trivialisation and Denaturalisation

The above enumeration of the new generation of rights is more than enough to show their breadth, heterogeneity and constant growth. Indeed, since the 1960s, human rights have been progressively increasing, and not always in the right direction. It is true that "[t]he catalogue of third generation rights (...) is still open,"[81] and understandably so in a world in constant transformation.

However, it is worth bearing in mind the dangers that a permanent creation of rights could entail. On the one hand, there is a certain risk of denaturalising human rights, especially in view of the nihilistic relativism prevailing in the current cultural framework. On the other hand, another certain danger is the impact that some 'new rights' or 'rights-desire' could have on the exercise of basic fundamental rights, which were the object of conquest in the two preceding generations. Let us now consider the first problem, leaving the second for another occasion.

Part of the doctrine has denounced that "this new generation is going beyond the limits of rights", giving rise to "an 'inflation' or a 'trivialisation' of rights; that, in short, not only are true rights no longer included but a concept and a category whose design has taken a long time to culminate has been dislocated."[82] In this line, it has been warned of the perverse effects that could be generated by the inclusion of some alleged rights called 'everyday rights':

> ...the picture becomes even more complicated if we take into account that rights that reflect the diverse multiplicity of demands that arise in affluent societies and that constitute the

---

[81] Martínez de Pisón (1997), p. 187.

[82] Martínez de Pisón (1997), p. 178, who quotes Haarscher (1991), pp. 41 ff, as well as Massini (1994), pp. 173 ff.

> majority of today's social demands are also often included in this category. They are 'everyday rights' because they arise directly from the everyday needs of individuals in developed societies. These rights refer to the diversity of concrete needs of citizens that are redefined and modified on a daily basis to the point that a claim can have an object and be the same or different depending on the person or the moment in which it is claimed. What matters is that the citizen does not appear in his generality, but that each individual becomes an interlocutor and petitioner of a right by the mere fact that he considers a claim to be opportune. Thus, the basis of these rights refers to the will, the desire, the arbitrariness of the individual. In reality, this is a perverse effect of the very success of the social state in its version of welfare, since it has committed itself to this objective to such an extent that a moment has come when any mere personal desire or whim seems to become an enforceable right, an 'everyday right.'[83]

How to argue, in a culturally relativistic society, that a certain claim of an individual or a collective cannot be considered a subjective right, or that it would even violate the minimum ethics that the Law must safeguard within a State or the international order? It is not easy, no doubt, but it is an unavoidable challenge if we do not want to trivialise Law and rights.[84]

To accept among the third-generation rights the so-called 'everyday rights' or the rights to eroticism, as well as the recognition of rights to non-human beings (animals, plants, nature, etc.), would mean the beginning of the end of the history of human rights. How to make justice and the protection of the most vulnerable and defenceless compatible with a supposed right to abortion? How to make respect for human life compatible, giving greater importance to the extinction of some animal species when thousands of immigrants lose their lives trying to cross the waters in the hope of being able to live a decent life?

It is not a question of undervaluing nature, animals or flora, but it would make no sense—"bordering on the absurd"[85]—to put their care before that of human beings. As has been said, animals and nature in general must be treated with care, but for this it is not necessary to grant them rights.[86] The duty of care that affects everyone is sufficient, using—if necessary—legal norms that sanction their mistreatment, which would not only be unjust but would even degrade those who inflict it.

---

[83] Martínez de Pisón (1997), p. 180.

[84] Martínez de Pisón (1997), pp. 180–181: "The same can be said of everyday rights, of everyday claims arising from personal whim disguised as legality, since, at bottom, they constitute as a group a perversion of the concept of rights, an involution of the historical process which, from positivisation to universalisation, has consolidated them as a new code of conduct for humanity and for the twenty-first century. In effect, this tends more to the loss of nature, to the trivialisation of human rights than to their full recognition and protection".

[85] Pérez Luño (1995), p. 117.

[86] Martínez de Pisón (1997), p. 180: "We speak of the rights of animals, of the rights of plants and, perfectly well, we could speak of the rights of rocks. In truth, we should rather speak of a special care or sensitivity towards other non-human beings, or towards nature. A sensitivity that can permeate the culture and customs of a people. But, from there, to making them subjects of rights as human rights there is an unbridgeable abyss. In view of these last considerations, we must reject outright the inclusion of the rights of non-human beings in this third category of rights by their very essence."

On the other hand, it is useful to distinguish those rights that reflect a real human need, from others that show mere individual desires or aspirations. It is important to distinguish between 'basic rights' (or 'need-rights') and 'rights-desire,'[87] or, if one prefers, between true rights and false rights.[88] This is no easy task, to be sure, but the stakes are high enough to pull out all the stops, pooling everyone's efforts, if we are to leave a legacy of rights that will adequately protect the human dignity of future generations.[89]

The 'trivialisation' or 'denaturalisation' of rights generated by the 'inflationary tendency' of "social demands that are assuming the status of rights", as well as by the emergence of "new sensibilities and new demands that claim to have access to the status of human rights", has been unequivocally denounced by some scholars. And the worst thing is that such rights (everyday rights, rights to eroticism—freedom of sexual relations, homosexuality, abortion, etc.—and the rights of the non-human matters—rocks, rivers, mountains, animals and plants), "in some cases, find recognition."[90]

---

[87] In this respect, see the study by Zimmerling (1990); in it the author provides a concept of necessity that is relevant for ethical discourse, since it demands that it meets the requirements of objectivity and universality. In the case of objectivity, she incorporates useful arguments to distinguish a "need" from a "desire" or a "preference" insofar as the former does not depend on thought or the functioning of the brain, but on "how the world is" (pp. 47 ff.); see also Rodríguez (2010), p. 383, where she states that the rights of the new generation, "...although they reflect moral claims that shape and limit Power, are channels of political and social participation and a means of resolving benefits for the satisfaction of basic needs, initially, they cannot be reduced to isolated individual claims and sometimes they are indissolubly linked to already consolidated fundamental rights".

[88] Ollero (2005), vol. I, pp. 595–598.

[89] Martínez de Pisón (1997), pp. 186–187: "I refer to the rights of future generations. Indeed, in the face of the above-mentioned risks, there is also growing concern for the continuity of humanity's historical and natural legacy which, to date, has remained almost unchanged, but which, increasingly, is in danger of being seriously impaired. In this sense, there is a growing concern to bequeath to future generations economic, social and natural conditions at least equal to those enjoyed by the present generation."

[90] Martínez de Pisón (1997), pp. 222–223: "Another trend that with unusual force is transforming rights is their inflationary tendency, the incredible increase in social demands that are assuming the status of rights, which require their recognition, protection and realisation. This phenomenon is also called the 'trivialisation' or 'denaturalisation' of rights and is connected with the previous statements on the impact of globalisation on the emergence of new rights, although, to be honest, the emergence of new categories follows other paths. The *inflation of rights* is, in fact, one of the most striking aspects of the current panorama, which is intended to indicate the tendency to increase the number and quality of rights. By now, it is well known that rights have emerged in generations: those of the first generation are civil and political rights; those of the second generation are economic, social and cultural rights; and those of the third generation are diffuse rights. And along with these, there are those who speak of a fourth and even a fifth. What is certain is that new sensitivities and new claims are emerging that seek access to the status of human rights: everyday rights, rights to eroticism (freedom of sexual relations, homosexuality, abortion, etc.) and the rights of the non-human matters (rocks, rivers, mountains and of animals and plants). And, in some cases, they find recognition."

It is precisely the legal recognition of some of these supposed rights that worries part of the doctrine, because "[a]ll this cannot but lead, in the order of human praxis, to the degradation of an idea that by dint of wanting to mean everything, ends up meaning nothing. Indeed, if we try to subsume under the concept of 'rights' freedoms, claims, legitimate aspirations, utopian desires, personal moral duties towards animals, instinctive drives and conservationist ideals, we should not be surprised at the vagueness, indefiniteness and—consequently—practical uselessness to which this concept will be thrown. And it will be very difficult for such a notion to be taken seriously, especially when its acceptance always implies obligations, sometimes very burdensome, for a subject or a group of subjects."[91]

This danger is particularly pressing if one takes into account the already diffuse nature of third generation rights. It is not in vain that part of the doctrine has qualified them as 'diffuse rights'. It has been rightly said that any increase in rights "undoubtedly affects their status, the definition of their basic elements: the subject, the object, the obligor, their basis and, finally, their protection."[92] If the first and second generation rights, whose statutes are much clearer and more precise than those of the third generation, have produced numerous conflicts, it is logical that with the third generation 'diffuse rights' the conflicts will increase considerably, especially when the new claims related to 'rights-desire' and other supposed rights (of non-human beings and inanimate beings) obtain legal recognition. Such recognition would contribute—or, rather, is already contributing—to the fact that "the profiles of rights have become blurred, that there is talk of denaturalisation and trivialisation, and not without reason."[93]

The fact that third generation rights can be referred to as 'diffuse rights' already shows that the concept of human right has been extended, to the point "that we do not know precisely who are the holders, what is the object (the legal interest being protected) and what is the nature of the legal protection they deserve."[94] In other words, if "[t]he concept of human right has a precise meaning when we can identify its holder or holders, its specific object, the mechanism that makes its claim possible, the passive subject(s) and some kind of sanction that its violation may entail,"[95] is it not that we have already gone too far, with "the possible affectation of the very concept of human right that its justification via the recourse of successive

---

[91] Massini (1994), p. 176 (text taken up by Martínez de Pisón (1997), pp. 223–224).

[92] Martínez de Pisón (1997), p. 223.

[93] Martínez de Pisón (1997), p. 223: "Already between the first and second generation there are notable differences, some being rights of freedom and others rights of equality. One implies a passive attitude of the State, the other, on the contrary, a decisive action with policies and social programs. For this reason, there are many clashes and conflicts. Third-generation rights are a category that presents even greater difficulties in defining their characteristic elements. Precisely for this reason, they are called diffuse rights. Not to mention the new claims that have to do with non-human beings or inanimate beings. All of this means that the profiles of rights have become blurred, that there is talk of denaturalisation and trivialisation, and not without reason".

[94] Rabossi (1997–1998), p. 50.

[95] Rabossi (1997–1998), p. 50.

generations entails"[96]? This is the danger of the thesis of generations of human rights in general, and of the third generation in particular:

> Introducing human rights that do not meet these conditions not only creates a dubious class, but casts a shadow of doubt over the entire class of human rights. Moreover, the strategy has the danger that it can continue to be used indefinitely to justify the incorporation of supposedly new 'rights.'[97]

"Greed breaks the camel's back", goes the popular saying, which might well apply to third generation rights: the objects and holders of these rights are so ambitious, abstract, diverse, all-encompassing and diffuse, that indeed more than "a shadow of doubt has been cast over the entire class of human rights". The strategy of permanent addition of new 'rights' is the order of the day,[98] and, as a result, the legacy of human rights for future generations is being seriously jeopardised. And not only for future generations. The consequences of this trivialisation or denaturalisation of human rights are already being experienced today. Hence the statement that "...we must pay as much attention to the new rights as to those which, long recognised and enshrined, have not yet found acceptable degrees of satisfaction."[99]

I think—with Bidart Campos and Rabossi—that we should rethink the conception of most third-generation rights, if we want to avoid the trivialisation of human rights. Such 'diffuse rights', with the problems they entail, should perhaps cease to be called rights, and look for other alternatives such as 'diffuse interests' or 'collective interests':

> Perhaps when we find neither a subjective right nor a right by analogy, but we are convinced that there is an obligation, we will have to forge a category of subjective legal situations that do not reach the profile of rights, but that will have to be elaborated, positivised, and protected, even by jurisdictional or any other means. And is it not possible to discover in the so-called diffuse or collective interests so many other subjective legal situations, in which subjectivity does not disappear, notwithstanding that the diffuse or collective (or supra-individual) interest is of a group or human group, but shared by each one of those who integrate the group and participate in common in the same interest?[100]

---

[96] Rabossi (1997–1998), p. 50.

[97] Rabossi (1997–1998), pp. 50–51; in facing this danger, perhaps Loewenstein's thesis contained in his work entitled 'Militant Democracy and Fundamental Rights' might be applicable (Loewenstein 1937).

[98] Martínez de Pisón (1997), p. 156: "...following this criterion, the generations of rights can be infinite if there is no kind of control or supervision. It would only be enough for new interests to emerge for a new right to emerge, which is, on the other hand, what has been happening in recent decades with the process of specification in which, when considering the new circumstances in which the human being finds himself in his vital context and in the different stages of his life, it is understood that new rights of provision emerge."

[99] Squella (2002).

[100] Bidart (1989), p. 160; see also pp. 349–350; in this respect, Rabossi points out—quoting Bidart Campos—that "it is possible to appeal to other strategies. For example, to stop speaking in these cases of 'rights' and use other notions, such as diffuse interests" (Rabossi (1997–1998), p. 51).

Human rights need to be taken more seriously. I do not share the view of those who think that the question of human rights "is not a philosophical problem, but a political one."[101] It is political, but also philosophical, ethical, legal, social—or sociological—and economic. To consider human rights as something merely political, or to leave them in the hands of the political class, would undoubtedly be a crass error, the consequences of which have already become present, with the legal recognition of 'impossible rights', incurring "in fantasies that detract from the seriousness of the science of human rights,"[102] or giving legal guise to "non-generalisable interests and valuations, that is, particular desires, private satisfactions or sufferings, non-objectifiable perceptions that are imaginations, fantasies and figurations."[103] It is therefore up to the philosophy of law and ethics to delve deeper into the axiological foundation and content of human rights.[104]

3.4 Epilogue: Critical Reflections on Some Alleged 'New Rights'

At the end of the 1980s, the renowned Italian jurist Norberto Bobbio called the present times "the age of rights."[105] Indeed, in the second half of the twentieth century, modern man has become more aware of human dignity and of his rights, the recognition and protection of which has been the responsibility of national legal systems and the international community. This recognition and protection of rights has, however, been the result of a long historical process. Over the course of history—"the master of life" (Cicero)—human society has learned that it is desirable to respect the rights of individuals in order to make peaceful coexistence possible.

The expression 'new rights' is inserted in a specific historical context, which includes the present moment. To qualify some rights as 'new' means to assume, on the one hand, that they did not exist before—or, at least, that they had not been recognised—and, on the other hand, that they are part of the current culture that has promoted—and continues to promote—their appearance and, where appropriate, legal recognition.

The history of human rights shows the close connection between law and human dignity, and how political power has been limiting its powers—or its sovereignty—

[101] Bustamante (2007), p. 15.

[102] Bidart (1989), p. 238.

[103] Bidart (1989), p. 271; in this regard, see also Pérez Luño (2000), p. 167.

[104] Bidart (1989), p. 271: "If positivity accuses and registers delays, the science of human rights has to go on opening paths, and the philosophy of law has a good part of the responsibility to seriously incite to that task. Modestly, we are trying to contribute something of our effort"; in this respect Rodríguez Palop, points out—in relation to the foundation of these rights - that "it is possible to relate them to the 'radical needs' and to the axiological content on which they are based" (Rodríguez 2010, p. 307).

[105] Bobbio (1996).

vis-à-vis its subjects or individuals. The history of human rights is, to a large extent, the history of the limits—imposed by law—of political power in order to safeguard and protect those fundamental rights that are rooted in the dignity of the person. The purpose of human rights is to establish a limit to the State or political power, which uses the Law to guarantee the recognition and protection of fundamental rights, those without which man would be deprived of his dignity, and political power would lose its *raison d'être*:

> The aim of every political association is the preservation of the natural and imprescriptible rights of man. These rights are liberty, property, security and resistance to oppression.[106]

In the history of human beings, four particularly relevant aspects or realities come into play, all of them within the framework of a given historical context: political power, law, human dignity and subjective rights.

- Political power
- The Law
- Human Dignity
- Subjective rights

Historical context

Although there are important medieval and modern precedents for human rights,[107] the emergence and recognition of civil and political rights—or, as they have also been called, first-generation rights—in the late eighteenth and early twentieth centuries is particularly illustrative in this regard, a context in which the modern notion of liberty appears in the transition from monarchical absolutism to political liberalism.

Faced with the absolutist political powers of the eighteenth century, political liberalism defended the existence of a private sphere of the individual in which the law did not allow any interference by the state. This sphere of freedom is what gave rise to a set of 'individual rights' or 'individual freedoms', both civil (religious, thought, expression, association and especially property and free market) and political (the right to vote and to stand for election, with notable—and well-known—limitations). Thus, with the passage of time, the different first, second and third generation rights were created and configured (although there is no unanimity in this respect):

- Civil and political rights (first generation) (late 18th to early nineteenth century.)
- Economic, social and cultural rights (second generation) (first half of the twentieth century)

---

[106] Art. 2 of the *Declaration of the Rights of Man and of the Citizen* (26 August 1789).

[107] As we have already seen: the Cortes of León of 1188, the Magna Carta of John without Land of 1215, the conquest of the Indies and the Second Scholasticism or the Treaty of Westphalia of 1648, are some examples.

- Rights to the environment, to peace, to development, to the self-determination of peoples, to the protection of the common heritage of mankind, etc. (third generation) (from the 60s of the twentieth century)

But where are the 'new rights' or 'emerging rights'? What rights are we referring to? What is their content?

As we have seen, there is no consensus regarding their specific content and scope. One part of the doctrine maintains—as we have seen—that all the other 'new rights' or 'emerging rights' would form part of the third generation[108]—or by the fourth, according to the opinion of others[109]—. For another doctrinal sector, certain 'new rights' would form a separate group, which would be—depending on each case—the fourth, fifth or sixth generation of rights. Along these lines, and as we have seen, for some, the *right to* information and communication technologies (ICT) would constitute the fourth generation,[110] while for others this same generation would be formed more by rights related to bioethics and biotechnology.[111] It is also known that non-human rights (those whose holders are machines, artefacts, robots and intelligent software) constitute fifth-generation rights, while rights related to transhumanism belong to sixth-generation rights.

As the reader will have noticed throughout these pages, I am not a great enthusiast for the generations of rights, although I understand that it is a pedagogical way of showing the historical evolution of human rights. That is why I have chosen to place all the 'new' or 'new generation' rights within the third generation rights, following in this respect the opinion of part of the doctrine.[112] Consequently, I have placed within this third generation not only the classic rights to the environment, to peace, to development, to the self-determination of peoples and to the protection of the common heritage of mankind, but also all the other *rights that have emerged in recent decades, that is, the rights related to information technologies, the rights of the human person, and the rights of the human person, rights related to* information and communication technologies (ICT), to bioethics and biotechnology, to non-humans (those whose holders are either animals, machines, artefacts, robots and intelligent software), to transhuman beings, as well as 'rights-desire', as I call them.

In the previous section we have warned of the danger and possible pernicious consequences of a permanent and arbitrary growth of human rights, especially when their object of protection and ownership are diffuse. In this final section we will briefly explain the emergence of non-human rights and, in particular, of 'rights-

[108] See, in this respect, footnote n. 7 and the corresponding main text.

[109] See, in this connection, footnote n. 4 and the corresponding main text.

[110] See, in this regard, footnotes nn. 5 y 58 and their corresponding main texts.

[111] See, in this regard, footnote n. 64 and its accompanying main text.

[112] See, in this connection, footnotes nn. 7, 11, 12, 81 and 108 and their corresponding main texts.

desire', which have experienced an unusual force and diffusion in the last five decades, specifically since the protests of May '68—or French May[113]—.

Among the 'new rights' or 'emerging rights'—including 'rights-desire'—one could mention a wide variety of alleged rights related to abortion ('women's right to choose'), euthanasia ('right to a dignified death'), reproductive health, gender and sexual orientation (including the right to enter into 'non-heterosexual marriage', right to adoption, etc.), genetic manipulation, animal care, and so on. One wonders why not claim and grant the right to have several wives or husbands (polygamy), or the right to marry relatives, if they want and wish to do so (incest), to give two examples that are being debated in some Western countries.

I am not opposed to a gradual, orderly and rational process of expansion of human rights. It would make no sense to adopt a position against the evolution of human rights, as long as their content does not imply an involution.[114]

The emergence of some so-called rights or 'rights-desire' is due to a modern cultural tradition whose bases or foundations make it difficult or prevent some 'new rights' or 'emerging rights' from presenting an axiological content in accordance with human dignity. Perhaps for this reason the recognition and protection of the fundamental rights of the first two generations were not able to prevent the horrors of the Second World War, just as the *Universal Declaration of Human Rights* (UDHR) of 1848—and its subsequent political covenants of 1963—are not sufficient to achieve a more just international order in accordance with the dignity of the human person.

What are the shortcomings that hinder a development of human rights more in keeping with the dignity of the human person? It is well known that the UDHR avoided addressing three particularly controversial questions: (1) the relationship of man to God, (2) the foundation of human rights, and (3) the limits of rights and their relationship to duties. Perhaps this explains why Pius XII did not want to sign the UDHR, although a few years later John XXIII changed his attitude, affirming—in his encyclical letter *Pacem in Terris* (1963)—that this text constituted a "great step for humanity".

What, in my opinion, should be the attitude of a citizen, a legal or political professional in the face of these supposed 'new rights', whose axiological content does not seem to be in accordance with human dignity?

First of all, one must acknowledge the positive and be aware of the negative, not only with regard to the possible—null or insufficient—substantiation, but also with regard to the content and scope of some rights. When arguing or showing the negative aspects, it is necessary to reason in a way that can be shared by those

[113]In this regard, see, for example, the study by Nieto (1971).

[114]I share, in this respect, the opinion of Gilbert K. Chesterton, who in his well-known essay *Orthodoxy* (Chesterton (1908), ch. VI, 2nd par. *in fine*) points out that "Evolution is only good if it produces good; good is only good if it helps evolution".

who do not think as one does.[115] In short, it is a matter of arguing more with reasons and less with authorities. Reasons unite if they are sensible, while authorities separate and distance if they are used without due caution. Human rights require the understanding of a plural community formed by individuals with different ideologies and visions, by believers and non-believers. And this understanding is, in my view, possible.

This understanding is possible because human rights pursue a common goal for believers and non-believers alike: peaceful and just social coexistence, public peace or tranquility, which is not possible without justice. And human rights, rooted in human dignity, are an indispensable condition for such social peace and justice.

The common mistake of most of the so-called 'new rights' consists in the loss of a sense of reality, if not in the rejection or disregard of reality. "Want is power." Technological advances have led man to think that he can do everything, that he is the measure of all things and that it is preferable to transform nature and reality than to know it. Robert Oppenheimer, for example, describes the invention of the atomic bomb as 'technology sweet', and for Rudolf Hess the concentration camps were a technical feat that allowed the crematoria and gas chambers to function uninterruptedly. "To will is to be able of." Technology and art reflect this idea, according to which the limit only comes from the ability of the craftsman or artist. In fact, the German expressions 'Kunst' and 'Techne' are closely related to the verb 'können'—'to be able'). In short, according to this conception, it would be the very limits of 'power' and 'capacity' that would determine the limit of willing.

What is the consequence of this conception? The contempt for reality, in this case, for the human condition—not to use the expression nature—and its dignity. What is the path that has led to this oblivion—or, in some cases, contempt—of reality? I list below some of the most important ones:

- The hypertrophy of one's own subjectivity, which distorts the perception of reality, which is not cognisable except through the sieve of one's own interests, ambitions or desires. This leads to a narcissistic conception of one's own life, which leads to seeing the other as an opponent, a rival or a competitor, given that he or she can become an obstacle or impediment to the realisation of my own self. Since the I and the you no longer have anything in common, 'tolerance' is required as an indispensable requirement for coexistence. If a common ground or dignity were to be glimpsed, the other would no longer be seen as an enemy, and this would allow tolerance to be replaced by cooperation, but this would require recognising the existence of a reality that transcends my self and challenges me, putting a stop to my desires, ambitions and whims. As human ambition is insatiable, but, at the same time, it is recognised that some limits are necessary, we opt for those that, although they can change completely according to the circumstances of the moment, have no other support than that

[115] Thus, for example, if one were a Catholic believer, it would be preferable to have recourse to the statements of the Magisterium of the Catholic Church only insofar as they could serve to exemplify, synthesise or summarise the reasons and social experiences that explain one's own way of thinking.

of consensus, embodied in a law that must be the expression of the general will. Consensus and the law therefore become limits that are more formal than material, more procedural than substantive, because, in reality, everything can change, nothing is permanent; and if reality contains nothing permanent, it is preferable to ignore reality, to ignore it, despise it and reject it. This contempt and rejection of reality allows us, in principle, to live and think without limits, except for those we want to impose on ourselves at any given moment, in which case we would always be dealing with 'self-referential limits';

- The exaltation of the self is a consequence of the hypertrophy of subjectivism, and is related to constructivism. According to this philosophical current, man makes himself, both physically and spiritually or personally (including affective, professional, social, etc.). Hence the thousands of web pages that any search engine detects when you search with the expression 'Reinvent yourself'; and.
- Utilitarianism and the search for one's own happiness (of course, alien to that of others). By denying the existence of parameters common to all human beings to achieve a happy life, this must be sought in an individual (or 'self-referential') way, trying to avoid that others prevent me or hinder the chosen path. This happiness, apart from reality, has consequences in language: words cease to refer to ideas or concepts that are found in reality. The connection between word-idea-reality vanishes; words begin to be used for concepts that have no connection with reality, or that contradict reality itself. It has been said that the degradation of language is the most pernicious aspect of modernity. Nietzsche said that as long as grammar is maintained there will be God, because words always refer to reality. Indeed, there are opinions that do not fit with reality: 'Interruption of pregnancy' (abortion/pre-embryo); 'Euthanasia' (as 'good death'); 'Morning after pill', 'Gender' (instead of sex, to reduce it to a merely cultural phenomenon), 'homosexual marriage' (to refer to an affective relationship to the union between two people of the same sex). And it is logical that they do not match reality, because that reality has been replaced by a freedom understood as autonomy, by a human will that, withdrawn and centred on itself, has raised desires to the level of rights, putting the law at the service of this new way of understanding human dignity, whose pillars are: (1) a freedom understood as quasi-unlimited autonomy (breaking with any bond), and (2) the search for pleasure or satisfaction of one's own desires (as we have seen, Peter Singer vindicates the rights of animals, whom he considers more worthy than the unborn—or *nasciturus*—the sick and the elderly); an example of this would be 'the right to passion or rapture', to which reference has already been made.

The second pillar explains why many of the 'new rights' are related to sexual morality: if personal fulfilment passes through the satisfaction of one's desires, what less than claiming a right to satisfy the drives of one's sexual rights! It is understandable that a human dignity based on a quasi-unlimited autonomy of will and on the gratification of one's own desires, pretends to guarantee the satisfaction of these desires, elevating them to the category of rights, thus preventing others from interfering in this area under the pretext that it is part of one's own intimacy or privacy, as is the case of some women: “I do what I want with my body” (one of the main arguments of the North American ‘pro-choice’ movement).

What should be said about all this? I think that only by understanding the logic of the other, we are in a position to rectify, retracing what needs to be retraced. What are, in my opinion, the errors that reflect some of the supposed ‘new rights’? Here is a summary of all of them:

1. they show contempt for the reality of man (natural, biological, anthropological and sociological);
2. they start from an exacerbated subjectivism that hinders or prevents just and peaceful social coexistence;
3. they put the immediate above the permanent, promoting a detached society, lacking those links (family, neighbourhood, friendship, village....), without which a society could hardly subsist (family and business);
4. they give primacy to the big over the small, leaving minorities unprotected, marginalised or ignored;
5. they elevate some desires to the category of rights, by defending a conception of human dignity based on the exercise of personal autonomy and its realisation in the satisfaction of one’s own desires. It does not seem that basing people’s rights on desires—sometimes capricious or spurious—, is an accurate criterion when it comes to creating the conditions that allow a peaceful and fair social coexistence;
6. they do not conceive that these ‘rights’ can be limited or prohibited by law, since this would imply—some argue—an undue interference in the individual’s private sphere (‘privacy’); and
7. these ‘rights’ are intended to be based on consensus, when this is not a sufficient legitimation if it is intended to justify the exercise of ‘rights’ which: (i) violate the fundamental rights of others (e.g. the right to life), and (ii) significantly curtail the exercise of first-generation rights and freedoms, with which the State’s power over the individual was limited (e.g. the right to freedom of conscience, freedom of religion and freedom of expression, among others).

As is to be expected, ‘new rights’, based on pure desire or autonomy of will, end up affecting the rights of others, those rights that are not the result of a desire, but of a human need, such as the right to life, freedom of thought and conscience, as well as the right to religious freedom, among others.

But how do we know which rights are more deserving of respect and protection: those that express a need or those that express a desire? For both need and desire are human realities, and are part of man. Common sense would seem to indicate that need should take precedence over desire. But how can one appeal to ‘common sense’ if one ignores or scorns the same reality? Are we not, perhaps, in a modern society in which man is the measure of all things and can, if he wishes, making the cloak a cloak, choose to exalt the ‘desire-rights’ and scorn, relegate or violate the basic rights (or the ‘need-rights’)?

This is what is happening in the western legal tradition: the vindication of some supposed ‘new rights’ is taking place which, being the expression of mere desires, could mean the end of the right to life, as well as of other fundamental rights and freedoms (religious, of conscience, of expression, of association, etc.), because in a detached and utilitarian society only opinions are admitted, but not convictions or permanent ideas which could limit the super-man who knows no limits and who can do anything. In spite of this, this supposed super-man ends up being satisfied with satisfying his most basic desires and instincts, those which are the object of enjoyment for the non-rational animals. And once we lose touch with reality, what do we want rationality for? Perhaps for the same reason it was used during the Second World War, thus satisfying a morbid 'technological seduction' ('technology sweet') put at the service of the death and extermination of millions of human beings.

I trust that our history will indeed serve, as Cicero said, to learn lessons that will be engraved in our collective memory and prevent certain episodes from being repeated.

Some Cited Normative Sources and Declarations

Textos básicos de la Historia constitucional comparada (1998) (ed. and prologue by J. Varela Suanzes). Centro de Estudios, Políticos y Constitucionales

Virginia Declaration of Rights (June 12, 1776).

Declaration of Independence of the United States (July 4, 1776)

Constitution of the United States of America (1787).

Declaration of the Rights of Man and of the Citizen (1789)

French Constitution of 1791.

Amendment to the American Constitution (December 15, 1791).

Charter of the United Nations (San Francisco, 26 June 1945).

American Declaration of the Rights and Duties of Man (May 2, 1948).

Universal Declaration of Human Rights (Paris, 10 December 1948).

Declaration on the Recognition of the Independence of Colonial Countries and Peoples, United Nations General Assembly, 14 December 1960.

General Assembly Declaration on Principles of International Law concerning Friendly Relations and Cooperation among States in accordance with the Charter of the United Nations (1970).

Charter of Economic Rights and Duties (1974).

International Covenant on Civil and Political Rights' and 'International Covenant on Economic, Social and Cultural Rights' (United Nations General Assembly Resolution 2200 A (XXI) of 16 December 1966, although the latter entered into force two months earlier (3.I.1976) than the former (25.III.1976).

Declaration on the Preparation of Societies for Life in Peace and *Declaration on the Right of Peoples to Peace (*United Nations General Assembly, Resolution 33 of 15 December 1978).

Universal Declaration on the Human Genome and Human Rights (1997).

Declaration on a Culture of Peace (UNESCO, 1999).

Cyberspace Bill of Rights (2008).

Some Charters and Declarations on Ecological Matters:

Water Charter adopted by the Council of Europe in Strasbourg (1968); *Declaration of the United Nations Conference on the Human Environment (*1972); *Declaration on Safe Drinking Water and Sanitation for the Decade* (1990); United Nations Conference on Environment and Development (*Earth Summit*), Rio de Janeiro (1992); International Conference on Water and Environment (Dublin, 1992); *Copenhagen Declaration on Social Development (*1995); *Marrakech Declaration*, First World Water Forum (1997); Kyoto Convention (1997); Rio +20 Summit (2012).

References

Doctrinal and Bibliographical Sources

Albers M, Hoffmann T, Reinhardt J (eds) (2014) Human rights and human nature. Springer, Dordrecht

Álvarez I (2009) Utilitarismo y derechos humanos: la propuesta de John S. Mill. Plaza y Valdés, Madrid

Andorno R (2009) Human dignity and human rights as a common ground for a global bioethics. J Med Philos 34:223–240

Andorno R (2012) Bioética y dignidad de la persona. Tecnos, Madrid

Andorno R (2014) Human dignity and human rights. In: Have HAMJ, Gordijn B (eds) Handbook of global bioethics. Springer, Dordrecht, pp 45–57

Arslan Z (1999) Taking rights less seriously: postmodernism and human rights. Res Publica 5:195–215

Ballesteros J (1992) Postmodernity: decadence or resistance. Emise, Pamplona

Ballesteros J (2002) Exigencias de la dignidad humana en biojuridica. Rivista Internazionale di Filosofia Del Diritto 79(2):177–208

Ballesteros J, Fernández M-A (2007) Biotecnología y Posthumanismo. Thomson-Aranzadi, Cizur

Bidart G (1989) Teoría General de los Derechos Humanos. Astrea, Buenos Aires

Bobbio N (1996) The age of rights. Polity Press, London. (reprinted by John Wiley & Sons, 2017)

Bostrom N (2005) A history of transhumanist thought. J Evol Technol 14:1–25

Bustamante J (2001a) Towards the fourth generation of human rights: rethinking the human condition in the technological society. Inter-Am J Sci Technol Soc Innov (September/December)

Bustamante J (2001b) Hacia la cuarta generación de derechos humanos. Revista electrónica CTS+I 1:3–24

Bustamante J (2007) Los nuevos derechos humanos: gobierno electrónico e informática comunitaria. Revista Venezolana de Información, Tecnología y Conocimiento 2(May–August):13–27

Chesterton G-K (1908) Orthodoxy. Chump Change

Corchete M-J (2007) Los nuevos derechos. Teoría y Realidad Constitucional 20:535–556

Cortina A (1986) Ética mínima: Introducción a la filosofía práctica. Tecnos, Madrid

Cortina A, Serra M-A (2015) Humanos o posthumanos? Singularidad tecnológica y mejoramiento humano. Fragmenta Editorial, Barcelona

Damour F (2015) La tentation transhumaniste. Éditions Salvator, Paris

de Prada J-M (2014a) Article, Alfa y Omega, 6.11.2014
de Prada J-M (2014b) Article, "Social Control", XLSemanal. http://www.finanzas.com/xl-semanal/firmas/juan-manuel-deprada/20141116/control-social-7835.html
de Prada J-M (2015a) Dinero, demogresca y otros podemonios. Temas de Hoy, Madrid
de Prada J-M (2015b) Interview in El Cultural, April 6th. https://www.elespanol.com/el-cultural/20150406/juan-manuelprada/23747672_0.html
de Prada J-M (2015c) Derechos sociales. ABC, April 29th
Gaylin W (1984) In defense of the dignity of being human. Hast Cent Rep 14:4
Gómez Y (2008) Derecho Constitucional Europeo: derechos y libertades. Editorial Sanz y Torres, Madrid
Haarscher G (1991) Philosophie des droits de l'homme, 3ème. Ed. Université, Bruxelles
Jonas H (1984) The imperative of responsibility. In: Search of an ethics for the technological age. University of Chicago Press, Chicago
Levinas E (1994) The rights of man and the rights of the other. In: Levinas E (ed) Outside the subject. Stanford University Press, California
Loewenstein K (1937) Militant democracy and fundamental rights. Am Polit Sci Rev 31(3):417–432
MacIntyre A (2001) Rational and dependent animals. Why humans need virtues. Paidos, Barcelona
Martínez M (2018) Una revisión del derecho fundamental a la protección de datos de carácter personal: un reto en clave de diálogo judicial y constitucionalismo multinivel en la Unión Europea. Tirant lo Blanch, Valencia
Martínez López-Sáez M (2018) Una revisión del derecho fundamental a la protección de datos de carácter personal. Tirant Lo Blanch, Valencia
Martínez de Pisón J-M (1997) Los Derechos humanos: historia, fundamento y realidad. Egido, Zaragoza
Masferrer A (2016) Taking human dignity more humanely: a historical contribution to the ethical foundations of the constitutional democracy. In: Masferrer A, García-Sánchez E (eds) Human dignity of the vulnerable in the age of rights: interdisciplinary perspectives. Springer, Dordrecht, pp 221–256
Masferrer A, García-Sánchez E (eds) (2016) Human dignity of the vulnerable in the age of rights. Interdisciplinary perspectives. Springer, Dordrecht
Massini C-I (1994) Los derechos humanos en el pensamiento actual. Abeledo-Perrot, Buenos Aires
Morello A-M (1998) Los derechos del hombre de las tercera y cuarta generaciones. In: Morello A-M, Estudios de derecho procesal - nuevas demandas - nuevas respuestas, vol 2. Platense / Abeledo-Perrot, Buenos Aires, pp 943–951
Mosterín J (1998) Vivan los animales. Temas de hoy, Madrid
Negro D (2009) El mito del hombre nuevo. Encuentro, Madrid
Nieto A (1971) La ideología revolucionaria de los estudiantes europeos. Ariel, Barcelona
Ollero A (2005) Verdaderos y falsos derechos. In: Europa: sé tú misma, vol 1. Fundación Universitaria San Pablo-CEU, Madrid, pp 595–598
Ortí J-M (2013) Oligarquía y sumisión. Ediciones Encuentro, Madrid
Peces-Barba G (1991) Curso de derechos fundamentales. EUDEMA, Madrid
Peces-Barba G (2004) Los nuevos derechos humanos y la ley. In: Aguilar R et al (eds) In Cicles Nous Drets Humans: 1998, 1999 i 2001. Ajuntament de Sabadell, Sabadell, pp 145–159
Pérez Luño A-E (1995) Tercera generación de Derechos humanos. In: Thetonio V, Prieto F (dirs) Los Derechos humanos. Una reflexión interdisciplinar. Etea, Códoba, pp 105–120
Pérez Luño A-E (1997) Estado Constitucional y derechos de la tercera generación. Anuario de Filosofía del Derecho XIV:545–570
Pérez Luño A-E (1998) Estado Constitucional y Generaciones de derechos. In: Corte IDH (ed) Liber Amicorum Héctor Fix-Zamudio, vol II. Inter-American Court of Human Rights, San José, pp 1241–1264
Pérez Luño A-E (2000) Derechos humanos, Estado de derecho y Constitución. Tecnos, Madrid
Pérez Luño A-E (2006) La tercera generación de derechos humanos. Aranzadi, Navarra

Pérez Luño A-E (2007) La concepción generacional de los derechos humanos. In: Academia de Ciencias Sociales y del Medio Ambiente de Andalucía (ed), Los nuevos derechos fundamentales. Academia de Ciencias Sociales y del Medio Ambiente de Andalucía, Sevilla, pp 33–54
Pérez Luño A-E (2013) The generations of rights. REDESG / Revista Direitos Emergentes na Sociedade Global vol 2, n 1: 163–196
Pope Francis (2015) Laudato Si': On Care for the Common Home, May 24th
Pope John Paul II (1981) Encyclical Letter Laborem Exercens
Pope John Paul II (1990) Message for the World Day of Peace 12: AAS 82
Postigo E (2009) Transumanesimo e postumano: Principi teorici e implicazioni bioetiche. Rivista Internazionale di Deontologia e Bioetica (Medicina e Morale) 2:267–282
Rabossi E (1997–1998) Las generaciones de Derechos humanos: la teoría y el cliché. Lecciones y Ensayos 69–71: 42–52
Rey J-L (2011) Discurso de los derechos: una introducción a los derechos humanos. Universidad Pontificia Comillas, Madrid
Riofrío Martínez-Villalba JC (2014) La cuarta ola de derechos humanos: los derechos digitales. Revista Latinoamericana de Derechos Humanos 15
Rodríguez Palop ME (2010) La nueva generación de derechos humanos. Origen y justificación. Dykinson, Madrid
Salter M (1996) The impossibility of human rights within a postmodern account of law and justice. Journal of Civil Liberties 1:29–66
Singer P (1975) Animal liberation: a new ethics for our treatment of animals. New York Review/ Random House, New York
Squella A (2002) Nuevos derechos humanos en el siglo XXI. ¿Y qué fue de los derechos de los siglos anteriores? Cuadernos Electrónicos de Filosofía del Derecho 5 (available at http://www.uv.es/cefd/5/squella.html)
Suñé Llinás E (2008) La ausencia de privacidad en Internet: Hacia una Constitución y Declaración de Derechos del Ciberespacio. Contrastes 50:66 ff
Tello Moreno LF (2012) El derecho al patrimonio común de la humanidad. Origen del derecho de acceso al patrimonio cultural y su disfrute. México
Vasak K (1977) The long struggle for human rights. UNESCO Courier:29–32
Vasak K (1984) Pour une troisieme génération des droits de l'homme. Essays on international humanitarian law and red cross principles in honour of Jean Pictet. Martinus Nijhofl, The Hague
Vidal Gil EJ (1993) Sobre los derechos de solidaridad. Del Estado liberal al social y democrático de Derecho. Anuario de Filosofía del Derecho 10:89–110
Zimmerling R (1990) Necesidades básicas y relativismo moral. Doxa Cuadernos de Filosofía del Derecho 7:35–54

Appendix

Decreta of Cortes of León (1188) [1]

The oldest documentary manifestation of the European Parliamentary System[2]

Decrees that Don Alfonso, King of León and Galicia, established in the Curia of León with the Archbishop of Compostela and all the bishops and magnates and also with the elected citizens of his kingdom.

[I]

In the name of God. I *Don Alfonso*, King of León and Galicia, having held curia in León, with the archbishop and bishops and magnates of my kingdom and elected citizens from each one of the cities, established and confirmed under oath that to all those of my kingdom, both clergy and laity, I would respect them the good customs that have been established by my predecessors.

[II]

Ditto. I decreed and swore that if someone had come to me with an accusation against another, without delay I will inform the accused of the accuser; and if he is unable to prove the accusation that he made in my curia, he will suffer the punishment that the accused would have suffered if the accusation had been proven.

[III]

Ditto. I also swore that, for the accusation that would be made about someone or for slander of him, I will never cause him harm or damage to his person or properties, until he is subpoenaed in writing to respond to justice in my curia in the manner that my curia determined; and if it is not proven, he who made the

[1] Source: see footnote n. 115 in Part I

[2] Declaration: see footnote 121 in Part I

A. Masferrer, *The Making of Dignity and Human Rights in the Western Tradition*,
Studies in the History of Law and Justice 29,
https://doi.org/10.1007/978-3-031-46667-0

accusation will suffer the aforementioned punishment and will also pay the expenses incurred by the accused in coming and going.

[IV]

Ditto. I also promised that I will not wage war nor make peace or make any agreement without the counsel of bishops, nobles and good men, by whose advice I must abide.

[V]

Ditto. I also established that neither myself nor anyone else other of my kingdom would destroy the house or invade or cut down the vineyards and trees of another, moreover he who has a grievance against someone should present the complaint to me or to the lord of the land or the justices appointed by me or through the bishop or the lord of the land; and if whoever is the object of the complaint wants to present a guarantor or give a guarantee according to the ancient law (*fuero*) he will not suffer any harm; and if he does not want to do that, the lord of the land and the justices would force him, as it is just; and if the lord of the land or the justices would not to do that, present me the complaint with the testimony of the bishop and of good men, and I will see justice done.

[VI]

Ditto. I also firmly forbid that anyone engages in any riots in my kingdom, instead of justice before me, as stated above. And if someone did cause such disturbance he would pay twice the damage done to me; and he would lose my favor, benefit and any land of mine if he possessed.

[VII]

Ditto. I also established that none dares to violently take either anything personal property or real property that would be in possession of another. And if this would be done, it is to be restored twice to whoever suffered the violence.

[VIII]

Ditto. I also established that none should pledge but through the justices and mayors designated by me; and they and the landlords do faithfully enforce the law in the cities and boroughs for those who seek it. And if someone else pledges in any other way, he would be punished as a violent invader. Similarly [is punishable] whoever pledges oxen or cows for ploughing, or whatever the villager had on him in the field, or the villager himself. And if someone pledges or seizes things, as stated above, he should be punished and also excommunicated. And whoever denies having acted violently to avoid such penalty, should present a guarantor according to the old law (*fuero*) and the ancient customs of the land, and immediately should be investigated if he committed violence or not, and according to the results of the investigation should be obliged to provide the given bail. The enquirers, however, be they by consent of the accuser and the accused, or if they fail to reach an agreement were those who were designated for the lands. If the justices and mayors or those that have my land were designated to do justice by consent of the aforementioned men, those should have seals, through which they should subpoena men to respond to the plaintiffs' demands and through them give me testimony about what complaints of the men are true or not.

[IX]

Ditto. I also decreed that if one of the justices denied justice to the plaintiff or delayed it maliciously or did not recognise his right by the third day, he should present witnesses before one of the aforementioned justices whose testimony stating the truth of the matter and compel the justice to pay the plaintiff twice as much of his demand and the costs. And if all the justices of that land deny justice to the plaintiff, he should take witnesses from good men by whom it is proven and give pledge without responsibility instead of the justices and mayors, as much for the demand as for the costs, so that the justices would satisfy twice and also concerning the damage, that would ensure whom guarantees, the justices would pay double.

[X]

Ditto. I also added that no one should appeal to the justices nor grab the pledges when he did not want to comply with the justice; and if he should do this, he should repay twice the damage, the demand and the costs and also pay the justices 60 *sueldos* [or wages]. If any of the justices require any of his subordinates to do justice and they should refuse to help him, they remain bound to the aforesaid penalty and also pay the lord of the land and the justices 100 maravedis; and if the defendant or the debtor were unable to pay the plaintiff, the justices and mayors without liability should seize his person and any assets he had, and deliver him with all his assets to the plaintiff, and if it were necessary, guard him under their protection, and if anyone were to take him by force, they would be punished as a violent invader. If any of the justices suffered any harm in carrying out the justice, all the men of that land will reimburse him for all the damage, in case he who did him harm should not have means to pay him; and if it happens, that one in addition may kill him, he would be taken as a traitor and a treacherous.

[XI]

Ditto. I stated that if anyone were summoned by the seal of the justices and he should refuse to appear before the justices, all this proven by good men, he should pay the justices 60 *sueldos*. And if anyone were accused of theft or other wrongdoing and the accuser should summon him before good men so that he would bring to justice, and he should refuse to come within 9 days, if it were proven that he has been summoned, he would be considered criminal; and if he were noble he should lose the 500 *sueldos* rank and those who capture him should have justice without any liability; and in the case that the noble at any time should make amends and satisfy all defendants, he should regain his nobility and then repossess the rank of 500 *sueldos*, as he had before.

[XII]

Ditto. I also swore that neither myself nor anyone else should enter by force the home of another or do any damage to it or to their assets; and if he should do this, he should pay the owner of the house twice its value and also to the lord of the land nine times the damage caused, if he does not promise to satisfy it, as it is written. And if it happens that he killed the home owner, man or woman, he should be declared treacherous and betrayer. And if it happens that the home owner, man or woman, or any of those who should help them to defend their home should kill him, they will not be punished as a murderer and the damage they caused they will never be required to answer for.

[XIII]

Ditto. And I established that if anyone should want to do justice to anyone who had a grievance against him and the aggrieved should not want to receive justice from him, as stated above, he should do him no harm; and if it should do, he should pay double, and if also he should kill him, he should be declared treacherous.

[XIV]

Ditto. I also established that if someone should wander by chance from one city to another or from one town to another or from one land to another and someone with seal should come from justices to justices from that land in order to detain him and to do justice to him, immediately and without delay they should not hesitate in detaining him and doing justice. If the justices should not do this, they should suffer the punishment that the wrongdoer should suffer.

[XV]

Ditto. I also forbid any man who possesses assets, for which he pays me taxes, should give them to any ecclesiastical establishment.

[XVI]

Ditto. I also ordered that nobody should go to trial in my curia or to trial in León unless for those causes for which he should go according to their own ancient laws (*fueros*).

[XVII]

Ditto. All the bishops also promised, and all the knights and citizens confirmed by oath to be loyal to my advice, to maintain justice and keep the peace in my kingdom.

The manufacturer's authorised representative in the EU is Springer Nature Customer Service Centre GmbH, Europaplatz 3, 69115 Heidelberg, Germany. If you have any concerns regarding our products, please contact ProductSafety@springernature.com

Printed and bound by CPI Group (UK) Ltd, Croydon, CR0 4YY
01/10/2026
02225865-0003